P9-AQM-835

Hilaire Belloc:
Edwardian Radical

Hilaire Belloc

Hilaire Belloc:
Edwardian Radical

John P. McCarthy

LibertyPress

Indianapolis

79-21657

Liberty*Press* is a publishing imprint of Liberty Fund, Inc., a foundation established to encourage study of the ideal of a society of free and responsible individuals.

The cuneiform inscription that serves as the design motif for our endpapers is the earliest known written appearance of the word "freedom" (*ama-gi*), or liberty. It is taken from a clay document written about 2300 B.C. in the Sumerian city-state of Lagash.

Copyright © 1978 by John P. McCarthy. All rights reserved, including the right of reproduction in whole or in part in any form. Brief quotations may be included in a review, and all inquiries should be addressed to Liberty Fund, Inc., 7440 North Shadeland, Indianapolis, Indiana 46250. This book was manufactured in the United States of America.

Library of Congress Cataloging in Publication Data

McCarthy, John Patrick, 1938–
  Hilaire Belloc: Edwardian radical.

  Bibliography: pp. 341–59.
  Includes index.
  1. Belloc, Hilaire, 1870–1953—Political and social views. 2. Great Britain—Politics and government—1837–1901. 3. Great Britain—Politics and government—1901–1936. 4. Radicalism—Great Britain.
PR6003.E45Z78   828'.9'1209   78–5635
ISBN 0–913966–43–6

To my wife Catherine and our children:
Lucy, Kathleen, Patrick, John, Michael, and
Mary Helen.

Contents

Acknowledgments

M y interest in Hilaire Belloc began when I read
The Servile State while a student. He was
scarcely alone in forecasting the growth of the all-
encompassing state, but was nearly alone in suggesting the close correlation between the growth in state
power and the enhancement of certain private interests.
In other words, he feared the prospects of state-
capitalism much more than socialism. Recent history
continues to validate his fears.

I am grateful to Professor R. K. Webb, who read
this work in its early stages and made many thorough
criticisms and useful suggestions that enabled me better to relate Belloc to the Edwardian political milieu.
I am also indebted to Professor Ross J. S. Hoffman,
who prompted my original interest in British history
and who gave me many valuable insights into the per-

sonality and character of Hilaire Belloc, with whom he was acquainted during Belloc's later American visits. Lastly, I must acknowledge the role of my wife Catherine, without whose encouragement, support, and patience this work would have been impossible.

Hilaire Belloc:
Edwardian Radical

Chapter One

Twilight of Radicalism, 1890–1901

Hilaire Belloc is chiefly known as a neomedievalist essayist-poet and Catholic apologetic historian, whose claim to admiration by our generation is compromised by his sympathy for authoritarianism and his anti-Semitism. But Belloc can be viewed in another light: as a radical-liberal in the tradition of Bright, Cobden, Morley, and the younger Joseph Chamberlain. Furthermore, he persisted in adhering to that tradition long after political, economic, and social changes (which in part were consequences of that tradition) had made it irrelevant or, at least, politically impractical. He detested the policies and political tactics of radicals like Chamberlain and Lloyd George, who did adapt themselves to a changing political milieu. He saw imperialist, protectionist, and collectivist departures from the radical ideal as largely motivated by the opportunity for private gain, and considered the yellow press and the disciplined mass political parties as the instruments used to advance such ends. From these convictions developed his disillusion with the British party system and, ultimately, with parliamentarianism itself.

Belloc's family credentials were legitimately radical. His maternal great-great-grandfather was the Unitarian philosopher Joseph Priestley, the "discoverer" of oxygen, whose house was wrecked by a mob because of his sympathy with the French Revolution. His maternal grandfather was Joseph Parkes, the Birmingham solicitor who served as an intermediary between the Whigs and the radicals of the Birmingham Political Union during the agitation for the passage of the 1832 reform bill and who, along with James Mill and Francis Place, sought to further the chances of the bill by creating, through journalism, public speaking, and personal influence with both the government and the popular organizations, an image of the imminence of revolution should the bill not be passed.[1] He became secretary to the commission which drafted the Municipal Corporations Act of 1835 and later worked as an electoral agent for the Liberals and as a parliamentary solicitor. Parkes' daughter and Belloc's mother, Elizabeth Rayner Parkes, a convert to Roman Catholicism, married

---

[1] Joseph Hamburger, *James Mill and the Art of Revolution* (New Haven: Yale University Press, 1963), pp. 49–51.

Louis Belloc of La Celle-St.-Cloud, a suburb of Paris. Louis Belloc's forebears included republican anticlericals (like his artist father) and an Irish colonel who served in the Napoleonic army (his mother's father). Belloc would probably have been raised and have lived permanently in France except for the early death of his father in 1872, just two years after Hilaire's birth. As a result the young widow returned with Belloc and his older sister to England, although close contact was maintained with the French relatives and many holidays were spent there.

Belloc went up to Balliol College, Oxford, in 1892, the year before its famous master Benjamin Jowett died. Belloc greatly admired Jowett and regarded his death as "a quite irreparable loss. . . . No one in Oxford had anything approaching his popularity and breadth. The others are all either silly men, or hated by the body of their fellows."[2] No doubt this regard traced to Jowett's championing of reforms at Oxford in the direction of removing religious qualifications, lessening the costs of education, updating the curriculum by including modern philosophers, and avoiding pedantic narrowness in an effort to make education relevant to society. Belloc's radicalism, however, was completely at odds with the essentially conservative attitude of

---

[2] Marie Belloc Lowndes, *The Young Hilaire Belloc* (New York: P. J. Kenedy & Sons, 1956), p. 126.

Jowett, who "believed in the virtue of an aristocrati-
cally framed society, though not in its exclusive character." In the master's eyes, privilege, whether inherited
or acquired, was legitimate, but it involved responsibility and hard work. It was within this framework of
assumptions that he sought to prepare his promising
students for important places in the existing establishment.[3]

Belloc attained notoriety at Oxford, especially
through his oratory at the Oxford Union, of which he
was elected president. He championed the liberal
position, which was decidedly in the minority at
Oxford at the time, against contemporaries like F. E.
Smith. He even led a small radical association called
the Republican Club. It had only two other members,
John S. Phillimore, afterward professor of classics at
Glasgow, and Francis Y. Eccles, who like Belloc had
an English and a French parent. Naturally there was a
decided Francophile character to the group.[4] In June
1895 he gained first class honors when he sat for his
schools, but was disappointed the next month in his
quest for a fellowship at All Souls. The bitterness with
which he reacted to this failure and his tendency to
attribute it to prejudice against him in large part be-

[3] Geoffrey Faber, *Jowett* (Cambridge: Harvard University Press,
1957), p. 40.
[4] G. K. Chesterton, *Autobiography* (New York: Sheed & Ward,
1936), pp. 299–301.

cause of his Catholicism perhaps foreshadowed a later inclination to ascribe a conspiratorial character to certain political developments.[5]

In late 1896, while still residing at Oxford where he was tutoring and writing poetry, Belloc and a group of colleagues collaborated in publishing a collection of *Essays in Liberalism*. Among the other contributors were J. S. Phillimore, his "Republican" friend; J. L. Hammond, the future social and economic historian; J. A. Simon, who would come to occupy cabinet positions under Asquith, MacDonald, Chamberlain, and Churchill; and F. W. Hirst, who would become the editor of the *Economist*. Sir T. Wemyss Reid, the editor of the *Speaker,* a Liberal weekly set up in reaction to the *Spectator*'s move toward Unionism following the Home Rule crisis of 1886, got the *Essays* published by Cassell & Company, which he managed. It was an ironic collaboration, for a few years later Reid, one of Rosebery's supporters, would turn over the faltering *Speaker* to the same group of young Liberals who, under Hammond's editorship, would be outspoken critics of the Boer War.[6]

The introductory essay by Belloc sought to assert

---

[5] Robert Speaight, *The Life of Hilaire Belloc* (New York: Farrar, Straus & Cudahy, 1957), pp. 95–97.

[6] Francis W. Hirst, *In the Golden Days* (London: Frederick Muller, 1947), pp. 155–60.

the essential principles of the liberal tradition, principles he feared were in danger of abandonment because
of the severe defeat the Liberals had encountered in
1895. Basic to liberalism, he insisted, was the theory
that "no association, especially no association of a
political kind, had a right to command the obedience
of its members unless those each had a part in the government of that which they were to obey." This principle was dependent on another idea, a "definition of
the citizen as a political unit."[7] Belloc's liberal individualism stressed "the representation of individuals
rather than corporate bodies, ranks, orders or interests," as was done in the Old Tory and Old Whig
traditions.[8] Such had been the radical impetus behind
the redistribution schemes and franchise extensions
from 1832 to 1885. With this political individualism
Belloc coupled the necessity that the enfranchised
citizen be "one whose economic and political independence was not, indeed, irresponsible." That is, he had
to possess "that faculty of self-restraint" which is "the
basis of all accumulation and of all sufficient material
happiness." This self-respecting and responsible citizen,
Belloc insisted (in accord with the standard liberal
doctrine), would not use his political power merely to

---

[7] Hilaire Belloc, "The Liberal Tradition," *Essays in Liberalism*
(London: Cassell, 1897), p. 7.

[8] Samuel H. Beer, *British Politics in the Collectivist Age* (New
York: Alfred A. Knopf, 1966), p. 34.

advance the interests of his class or himself, but could instead, because of his economic freedom and self-sufficiency, "be counted upon not to give his vote upon a general issue for purposes lower than those of the common good."[9]

In the case of radical Liberals like Belloc, this theory of the responsible propertied voter cannot be interpreted as simply the advocacy of the cause of the middle classes, who, upon their admission to the political life of the nation by the earlier Reform Acts, should then be conservative and satisfied. Instead, the self-responsible middle-class voter would broaden his vision beyond that of class interests toward the well-being of all of society, in contrast to the specific class consciousness of the various orders represented prior to liberal reform. Furthermore, the liberal ideal aimed at a broadening of the middle class so that most individuals in society could become their own economic masters.[10] The main impediment that radical Liberals saw to the attainment of this ideal was the continued existence of various privileges and monopolies in society, especially in the ownership of land, in local government, and in the religious establishment. Hostility to these vested interests had inspired the more ardent Liberals—those unsatisfied with simply the enfranchisement of the middle classes and the achievement of free trade—in

---

[9] Belloc, "Liberal Tradition," p. 8.
[10] Beer, *British Politics,* pp. 36–37.

the formation of a mass party organization, the National Liberal Federation, for more effective political
action.

The types of issues that attracted radicals like John
Bright, Joseph Chamberlain, John Morley, and Henry
Labouchere were church disestablishment in Wales and
Scotland (and probably ultimately in England), restriction of the powers of the House of Lords, democratic
local government in the form of district and parish
councils, reforms in land law, and a nonsectarian or
secular national education system. The last famous
collective proclamation of these radical objectives prior
to Belloc's writing had been the Newcastle program of
the National Liberal Federation in 1891. Much of the
successful campaigning that resulted in the Liberal
victory and the formation of the fourth and last Gladstone ministry in 1892 was based upon it. Much of the
Newcastle program, however, especially its most controversial item, Irish Home Rule, was not attained
during Gladstone's ministry. When he resigned following differences with his own cabinet, he was succeeded
by the Liberal-Imperialist Lord Rosebery, who was
particularly hostile toward the radicals. The cabinet
resigned after a year filled with internal dissension in
the ministry and shortly afterward the general election
of 1895 returned a Conservative-Unionist majority of
152. Belloc and his colleagues insisted that these difficulties of the Liberal Party resulted from its lukewarm
attitude toward the radical principles, and asserted that

its abandonment of them would bring about the party's disappearance.[11]

Actually the cause of the Liberal Party's failure in the political arena was much more likely the very radicalism that Belloc professed, or at least the disunity it had created within the party. The Whigs in the party, that is those connected with the landed and titled elements of society and the moderate Liberals, whose "doctrine of individual freedom . . . demanded free trade for British commerce, freedom of contract for British employers," and for whom the 1884 Electoral Reform Act "was to be the last great contribution of the party toward a democratic Britain,"[12] naturally feared the radicals as a threat to the status quo. This fear drove many of them into the ranks of Conservatism.

The specific issue which sparked their departure was Gladstone's endorsement of Irish Home Rule. Such a concession to the rebellious and often violent Irish was regarded as a betrayal of those principles—"security of person and property and the reasonable enforcement of contracts"—that were deemed basic "for liberty and civilization."[13] Paradoxically, one of the most celebrated

---

[11] Belloc, "Liberal Tradition," p. 3.

[12] Gordon Goodman, "Liberal Unionism: The Revolt of the Whigs," *Victorian Studies* 3 (December 1959): 175.

[13] R. C. K. Ensor, "Some Political and Economic Interactions in Later Victorian England," *Transactions of the Royal Historical Society,* 4th ser. 31 (1949): 25–26.

Liberals to take the Unionist walk toward Conservatism was the very radical leader who had inspired the most fear in the hearts of the Whigs, Joseph Chamberlain. Despite this celebrated defection, Liberal Unionism has to be interpreted primarily as an antiradical movement based upon fear of a radical assault on established property, which was how—with some justice—the Whigs saw Home Rule and land-reform agitation in Ireland. At almost the same time that the Liberal Party was abandoned by the more conservative-minded who feared the radicals, there came the loss of significant working-class support, resulting in the appearance in 1895 for the first time in a general election of the Independent Labor Party. A major reason for the development of the ILP and the withdrawal from the Liberal Party of many working-class activists, like Ramsay MacDonald, was the persistent hostility of the Liberal associations to the nomination of working-class candidates.[14]

The development of the ILP points to an important characteristic of traditional radicalism, which goes a long way to explain its political decline as well as the decline of liberalism in general: liberalism seemed irrelevant to a changing economic structure as well as to the foremost social problems of the day. As late as the 1880s and the 1890s, the radicals, including Chamber-

---

[14] Henry Pelling, *Origins of the Labor Party,* 2d ed. (Oxford: Oxford University Press, 1965), pp. 164–66.

lain at the time of his "Unauthorized Program" of 1884, clung to the essential premises of laissez-faire.[15] What the radicals hoped to achieve was the extension of the economic freedom attained by the middle-class entrepreneur to the population at large. They sought to correct the economic plight of the poorer classes while remaining within the laissez-faire system. The state actions they desired were primarily geared toward placing the poorer classes and the workers in a more competitive position in relation to their employers as well as in a position of self-reliance. Belloc and his young radical colleagues accordingly could approve certain state actions—such as factory acts, graduated income taxes, and workmen's compensation laws—that aimed at enhancing the economic freedom of the worker. Such programs were not designed to subordinate enterprises and workers to state control as socialism would. Nor were they intended to penalize or discourage savings and enterprise.[16] These young radicals tended to see the lingering force of privileged monopoly as underlying most of the economic injustices of society. From such an assumption it could be argued that laissez-faire had not been completely established, and therefore had not been adequately tested.

This animosity toward privilege applied most espe-

---

[15] Peter Fraser, *Joseph Chamberlain* (London: Cassell, 1966), p. 49.

[16] Francis W. Hirst, "Liberalism and Wealth," and J. A. Simon, "Liberals and Labour," *Essays in Liberalism,* pp. 87–90, 113–14.

cially, from the radical perspective, to landownership. Belloc feared that liberalism was not pursuing its heritage with regard to the soil, "the most important of all the means of production," where "restrictions made for the benefit of a small class" and "the partial monopoly which these restrictions created" must be removed. He seemed not to take into account the extensive land legislation that the Liberals had produced for the explicit purpose of protecting the tenant from exploitation by the landlord. For instance, the Irish Land Act of 1880, passed under Gladstone, sought to provide fixed rents and security from eviction. In 1886 Gladstone introduced another measure providing state loans for Irish peasants to purchase lands. It failed to pass, but the Unionists subsequently enacted a series of measures to facilitate peasant proprietorship in Ireland, largely with the hope of dampening Home Rule enthusiasm. But Belloc wanted further steps taken to create the "free trade in land" that could revive an English peasantry destroyed by "two centuries of landlord encroachment." He specifically wanted those objectives of both Chamberlain's 1884 program and the 1891 Newcastle program: to remove primogeniture and entail and to cheapen the legal costs for the transfer of land.[17]

Late Victorian economic developments, however,

---

[17] Belloc, "Liberal Tradition," pp. 18–20.

made many of these radical objectives irrelevant. The desire for free trade in land and the hostility toward the privileged position of the landed aristrocracy and gentry had become dated as a result of the agricultural depression that commenced in the 1870s. The depression was particularly felt by grain farmers, who were confronted with the competition of transatlantic imports. One result was an enormous migration of agricultural laborers to the cities, thereby eliminating much of the potential peasantry to whom the radicals would have extended ownership. Similarly, a landowning class, prompted by declining rents and general despondency over the future of agriculture to sell considerable amounts of real estate, could scarcely be the ominous power pictured by the radicals.[18] Of course, much of the agricultural depression was more apparent than real, for while the wheat farmer suffered, other forms of agriculture, like stock farming, to which many adjusted, did very well and even benefited by the urbanization of Britain. Even the position of the agricultural laborers improved as a result of the migration of so many of their fellows to the cities, largely because of the better bargaining position belonging to those who remained in the countryside. Nonetheless, agriculture as a whole did decline in respect of the phenomenal rents and profits it had been receiving in midcentury

---

[18] F. M. L. Thompson, *English Landed Society in the Nineteenth Century* (London: Routledge & Kegan Paul, 1963), p. 318.

and in relation to the growing incomes in the industrial sector.[19]

In addition to these developments in agriculture, industrial and commercial changes had also worked against the radical ideal of the economically independent citizen, perhaps best typified by the mid-Victorian manufacturer but also including the small merchant and the independent artisan. This was evidenced by the increasing conversion to and appearance of joint-stock or public companies after 1870. The family or private firms so identified with the radical ideal were often faced with the alternative of becoming public, and thereby replenishing themselves with managerial talent or collapsing. Probably even more disheartening to the radicals than the decline of the private firms were the changing attitudes of the younger generations of these entrepreneurial families, who, after public school and university education, pursued their social climbing by adopting specifically anti-middle-class, antibusiness attitudes similar to those patronizing social concerns that radicalism despised in the aristocracy.[20] The newer public companies tended to be larger than

[19] W. H. B. Court, *British Economic History, 1870–1914, Commentary and Documents* (Cambridge: At the University Press, 1965), pp. 33–36; T. W. Fletcher, "The Great Depression of English Agriculture, 1873–1896," *Economic History Review,* 2d ser. 13 (April 1961): 417–32.

[20] Charles Wilson, "Economy and Society in Late Victorian Britain," *Economic History Review,* 2d ser. 18 (August 1965): 197–98.

the old private and family companies. An even greater departure from radical principles, however, was the tendency toward industrial amalgamations or, at least, trade associations. These monopolistic tendencies were justified as means of lessening costs, including that of labor, eliminating "cutthroat" competition, and stabilizing trade fluctuations.[21]

Another aspect of the tendency toward economic amalgamation at the expense of the individual entrepreneur resulted from the increase in real wages that accompanied the depression. That aspect was the increasing mass production of consumer goods, whereby factories produced "the branded, packaged, standardized, advertised products" previously supplied, if at all, by the village or town craftsman.[22] Belloc lamented such developments in his essay, observing that conditions had been brought about in England which he regarded as the very antithesis of the liberal ideal:

> capital held in large masses and in a few hands; men working in large gangs under conditions where discipline, pushed to the point of servitude, is almost as necessary as in an armed force; voters whose most immediate interests are economic rather than political; citizens who own, for the greater part, not even their roofs.[23]

---

[21] W. H. B. Court, *A Concise Economic History of Britain: From 1750 to Recent Times* (Cambridge: At the University Press, 1962), pp. 213–16.

[22] Wilson, "Economy and Society," p. 191.

[23] Belloc, "Liberal Tradition," p. 29.

The object of Belloc's regret was a development in political psychology whereby the spirit of British politics became less characterized by the individualist voter and more by the institutional or collectivist voter. The former, usually an employer, self-employed, or an employee in a small enterprise, was a voter whose economic needs or hopes did not generally require political assistance, but would be more likely bettered by voluntary or individual action. Consequently, his vote was based on something broader than personal economic interest, even if it was nothing more than a hatred of the establishment or an attempt to demonstrate that he could have a say in society. The latter voter, usually the industrial worker, tended to base his vote and attitude on national questions on "practical objects conceived in material terms," such as labor or welfare legislation. The difference between the Victorian radical and the twentieth-century Laborite can often be seen in these terms.[24]

In addition to these economic factors, there were also many political forces making the radical ideal unfeasible. For one thing, the National Liberal Federation had very early in its history begun to lose its purely radical character. Instead it came to serve a principle of organization concerned more with Liberal electoral

---

[24] J. R. Vincent, *Pollbooks, How Victorians Voted* (Cambridge: At the University Press, 1967), pp. 43–45.

victories than with radicalism.[25] This process was intensified when the organizational genius of the National Liberal Federation, Francis Schnadhorst, began to lose the earlier radical enthusiasm of his Birmingham days and concentrated instead on such matters as organizational efficiency and party finance. This became especially pronounced after he moved the NLF headquarters from Birmingham to London, and accepted, simultaneously with his NLF position, the post of secretary to the Liberal Central Association, the parliamentary party's organization. This priority of organizational needs over radical aspirations became so great that after 1895, such radical MPs as Charles Dilke, Henry Labouchere, and Wilfrid Lawson began criticizing the subordination of the NLF to the LCA.[26] But this was only one aspect of a more general increase in the power of the leadership of both parties. In addition to the subordination of the popular organizations to leadership needs, there was the increasing domination of Parliament by the ministry through changing procedural rules that limited the power of the private member and through the disciplinary power that resulted from the individual MP's dependence on the

---

[25] Francis H. Herrick, "The Origins of the National Liberal Federation," *Journal of Modern History* 17 (June 1945): 129.

[26] Barry McGill, "Francis Schnadhorst and the Liberal Party Organization," *Journal of Modern History* 34 (March 1962): 38.

party organization and funds at election time. Hostility to front-bench control of British parliamentary politics would become a central preoccupation of Belloc after he entered Parliament.

Not only did the Liberal organization appear hostile to radicalism, but a rival program developed within the party. That was Liberal-Imperialism, which became so hostile to radical Little Englandism at the time of the Boer War that a schism comparable to the Unionist secession over Home Rule was almost provoked. The central figure in the Liberal-Imperialist movement was the articulate, learned and extremely wealthy Earl of Rosebery. He had become a convinced imperialist after a world tour in 1883 on which his imagination had been stirred by his contact with the diverse races and lands under British control and influence. He had visions of these territories maturing into nations, but not of their "leaving the empire, because the empire is a commonwealth of nations." His own definition of an advocate of the apparently contradictory views of liberalism and imperialism was "a Liberal who is passionately attached to the empire . . . who believes that the empire is best maintained upon the basis of the widest democracy, and that the voice is most powerful when it represents the greatest number of persons and subjects." Preoccupied with imperial concerns during his period as Foreign Secretary in the third and fourth Gladstone ministries (1886 and 1892–94), he essentially carried on the policies of his Conservative predecessor, Lord Salisbury. That policy was careful isolation from Europe and reliance upon British seapower to maintain the status quo. He admitted as much in 1892, when he noted that "our great empire has pulled us, so to speak, by the coattails out of the European system."[27] During the last Gladstone ministry, he infuriated the radicals by his insistence on independence in conducting foreign affairs. Certain specifically imperialist policies of his, such as the maintenance of a British presence in Uganda even after the chartered proprietary colonizers, the British East Africa Company, had declined financially, particularly annoyed them.

There was a domestic aspect to Liberal-Imperialism that was equally alien to the radical tradition. Liberal-Imperialism did not have a Conservative or Whiggish hostility toward social reform, but instead tended to outbid the radicals, whose approach was primarily a negative assault on privileged monopoly, by advocating more positive governmental action aimed at social improvement. Rosebery's record in this regard while serving as the nonpartisan chairman of the London County Council in 1889 drew the interest of many younger Liberal MPs, who were not attracted by the negative character of the traditional radical rhetoric

---

[27] Robert Rhodes James, *Rosebery* (New York: Macmillan, 1963), pp. 156–58, 201.

voiced in Parliament. Among them were H. H. Asquith, Edward Grey, and R. B. Haldane. Considerable political intimacy developed between Haldane and Rosebery, and they came together in an ambition to create a group within the Liberal Party that aimed at "gaining the confidence of the public by its constructive propositions, and . . . gaining a position from which to criticize with the utmost frankness and firmness the people with whose ideas we were at present associated."[28] They were referring to the more traditional radicals.

Liberal-Imperialists occupied significant positions in Gladstone's last ministry, and Rosebery succeeded the GOM as Prime Minister and party leader in 1894, but they faced considerable opposition within the party in those years. The most formidable opposition came from the curious and not very cohesive alliance of Sir William Harcourt, the Chancellor of the Exchequer, and John Morley, the Chief Secretary for Ireland. Their hostility toward Liberal-Imperialism did not submerge the basic differences between them. Harcourt was a Whig, with considerable hereditary credentials, while Morley came from the Lancashire middle class. Furthermore, Harcourt concerned himself primarily with day-to-day party and parliamentary struggles rather than with comprehensive programs and philosophies. Morley, on the other hand, had been an intellec-

---

[28] Dudley Sommer, *Haldane of Cloan* (London: George Allen & Unwin, 1960), p. 76.

tual disciple of John Stuart Mill and Auguste Comte and a political follower of W. E. Gladstone. He had obtained a reputation as an intellectual journalist, editing the *Fortnightly Review,* and approached political questions first from a theoretical or philosophical basis.

The Liberal-Imperialist Asquith commented on this incongruous pair who

> belonged not only to different generations, but in all essentials, except that of actual chronology, to different centuries. . . . They had hardly even a prejudice in common. Their intercourse, once they became friends, was checkered by periodic misunderstandings. . . . Had they a common faith? It is hard to say—except that, from different points of view, they were equally ardent disciples of what used to be called the anti-imperialist and "Little England" school.[29]

Morley and the Roseberyites were able to maintain good relations in spite of their political differences because of their sharing the temperamental affinity between intellectuals. As a result, Morley was able to act as an intermediary between the Liberal-Imperialists and Harcourt, whose irascible and contentious nature made him an almost impossible colleague. This fractious personality of Harcourt caused even his ally Morley to prefer Rosebery as a successor to Glad-

---

[29] Earl of Oxford and Asquith, *Fifty Years of the British Parliament,* 2 vols. (Boston: Little, Brown, 1926), 1: 246–47.

stone, a preference shared, more significantly, by the queen.[30]

Keeping alive the radical faith against the Liberal-Imperialists in a more vehement manner than Morley was Henry Labouchere, the MP from Northampton and publisher of the radical weekly *Truth,* who had assumed the leadership of the declining group of traditional radicals in the House of Commons. He personified many of the Little England and radical attitudes that were unacceptable and unpleasant in the sight of both the establishment and the increasingly imperially conscious public. Many parallels can be seen in the political views, temperaments, and tactics of Labouchere and Belloc, despite the former's religious skepticism and the latter's Catholicism. Labouchere had disqualified himself from a cabinet position in the fourth Gladstone government because of the offense his "unrespectable and antinational" positions had given to the Queen. He was a persistent critic of all privileged establishments, the nobility, the church, and even the royal family. This hostility had the penurious air of French peasant radicalism, as he was particularly incensed over the elaborate expenses involved in maintaining these establishments. He was cynical about

---

[30] Peter Stansky, *Ambitions and Strategies* (Oxford: Oxford University Press, 1964), pp. 43–46.

politicians in general, and consequently was unsympathetic to granting any significant increases in pay to ministers. He desired further democratization of the House of Commons through more frequent elections and the payment of members. The House of Lords was his particular *bête noire:*

> Members of the House of Lords were neither elected nor selected for their merits. They sat by the merits of their ancestors, and, if we looked into the merits of some of those ancestors, we should agree that the less said about them the better. The House of Lords consisted of a class most dangerous to the community—the class of rich men, the greater part of whose fortune was in land. . . . They consisted generally of two classes—of those who were apparently successful politicians, and of those who were undoubtedly successful money grabbers.[31]

In addition to his traditional radical dislike of privilege and extravagant government expenditure, Labouchere was also hostile toward collectivism. In a debate with H. M. Hyndman, the leader of the Social-Democratic Federation, he insisted on the necessity for respecting private capital in view of the long-range and benevolent distribution that results from it when controlled by competition. He warned against state owner-

---

[31] Algar Labouchere Thorold, *The Life of Henry Labouchere* (London: Constable, 1913), pp. 217–18.

ship of the means of production, which would destroy individualism and self-reliance and give a body of men "the power of destroying and ruining, at one fell blow, the entire nation."[32]

As would be the case in Belloc's career, Labouchere's outspokenness, especially as a journalist, particularly embittered the establishment. The weekly radical journal that he owned, *Truth,* was given to blunt criticism and exposure, which often involved it in libel suits. Its attacks on Lord Rosebery, and especially on his imperial policies, intensified Rosebery's hostility to Labouchere. As Foreign Secretary, Rosebery opposed granting Labouchere the ambassadorship he had requested. No justification for the award, either as compensation for Labouchere's not getting a cabinet position or as a means of ending his troublesome presence in the House of Commons, would induce Rosebery to grant it.[33]

Naturally, Labouchere was quite unsympathetic to Rosebery, a peer, being the Liberal Prime Minister, and was responsible for the first great embarrassment of that short-lived ministry. On March 13, 1894, Labouchere successfully moved, over the ministry's opposition, an amendment to the address which practically called for the abolition of the power of the House of

[32] *Ibid.,* p. 434.
[33] James, *Rosebery,* pp. 256–58.

Lords. It passed mainly because it was made at dinner-time when the size of the House was small.[34]

While Labouchere's personal eccentricity might account for the limitations on his influence and popularity, there remained no doubt that radicalism in general was out of favor, especially following the Unionist victory of 1895. Popular enthusiasm and imperial interest became focused on the man who had once been the great hope of the radicals, Joseph Chamberlain. By 1899, in fact, Chamberlain could contemptuously refer to Labouchere as "a bundle of old rags," even though Labouchere had been his old ally and an intermediary between himself and Gladstone in efforts at reconciliation over the Home Rule issue.[35]

Belloc, therefore, began his literary and journalistic career in a very hostile political climate. Furthermore, his personal disappointment in not obtaining the All Souls fellowship had intensified his disenchantment

---

[34] *Ibid.,* pp. 337–39. The success of Labouchere's motion was assisted by the votes of many Irish members, who were annoyed at a remark Rosebery had ineptly made the day before in the House of Lords to the effect that Home Rule ought not to be carried unless a majority of the English MPs, not simply a majority of the whole House of Commons, approved it. Such would have ruled out Home Rule since the majority of the English members were hostile to it, and its passage, like the Liberal majorities, was dependent upon the Celtic fringe.

[35] Winston S. Churchill, *Great Contemporaries* (London: Thornton Butterworth, 1937), p. 73.

with the prevailing temperament of the political, literary and academic establishment. In place of the fellowship and the subsequent career as an historian that he had expected, he was confronted upon finishing his studies at Oxford with blunt economic necessity that required his turning toward tutoring and university extension lecturing. He traveled to the United States in 1896 and again in 1897. The first visit was to woo Elodie Hogan, a young Irish-American from California, whom he had met in London five years earlier. On both trips he gave numerous lectures. Within the next five years, he published several collections of humorous verse, short prose satires, as well as two biographies. Appropriately, the young biographer wrote about the French revolutionaries Danton and Robespierre, for, in addition to his English radicalism, there was much of the Jacobin or radical republican in Belloc. Having maintained his French citizenship, he even fulfilled his required tour of duty in the French army in the year before he went to Oxford.

Although most of his French relatives were conservative republicans, Belloc had developed great enthusiasm for his family friend and neighbor, Paul Déroulède, and had even become a member of the Ligue des Patriotes.[36] This organization, which Déroulède had founded in 1882, was primarily concerned with the

---

[36] Marie Belloc Lowndes, *Where Love and Friendship Dwelt* (New York: Dodd, Mead, 1943), p. 59.

French recovery of Alsace-Lorraine, and, to that end, sought to mobilize a mass of followers for extrapolitical and extraparliamentary street action against the existing parties and the National Assembly. Déroulède and his movement, like much of the support for General Boulanger in the late 1880s, was a prototype of the curious left-right revolutionary amalgam that had developed in the name of French nationalism against the established republican center. Historically, French nationalism had been a revolutionary force, and Déroulède himself was basically a republican.

Disappointment with the Third Republic, however, had prompted an alliance of radical republicans, Bonapartists, and legitimists. This alliance could therefore make various appeals to diverse elements: as socialist to the poor, as radical to the lower middle class, and as defender of order to the richer conservative classes. These French nationalist associations would not become exclusively conservative until after the turn of the century, when the development of internationalist-minded socialist organizations would lessen their appeal to the left. Partly for this reason, the Ligue des Patriotes was a type of movement entirely different from the royalist Action Francaise movement founded in 1899 by Charles Maurras.[37]

---

[37] Eugen Weber, "France," *The European Right,* ed. Hans Rogger and Eugen Weber (Los Angeles: University of California Press, 1966), pp. 85–94; D. R. Watson, "The Nationalist Movement in Paris, 1900–06," *The Right in France, 1890–1919,* ed. David Shapiro, 2d ed. (London: Chatto & Windus, 1962), pp. 83–84.

Belloc's own political outlook duplicated this left-right ambivalence of French nationalism in the late nineteenth century. A particularly unpleasant characteristic that he derived from French nationalism was anti-Semitism. Significantly, Belloc sympathized with the anti-Dreyfusards, a position which attracted very few followers in England.[38] But anti-Semitic feelings remained strong in Belloc long after the heated atmosphere of the Dreyfus case had passed from public interest. His novels and some of his poetry were notorious for it as Jewish characters appeared in a rather unpleasant light in his works. Furthermore, his radical political criticisms would view the Jewish presence as disproportionately high in the more unpleasant activities of the Edwardian plutocracy, especially in matters like the purchase of government policies and honors. His anti-Semitism was closely connected with his hostility to finance capitalism, which he appraised as highly subject to Jewish influence.

His French connection, especially his French political sentiments, made Belloc something of an outcast in the England of the 1890s. The French and France were not highly regarded in England; even more distressing to Belloc, the nation which seemed to evoke the most favorable English attitude was Germany. As mentioned before, British foreign policy in the 1880s

---

[38] Hilaire Belloc, *The Cruise of the "Nona"* (Westminster, Md.: Newman Press, 1956; first published 1925), pp. 214–15.

and 1890s, under both Conservatives and Liberals (especially Rosebery), was based on isolation from the Continent. If there was any European power with which Great Britain would ally itself it was Germany, a conservative status-quo power.[39] This was despite temporary antagonism arising from Kaiser Wilhelm's telegram of support to President Kruger of the Transvaal at the time of the Jameson raid early in 1896. The reason was that Germany was not in a serious position to interfere with Great Britain's position in South Africa, and agreement had been reached between them on other potential imperial disputes such as the accord in 1890 on African territories.

The minimum of contention Great Britain had with Germany contrasted greatly with its rivalry with France over imperial designs in Africa and Asia. Also disturbing in England were those revanchist desires that moved such French elements as the Ligue des Patriotes. The anti-French and pro-German sentiments in British policy and national temperament peaked by late 1898. Before that the instances of accord with Germany had been of a limited nature in keeping with Lord Salisbury's isolationism and distrust of overextensive and unrealistic commitments. However, his Colonial Secretary, Joseph Chamberlain, the ex-leader of the radicals, began advancing suggestions for ending diplomatic

---

[39] Lillian M. Penson, "The New Course in British Foreign Policy, 1892–1902," *Transactions of the Royal Historical Society,* 4th ser. 25 (1943): 121.

isolation and establishing a comprehensive Anglo-German alliance. Being much more responsive to and aware of what could excite the popular imagination than Salisbury, Chamberlain spoke in terms of an ethnic identity between the Teutonic people of the world.[40] This was simultaneous with the Fashoda crisis in which Great Britain and France almost went to war with each other following the meeting of their respective military contingents that were advancing into the Sudan in the quest for hegemony over that territory. War was avoided when the French withdrew and yielded the territory to English authority.

At the time Francophobia was greatly inflamed by the mass press with its sensationalist and jingoist presentation. The most notorious example was the *Daily Mail,* which Alfred Harmsworth, later Lord Northcliffe, began in 1896. But Germanophile and anti-Latin sentiments had been developing for some time on a much higher level than that of popular journalism. In the academic world, particularly among philosophers, the influence of German philosophy had been increasing and Kantian and Hegelian thought for a while replaced utilitarianism and empiricism as the prevailing philosophical position. Belloc's college, Balliol, was a foremost center for this development. Benjamin Jowett himself had encouraged the studying of modern Ger-

---

[40] J. L. Garvin, *The Life of Joseph Chamberlain,* vol. 3, *Empire and World Policy* (London: Macmillan, 1943), pp. 507–8.

man philosophy, although later he lost such enthusi-asm.[41] But one of his students, Thomas Hill Green, who became a fellow of Balliol and professor of moral philosophy at Oxford in the 1870s, was the central figure in the development of idealism in England. Jowett's successor as master of Balliol, Edward Caird, was another major proponent of this school.

While Hegelianism can be used to support an au-thoritarian and conservative political stance, English idealism was primarily associated with liberalism and radicalism. However, it did work to bring about a for-midable transformation in liberalism away from its in-dividualist foundation toward a more collectivist basis. This was because idealism emphasized the social char-acter of man, arriving at its political and social concepts from the starting point of man as part of society rather than as an isolated individual, as the utilitarians saw him. In the teleological view of idealism man attained his perfection as part of society and through society. Hence, there was a need to create the social environ-ment whereby that perfection could be approximated. This highly social view of man naturally emphasized the theme of duty and responsibility as much as liberty and rights. Idealism influenced many of the brighter young liberals of the late 1870s, the 1880s, and the 1890s, including many Balliol students, who would

---

[41] Melvin Richter, *The Politics of Conscience* (London: Weidenfeld & Nicolson, 1964), p. 71.

come to play a very important part in this more collectivist transformation of liberalism and the decline of the older radicalism.[42]

The administrative and organizational efficiency of Germany, of Prussia especially, served as an example for many of the newer liberals of the direction their efforts must take to create by state action the proper social environment whereby individuals could realize their full human potential. But some admiration for Germany, especially on a more popular level, was based on grounds that were not very liberal. The latter were the external, or racial, social Darwinist views put forward by writers like Benjamin Kidd. Unlike Herbert Spencer and his early Social Darwinism, by which he viewed the struggle for survival between individuals as a justification for laissez-faire, Kidd viewed the struggle as taking place between races or nations. In the struggle the Teutonic races (the English and the Germans) would triumph because of such qualities as

---

[42] *Ibid.*, pp. 283–94. Green's philosophical teachings had a formidable effect in moving liberalism in a "statist" direction. However, it must not be forgotten that his thought had its greatest influence between 1890 and 1914, whereas he had died in 1882 and had formed his position in the heart of the Victorian era. Therefore, despite the "collectivist" implications that came to be drawn from his theories, Green himself accepted most of the concepts of the Bright-style liberalism with its emphasis on self-reliance, private property, and middle-class moralism. Obviously he had not worked out in his own mind the full implications of his philosophy with regard to specific social policies.

"reverence, . . . great mental energy, resolution, enterprise, powers of prolonged and concentrated application, and a sense of simple-minded and single-minded devotion to the conception of duty." This contrasted with the intellectually gifted Celtic races (for example, the French) whose intellectuality prompted self-seekingness at the price of racial solidarity.[43]

It was against such a variety of attitudes, as philosophical idealism, Francophobia, and Anglo-Saxon racism, that Belloc first directed his literary wit. He wrote a satirical tribute to an imaginary don, J. A. Lambkin, "Sometime Fellow of Burford College," Oxford, whose "learning and scholarship, so profound in the dead languages, was exercised with singular skill and taste in the choice he made of modern authors." This was reflected in the fact that "of the European languages he would read German with the greatest pleasure, confining himself chiefly to the writings of Lessing, Kant, and Schiller." Naturally, "He was ignorant of Italian," although thoroughly acquainted with French classics, or at least their "admirable translations" in the Half-Crown Series.[44]

In an obvious jibe at the philosophical idealists, especially their abstruse style, Belloc satirized certain

---

[43] Bernard Semmel, *Imperialism and Social Reform* (London: George Allen & Unwin, 1960), pp. 31–35.

[44] Hilaire Belloc, *Lambkin's Remains* (London: Duckworth, 1920; first published 1900), pp. 184–85.

of the central features of their system in "Lambkin's Essay on 'Success'" and in "Lambkin's Lecture on 'Right.'" For instance, their teleological approach is caricatured in Lambkin's definition of success ":as the *successful consummation of an imagined good* or more shortly as the *real*ization of an *imagined good.*"[45] The ethics of the idealists, having a teleological basis, grounded morality on "the consciousness that there remains a perfection to be attained." This implied a vocation that had to be fulfilled in order to reach something absolutely desirable, regardless of whatever might be a temporary individual desire. Furthermore, the idealists sought proof or "witness" of man's progress toward this perfection, or development, in the history of human institutions.[46] Belloc had Lambkin complicate this philosophical approach to the point of ridicule in his pronouncement of two formulas: "The involute of progression is the subconscious evolution of the particular function," and "the sentiment of right is the inversion of the subconscious function in its relation to the indeterminate ego." Such, he insisted, was "the final summing up of all that is meant by development," and was "admitted by all European philosophers in Germany."[47]

Belloc also had Lambkin serve as a foil for his other

[45] *Ibid.,* p. 196.

[46] Richter, *Politics of Conscience,* pp. 199–200.

[47] Belloc, *Lambkin's Remains,* p. 214.

animus, the popular press, by having him write for a popular Sunday newspaper (owned, appropriately in a Bellocian satire, by a Mr. Solomon). In his article, Lambkin boasted that "the English-speaking race has —if we except the Dutch, Negro, and Irish elements— a marvelous talent for self-government." This was very plain, although the don-turned-journalist could not tell "why, in the inscrutable designs of Providence, our chosen race should have been so specially gifted."[48]

It was as an opponent of imperialism that Belloc received his first significant notoriety as a satirical writer. The term *imperialism* had not been used in the middle of the nineteenth century to describe existing British policy or the existing British overseas territories. If anything, it was an unfavorable term applied to the system and policies of Napoleon III. Even mid-Victorian critics of the overseas policies of the British government did not ascribe to the government any theoretical commitment to imperialism.[49] By the late 1880s and the 1890s, however, the concept of imperialism was becoming the prevailing political orthodoxy of England, except for a declining minority of radicals whose tradition Belloc followed. This late Victorian imperialism was not simply of British self-interest

---

[48] *Ibid.*, p. 234.
[49] Richard Koebner and Helmut Dan Schmidt, *Imperialism* (Cambridge: At the University Press, 1964), pp. 29–31.

against other powers, as the older Tories like Lord Salisbury and others in Disraeli's tradition viewed and practiced it. Instead, a newer breed, such as the Liberal-Imperialists like Rosebery, Grey, Haldane, and Asquith, as well as the younger Conservatives like Curzon, Balfour, and Wyndham, had a more elevated concept of imperial mission.[50]

This took a variety of forms—from the desire for a racial unity of the scattered Anglo-Saxon peoples throughout the world, through the interest in an imperial federation of self-governing nations, to the advocacy of greater unity in the form of an imperial parliament. In addition, British control of less developed areas that were believed incapable of self-government, such as India, Egypt, and the increasing African territories, was justified as a kind of missionary or civilizing task. This task, which was to be done not just for the benefit of Great Britain but also for the people of the territories themselves, was to be performed by the administrators and soldiers of the "imperial service." A typical example was Alfred Milner, who served as undersecretary for finance in Egypt from 1889 to 1892 before becoming the High Commissioner for South Africa.

Milner, for many reasons—not the least being his German birth and paternal antecedents—was the per-

---

[50] A. P. Thornton, *The Imperial Idea and Its Enemies* (London: Macmillan, 1959), pp. 88–89.

sonification of the attitudes which Belloc despised. A student at Balliol—that nest of much of the new liberalism that despised the older radicalism—Milner broke with the Liberals on the Home Rule issue. Although he served under the Conservatives, he was much more at home with the Liberal-Imperialists. He combined his sense of imperial mission with a sympathy for "collectivism," or the vigorous use of state power to enhance the quality of national life. He was typical of that political phenomenon known as social imperialism, and illustrated how imperialism was very much a new kind of radical idealism.[51] What had developed was a curious combination of Tory paternalism and collectivism that sought to use political power to correct and ameliorate conditions at home and abroad which, it was argued, would be left uncorrected or allowed to worsen under the laissez-faire and Little England approach of the older radicalism.

Significantly, imperialism drew the support of important members of the Fabian Society. For instance, George Bernard Shaw could defend the Boer War. He did so, not in a jingoist sense, but on the grounds that since the cause of international civilization must prevail over romantic nationalism, it was appropriate that a backward, retrogressive society, like that of the Boers,

---

[51] Semmel, *Imperialism and Social Reform*, pp. 177–87; A. J. P. Taylor, *The Troublemakers* (London: Hamish Hamilton, 1957), pp. 90–91.

be absorbed by the modern and liberal British Empire. This position did not commit him to unreserved support of the government or of actions taken in the name of imperialism, especially should they contradict what should be the civilizing and progressive consequences of imperialism. While Shaw's views were published in a Fabian pamplet, *Fabianism and the Empire,* the nearest the society itself came to an endorsement of imperialism was the narrow defeat, in a referendum of the membership, of a proposal that a condemnatory resolution be made about imperialism and the war. Anti-imperialist sentiments were expressed within the society by G. N. Barnes, Ramsay MacDonald, and S. G. Hobson, whose resolution condemning the war was rejected at a Fabian meeting along with a prowar amendment offered by Shaw.[52]

There remained during the "zenith" of imperialism a number of persistent critics, whose ranks would increase and become more articulate after 1900 as the Boer War became much more costlier in lives and effort than had originally been expected. Two who criticized vehemently at a time when imperialism was not as costly or as in disfavor were Henry Labouchere and Wilfrid Scawen Blunt.

The radical leader Labouchere, unlike Chamberlain,

---

[52] A. M. McBriar, *Fabian Socialism and English Politics, 1884–1918* (Cambridge: At the University Press, 1962), pp. 119–30.

kept the Bright-Cobden faith in his hostility toward empire building. Much of his hostility was based upon the traditional radical fear that overseas and imperial commitments would involve enormous public expenditures and increase the executive power in areas free from direct parliamentary surveillance. An example was the virtual independence from the rest of the government that Rosebery had as Foreign Secretary. The development of Liberal-Unionism and Liberal-Imperialism confirmed Labouchere's view that the Whigs and the Tories were virtually identical. Imperialism and its consequence—an executive free from parliamentary and fiscal control—enhanced the Whig approach to politics, which he regarded as simply "a game between two rival aristocratic bands," as well as the Tory approach, which insisted on the necessity for a superior class to govern the people who could not govern themselves.[53]

A more remarkable antiimperialist was Wilfrid Scawen Blunt, near whose Sussex estate Belloc came to live in 1902. Blunt came from the very landed gentry that Labouchere-type radicals despised. His father was a squire who possessed four thousand acres, a justice of the peace, a deputy lieutenant of Sussex, master of the local fox hounds, and a devoted follower of the Duke of Wellington. Like Labouchere, Blunt served for a while in the diplomatic service, but after the death of

---

[53] Thornton, *Imperial Idea,* pp. 84–88.

his elder brother settled down with his wife on his ancestral estates and turned his attention to architecture, sculpture, and poetry. Then in 1875 he and his wife commenced a series of journeys through the Arabic world, from which he developed a kind of identification with Islam, having lost his Roman Catholic faith. Blunt began to break with officialdom about the time of the Egyptian occupation in 1882, which he was almost alone in opposing, as he sided with the cause of the Egyptian nationalists. Later he would sympathize with Home Rule, and even incur imprisonment for his efforts to oppose the policy of coercion in Ireland. The rest of his years he devoted to criticism of European imperialism, especially its more brutal and legally questionable deeds, and to fulfilling what he regarded as his "mission in life, that of pleading the cause of the backward nations of the world, and especially those of Asia and Africa, from their slavery to Europe."[54]

From such critics came a vision of imperialism quite different from that missionary or civilizing picture painted by the mass press and popular writers, like Rudyard Kipling, H. Rider Haggard, and G. A. Henty, which had become part of the code inculcated into the British ruling class, especially during their public school days.[55]

---

[54] Wilfrid Scawen Blunt, *My Diaries, 1888–1914* (London: Martin Secker, 1932; first published in 2 vols., 1919–20), p. 1.

[55] Thornton, *Imperial Idea,* pp. 90–94.

The radicals, instead, tended to view imperialism, especially the expansion of European authority over undeveloped areas in Africa and Asia, as having been inspired in large part by the opportunities for private profiteering. This profiteering consisted of either outright plundering and robbery of the natives or speculative gains in the shares of enterprises set up to finance overseas ventures. The British intervention in Egypt in 1882, for instance, was a move to save the private investments of the Suez Canal Company shareholders, as well as the bondholders in the indebted Egyptian government, lest they should lose all following a repudiation of debt by a revolutionary nationalist government in Egypt. Labouchere's journal, *Truth,* likewise paid great attention to the rapid climb and then decline in the value of South African mining shares just before the Jameson raid at the end of 1895.

Belloc became a major poet of this cynical view of imperialism. Naturally, an English member of the Ligue des Patriotes would interpret the financial and speculative aspects of British imperialism in a way somewhat similar to the response of French nationalists to the Panama Canal Company scandal of 1892 and 1893, that is, as a form of profiteering against the public good by a handful of cosmopolitan financiers who were, in significant numbers, Jewish. He turned his pen against the financial conspirators and their major servants, whether they were bankrupt aristocrats trying to restore their position by speculative ventures, or journalists and men of letters glorifying the empire, or freebooting adventurers whom others glorified as the makers of the empire.

For instance, in his mock-heroic poem "The Modern Traveller," the narrator gave an account to a journalist from "The Daily Menace" of his recent expedition to Africa. His colleagues were Commander Henry Sin, a mercenary adventurer, who was

> Untaught
> Lazy, and something of a liar,
> . . . .
> A little slovenly in dress,
> A trifle prone to drunkenness;
> A gambler also to excess,
>   And never known to pay,

and William Blood, a man of a different stamp, who in other times would have been a political leader or a warrior. However, fortune

> Had marked him for a great career
> Of more congenial kind—
> A sort of modern buccaneer,
> Commercial and refined.
> Like all great men, his chief affairs
> Were buying stocks and selling shares.[56]

The tale of "The Modern Traveller" concerned an effort to swindle some African natives. However, the

---

[56] Hilaire Belloc, "The Modern Traveller" (first published 1898), *The Verse of Hilaire Belloc,* ed. W. N. Roughead (Holland: None-such Press, 1954), pp. 166–67, 171.

attempt was less than successful as the narrator had to sacrifice his companions to save his own skin. Cowardice, deceit, and treachery dominated their adventures and contrasted decidedly with the energetic, fearless, adventurous, and noble empire builders of the G. A. Henty and H. Rider Haggard novels.

The Boer War acted as a great stimulus to the expression of traditional radical Little England feelings. The radical position was brought to light more through the weekly reviews and the press than by statements in Parliament, thanks in part to the effect of increasing popular literacy on the styles of journalism—papers seeking a broad readership tended to drop the printing of parliamentary debates. The radical bypassing of Parliament also resulted from another development which Belloc would come to lament—the declining importance of the independent MP.[57]

A major advocate of the antiimperialist position was H. W. Massingham, the editor of the *Daily Chronicle* until a change in ownership in 1899 forced out the pro-Boers. They conveniently moved over to the previously imperialist *Daily News,* the purchase of which by a pro-Boer syndicate had forced the ouster of the imperialist editor, E. T. Cook, at about the same time. Another center for pro-Boer writing was the *Speaker,* the Liberal weekly that had been taken over by Belloc's

[57] Taylor, *The Troublemakers,* pp. 95–96.

Oxford collaborators in the *Essays in Liberalism,* with J. L. Hammond assuming the editorship. The success of and *raison d'être* for the *Speaker* traced in large part to hostility to the war, and upon the conclusion of the war the paper declined and its contributors scattered.[58] Later it was taken over by Massingham, under whom it was renamed the *Nation,* and it attracted many of the pro-Boer antiimperialist writers of the *Daily News* and the *Speaker.*

It was through the *Speaker* group that Belloc first met G. K. Chesterton, formerly a writer for the *Daily News,* and very rapidly they developed a rapport. Belloc and Chesterton, with others of the *Speaker* group, especially its literary editor, F. Y. Eccles (one of Belloc's colleagues in the Oxford Republican Club), opposed the war because they were sympathetic with the Boers. Rather than object on pacifist grounds, they condemned the war as an immoral abuse of the English fighting forces and national treasure for the benefit of alien financiers. Chesterton noted the "subconscious sympathy" that had developed in his first meeting with Belloc: "We were both pro-Boers who hated pro-Boers. Perhaps it would be truer to say that we hated a certain number of unimaginative, unhistorical anti-militarists who were too pedantic to call themselves pro-Boers."[59] This attitude would in a few years put Belloc and

---

[58] Hirst, *In the Golden Days,* pp. 204–5.
[59] Chesterton, *Autobiography,* p. 115.

Chesterton completely at odds with so many of those who were their allies at the time of the Boer War, but who would be their antagonists on the issue of the Entente and World War I.

Belloc's anger at the idea of England being used by alien financiers appeared in "To the Balliol Men Still in Africa," his lament for his college mates who were in the imperial services:

> I have said it before, and I say it again,
> There was treason done, and a false word spoken,
> And England under the dregs of men,
> And bribes about, and a treaty broken:
> . . . .
> Rare and single! Noble and few! . . .
> Oh! they have wasted you over the sea!
> The only brothers ever I knew,
> The men that laughed and quarreled with me.[60]

He employed his satirical talents for the *Speaker* in a series of articles that were ostensibly a handbook for aspiring writers. Entitled *Caliban's Guide to Letters,* it was the effort of Thomas Caliban, the very type of popular journalist who had helped create the popular imperialist fervor, to impart the secrets of his trade partly by providing examples of his own work. One example was an interview by Caliban of a Kipling type: "a man here who should *count,* who should *tell* . . . a

---

[60] Hilaire Belloc, "To the Balliol Men Still in Africa," *The Verse of Belloc,* p. 44.

man with something in him quite peculiar and apart.
. . . It is England through and through, and the best of
England." The subject of the interview described his
effort "to imprint this idea of the law upon the mind of
the English-speaking world." The idea of the law, he
insisted, was "the strongest thing in modern England."
He summarized the law in the simple admonition, "Do
this because I tell you, or it will be the worse for you."
Such was all that need be known to have a great
civilization.[61]

At the time of the Boer War there appeared a more
theoretical or analytical criticism of imperialism, which
complemented the less analytical attacks such as Belloc's or Labouchere's. This was the work of J. A.
Hobson, who tried to refute the economic justifications
given for the late nineteenth-century imperial expansion: that it provided new markets for British foreign
trade and served as an outlet for a growing British
population. He argued that imperialism had not
brought such benefits, but, because of its enormous
expense, had "jeopardized the entire wealth of the
nation." While the nation as a whole suffered from
imperialism, he noted that there were certain vested
interests that had profited tremendously by it. These

[61] Hilaire Belloc, *Caliban's Guide to Letters* (London: Duckworth,
1920; first published 1903), pp. 85, 93.

included the professional imperialist services such as the military and the diplomatic corps, the manufacturers of those products essential for imperial endeavors, and the shipping industry. But the most important beneficiaries, he reckoned, were the investors who profited at a high rate from loans to foreign and colonial governments and from investments in communications services, lands, and mines in foreign and colonial territories. He attributed the imperialist policies of Great Britain primarily to the desire of the investing classes for new areas of investment. But he regarded the investors themselves as "the cat's paw of the great financial houses," who were interested in investment not so much for interest as for speculative purposes. Calling the financial houses "the central ganglion of international capitalism," Hobson described their role as follows:

> United by the strongest bonds of organization, always in closest and quickest touch with one another, situated in the very heart of the business capital of every state, controlled, so far as Europe is concerned, chiefly by men of a single and peculiar race, who have behind them many centuries of financial experience, they are in a unique position to control the policy of nations.

He admitted that there were other factors, such as patriotism, adventure, military enterprise, political ambition, and philanthropy, which provided the motor power and the fuel for imperialism. But he insisted that finance was "the governor of the imperial engine, directing the energy and determining its work."[62]

Belloc gave literary expression to this view of imperialism in his satirical novel *Emmanuel Burden* (which had originally appeared in the *Speaker*). The central character, Emmanuel Burden, was an iron merchant who was duped by his son's creditors into becoming one of the original subscribers of a company organized ostensibly to develop a river delta in Africa but in reality to develop a scheme for speculative profits. Among the cabal running the scheme were an "international" Jewish financier, I. Z. Barnett, and a noble, Lord Benthrope. The latter was the stereotype of an aristocracy losing much of its social and political power because of declining economic circumstances ever since the great agricultural depression of the 1870s, and seeking to recoup through speculative ventures connected with imperialism. The cabal was able to enlist the aid of clergymen, academicians, and journalists especially in the glorifying of their venture as part of Britain's imperial destiny. The most admirable character in the novel was a shipping merchant friend of Burden's, a Mr. Abbott, who rejected all requests, plus intimidation, to lend his entrepreneurial prestige to the scheme. He personified the Victorian middle-class type that had been debunked by writers, especially

---

[62] J. A. Hobson, *Imperialism: A Study,* 3d ed. (London: Duckworth, 1938; first published 1902), pp. 56–59.

the poets of imperialism, as his views were basically that traditional radicalism that Belloc admired. He believed in free trade, the gold standard, and had a Little Englander's disregard for "foreigners." He did not share the imperial vision, but loved "the soil, the air, the habit" of England. Unlike Burden, he had continued to support Gladstone after his endorsement of Home Rule. Furthermore, he shared "every illusion a belated radical can nourish," as he viewed the occupation of Egypt as having been "provoked by a group of bankers and scripholders," and was convinced "that the problems of Irish land were principally due to the greed of English moneylenders."[63]

Recent historians have tended to deemphasize the purely economic interpretation that the radicals made of imperialism. It is argued, instead, that late Victorian policy in Africa was dependent more on the Foreign Office's conception of Britain's strategic and political requirements than on any pressure by finance capitalism. The Foreign Office simply adhered to the traditional precept that "British strength depended upon the possession of India and preponderance in the East," and African policy was formulated primarily with that consideration in mind.[64] Further proof of the insignifi-

---

[63] Hilaire Belloc, *Emmanuel Burden* (New York: Charles Scribner's Sons, 1904), pp. 197–99, 272.

[64] Ronald Robinson and John Gallagher, with Alice Denny, *Africa and the Victorians* (New York: St. Martin's Press, 1961), p. 464.

cance of economic considerations in imperial policy was the relatively small percentage of the total British overseas investment that went to the Afro-Asian areas annexed after 1870.[65]

The controversy over the Boer War gave new life to the forces of radicalism. Naturally, the pro-Boers or Little Englanders, like Morley, Labouchere, and young Welsh radical MP David Lloyd George, had to undergo the taunt of their being "unpatriotic" during the Khaki election of October 1900, a contest in which the Unionist government was able to benefit from numerous victories in the war which suggested that it was all but over. Even with this asset, however, the government's victory was not that impressive, for its parliamentary majority, although substantial (134), was smaller than the majority after the 1895 election. Furthermore, in the popular vote the Unionist majority was only 300,000 in a total vote of four and a half million. The radical position improved much more the next year when the supposedly defeated Boers commenced their guerrilla warfare. The campaign against them became increasingly unpopular and distasteful as objections were raised not only to the unexpectedly high costs of the war in British manpower and treasure, but also to the tactics used to suppress the Boers.

---

[65] D. K. Fieldhouse, "Imperialism: An Historiographical Revision," *Economic History Review,* 2d ser. 14 (December 1961): 197.

The decline in imperialist fervor as a result of the war, which ended in 1902, was followed by divisions and dissensions within the Unionist camp over the issues of protectionism and education. This opened the way for a great Liberal and radical resurgence. However, this resurgence was complicated by the continuance of differences within the Liberal Party, differences that almost reached the point of schism during the Boer War, between the radicals and the Liberal-Imperialists. Even after the was was over, the division over differences continued, especially in the approach to domestic issues. The presence in the Liberal government of 1905 of Liberal-Imperialists made unlikely the thorough pursuit of a traditional radical policy that would appeal to those like Belloc. Was the failure of the traditional radical measures proposed by the Liberal government elected in 1906 a proof of the insincerity of party politics, as Belloc came to believe? Was the election of 1906 a mandate for traditional radicalism, or was it more a call for a newer radicalism, or collectivism, concerning which policy the Liberal-Imperialists were more adaptable?

Chapter Two

Liberal Revival, 1901–05

The division of the parliamentary Liberal Party into nearly equal groups of radical pro-Boers and Liberal-Imperialists almost brought about the dissolution of the party. Differences on the question of the war were intensified by the determination of the Liberal-Imperialists to challenge the basic laissez-faire principles of traditional radicalism. But Liberal disunity was temporarily smothered when the prospects for a return to office brightened because of the number of lively controversial issues within the Unionist camp. These were Joseph Chamberlain's espousal of tariff reform, the 1902 Education Act, and the 1904 licensing legislation. Furthermore, the Liberal position on protection, education, and licensing was formulated in accord with the central themes of nineteenth-century liberalism and radicalism: free trade, religious disestablishment, and Nonconformist temperance reform. Indeed, a contemporary or a superficial observer of the spirit of British

politics in the early years of this century might easily
have interpreted it as a continuation of the nineteenth-
century struggle between church and chapel, privilege
and radicalism.

Hilaire Belloc entered the political arena sharing this
radical enthusiasm. He saw his personal electoral success and the general Liberal victory in 1906 as a mandate for a final assault on the privileged establishment.
There were other things, however, troubling an electorate which found the radical causes increasingly irrelevant. This diversion became manifest before the decade
was out, and explained both the Unionist success in
blocking radical legislation and the Liberal government's reluctance to push its program very far. But
Belloc interpreted the failure of traditional radicalism
as a betrayal of the electors and an example of the
essentially corrupt character of British party politics.

During the Boer War the Liberal MPs had divided
three ways. The pro-Boers, such as Harcourt, Morley,
Labouchere, and Lloyd George, were totally opposed
to the war and blamed Great Britain for causing it.
They were about equal in number to the Liberal-
Imperialists, such as Asquith, Grey, and Haldane, who
believed the ultimatum of the Boers to have caused
the war and regarded British annexation of the Transvaal and the Orange Free State as an ideal outcome of
the war. A smaller center group, which followed the
party's leader, Henry Campbell-Bannerman, who

sought to maintain party unity, tended to blame Great Britain for the outbreak of the war, but once it had started supported the government in its efforts to annex the Boer states. Despite these differences, all Liberal candidates were branded as "pro-Boers" by the Unionists during the 1900 Khaki election. The Liberal Imperial Council sought to dissociate the Liberal-Imperialists from the rest of the party and thereby to save itself from the opprobrium of treason, but was in turn condemned by Campbell-Bannerman for being divisive. The inner party feuding intensified in the spring of 1901, following the return to England of Alfred Milner, the High Commissioner of South Africa, whose diplomatic tactics were regarded by the pro-Boers as a major cause of the war. The attendance of leading Liberal-Imperialists like Grey and Henry Fowler at testimonial dinners for Milner, incurred the strong disapproval of such pro-Boers as James Bryce and John Morley, who labeled Milner an "imitation Bismarck." About this time Campbell-Bannerman was drawn more to the radical side when he condemned as "methods of barbarism" the concentration camp tactics used by the government against the guerrilla warfare of the Boers. The famous "war to the knife and fork" was launched within the party as the various factions held dinners at which the speakers condemned the other factions. Efforts at stemming party disunity were eventually made by Campbell-Bannerman, who summoned a special party meeting at which he was able to secure

a unanimous vote of confidence in his leadership, and
by Asquith, who, while insisting that the existence of
differences within the party could not be smothered,
sought to disclaim any Liberal-Imperialist intention to
secede.[1]

The efforts at conciliation were complicated by the
return to the political wars of the leading Liberal-
Imperialist, the former Prime Minister, Lord Rosebery.
Following his resignation from the party leadership
in 1896, Rosebery, to the dismay of many of his
younger admirers in the party, had absented himself
from politics except for making a few proimperialist
statements and endorsing a Liberal-Imperialist candidate in the 1900 election. Then, in a letter to the *Times*
on July 17, 1901, he insisted that the Liberal Party
"must make up its mind about the war. . . . One school
or the other must prevail if the Liberal Party is once
more to become a force." But, just as startlingly, he
again disappointed the Liberal-Imperialists, who might
have been willing to follow his lead in secession. He
decided to remain aloof from any active political role,
asserting that "for the present, at any rate, I must
proceed alone. I must plough my furrow alone." But
the following December 15, in a speech at Chesterfield,
Rosebery returned to the fray. Taking a new turn, he
devoted some of his talk to criticizing the Unionist
government, and Milner especially, for inept handling

---

[1] Roy Jenkins, *Asquith* (London: Collins, 1964), pp. 137–39.

of negotiations with the Boers. Then, turning to domestic questions, he labeled the radicals within the Liberal Party as really being "Tory in the pejorative sense of the word" in that they "sit still with the fly-blown phylacteries of obsolete policies bound round their foreheads, who do not remember that while they have been mumbling their incantations to themselves, the world has been marching and revolving. . . ." The traditional radical causes, such as those of the Newcastle program, especially Irish Home Rule, should be abandoned, as he urged the Liberals to write on their "clean slate . . . a policy adapted to 1901 or 1902, and not a policy adapted to 1892 or 1885."[2]

The speech was notable on two counts. For one thing it reflected increasing impatience even by the professed imperialists with the war, or at least its expensive and inconclusive duration. It automatically caused consideration of Rosebery as an alternative Prime Minister of a possible coalition government that was not pro-Boer, Little Englander, or "unpatriotic." For instance, the *Times,* which had intensified its criticism of the Unionist government's inefficient waging of the war, was naturally hopeful that Rosebery would insist that the Liberal leadership dissociate itself from the extreme pro-Boer radicals.[3] Second, Rosebery's attitude drew

---

[2] Robert Rhodes James, *Rosebery* (New York: Macmillan, 1963), pp. 425–26, 432.

[3] S. Maccoby, *English Radicalism, 1886–1914* (London: George Allen & Unwin, 1953), p. 326.

support, not just from conservatives anxious for a more efficient imperialist government, but also from the more scientific and less dogmatic radicals like the Fabian socialists Sidney and Beatrice Webb. Writing in the *Nineteenth Century,* Sidney Webb had seen in Rosebery a possible opposition to the Unionists who could present an alternative other than "a defunct liberalism." He had taken the first step in this direction by having "turned his back on Houndsditch and called for a complete new outfit" in contrast to Campbell-Bannerman's efforts at "piecing together the Gladstonian rags and remnants, with Sir William Harcourt holding the scissors, and Mr. John Morley unctuously waxing the thread."

They saw the older liberalism as putting various political, religious, and social impediments in the way of progress, as having outlived its usefulness. Furthermore, its concepts of "freedom of contract," "supply and demand," and "voluntaryism" had actually worked out disastrously for the masses, whose economic power was insufficient to obtain "even the minimum conditions of physical and mental health necessary to national well-being." The new age required men to think about community relationships, as their well-being could be realized, not by individual action, but only by the collective endeavors of unions, municipal enterprises, cooperative societies, and the state. In this regard, the views of the older radicals were quite inadequate.

Their conception of freedom means only breaking somebody's bonds asunder. When the "higher freedom" of corporate life is in question, they become angrily reactionary, and denounce and obstruct every new development of common action.

Optimistic because of the Roseberyite diagnosis of the weakness of traditional radicalism, Webb urged the Roseberyites to launch a campaign to win the country to "a policy of national efficiency," whereby the government would "ensure the rearing of an imperial race." This policy would aim at correcting the condition of the sweated trades, stimulating municipal enterprises, and promoting comprehensive national education. At the time, however, they did not expect the Roseberyites "to declare themselves in favor of our measure of collectivism, although they held no views that are inconsistent with it."[4]

The already imminent Liberal split became even more imminent in February 1902 with the formation of the Liberal League, an extraparty organization, for the purpose of promoting Liberal-Imperialist ideas, including the desire for a "clean slate" of Liberal doctrine. Rosebery was its president, and Asquith, Grey, and Haldane were vice presidents. It attracted the political sympathy of such diverse sources of anti–

---

[4] Sidney Webb, "Lord Rosebery's Escape from Houndsditch," *Nineteenth Century* (September 1901), in Beatrice Webb, *Our Partnership* (London: Longmans, Green, 1948), pp. 220–24.

Little Englandism as the Fabians and the Harmsworth press. As the same time, Campbell-Bannerman moved more and more toward the radical side. After unsuccessful attempts at reconciliation with Rosebery, he announced that he was "not prepared to erase from the tablets of my creed any principle or measure or proposal or ideal or aspiration of liberalism."[5] The impending schism was soon overshadowed, however, by developments over which the Liberal Party had no control, but from which it would benefit considerably. For one thing, the Boer War, the major *raison d'être* of the schism, came to an end on May 12, 1902, with the signing of the Peace of Vereeniging. During the preceding two months, moreover, the Unionist government had introduced into Parliament two measures which would ultimately rally the feuding Liberal factions and split the forces of Unionism. These were the education bill, introduced on March 24, 1902, which raised again the specter of church versus chapel, and the introduction, on April 14, as part of the budget, of a one-shilling duty on corn. The latter, which the Chancellor of the Exchequer, Sir Michael Hicks Beach, reluctantly agreed to against his free-trade principles, was strictly for revenue purposes since increasing government expenses had exhausted all other means of indirect taxation. In the following year the Colonial Secretary, Joseph Chamberlain, completely altered the

---

[5] James, *Rosebery,* p. 437.

ground rules of political discussion and almost wrecked his party by his proposal to broaden this duty into a thorough system of imperial preference.

It was into this changed political arena that Hilaire Belloc threw his hat, at first as a Liberal propagandist and later as an actual candidate for Parliament.

Following the advice of Edward Caird, Jowett's successor at Balliol, that he not seek a professorship at Glasgow University where, he had been informed, his religion would bar his selection, Belloc abandoned any remaining ambition for an academic career and moved to London in 1900 to be in closer contact with the literary and journalistic world.[6] Within the next five years he intensified his literary output. In addition to the biographies, collections of verse, and satires already mentioned, he wrote essays and articles for the *Speaker,* the *Daily News,* and even the *Daily Mail.* The last he regarded as comparable to making friends with the devil, who, he noted, paid "exorbitantly well."[7] Anxiety about an income to support his family, which by this time had grown to five children, persisted with Belloc, even after he had attained great success. This was probably the reason for many of his prolific and often redundant writings, and explains "why so much of his

[6] Robert Speaight, *The Life of Hilaire Belloc* (New York: Farrar, Straus & Cudahy, 1957), pp. 121–22.

[7] Belloc to Maria Lansdale, March 14, 1903, Princeton University Library.

work has melted away."[8] Still, some of his most lasting work was produced in this period, such as his translation of J. Bédier's French version of *The Romance of Tristan and Iseult,* and *Avril,* a collection of critical essays on the literature of the French Renaissance.

In 1902 he published what many regard as his most enduring and most typical book. It was the notebook of experiences and reflections on a pilgrimage made on foot the previous spring from Toul in France to Rome. In *The Path to Rome* there was manifest another aspect of Belloc's *weltanschauung* that was very different from his own nineteenth-century radicalism, but equally, if not more, hostile to the doctrine of social efficiency called for by the Fabians and groped toward by the Liberal-Imperialists. Belloc's work had a spirit of romantic neomedievalism which idealized a precapitalist, prenationalist Christian Europe where the social Darwinist concepts of racial politics were nonexistent. Naturally, he admired the prevailing Catholicism of that time when "once all we Europeans understood each other" in contrast to his own era when "we are divided by the worst malignancies of nations and classes."[9]

Belloc differed from other reformers and critics, like

---

[8] Hesketh Pearson, *Lives of the Wits* (New York: Harper & Row, 1962), p. 279.

[9] Hilaire Belloc, *The Path to Rome* (Garden City, N.Y.: Doubleday, Image Books, 1956; first published 1902), p. 66.

the Fabian socialist Graham Wallas who, in his *Great Society,* saw the major challenge for mankind to be the scientific and psychological adjustment of its instincts and habits to a highly technical, interdependent, and urbanized society in a way that would best approach rational and humanist ideals.[10] Instead, Belloc believed that man could "be fairly happy . . . and, what is more important, decent and secure of our souls," only by gaining that "feeling of satisfaction" which results from doing what "is buried right into our blood from immemorial habit" and "what the human race has done for thousands upon thousands of years": traditional and natural activities such as hunting, drinking "fermented liquor with one's food—and especially deeply upon great feast days," going to sea, dancing, and singing in chorus. Another wise thought, he insisted, was that "every man should do a little work with his hands."[11]

Belloc, not content to limit himself to a literary career, prepared himself for the bar. Upon presenting himself for the examination, however, he was discouraged by one look at the test papers and departed. He decided to substitute politics for the abandoned legal

---

[10] Graham Wallas, *The Great Society* (New York: Macmillan, 1914).

[11] Belloc, *Path to Rome,* p. 39.

ambitions. His quest for a parliamentary candidacy was satisfied in May 1904 when the local selection committee of the constituency of South Salford, an industrial suburb of Manchester, accepted the National Liberal Association's recommendation of him as a candidate. It was a predominantly working-class district, having, like much of Lancashire, a significant Irish Catholic component in its population. The Conservatives had held the seat since 1886, partly because in both 1892 and 1895 the presence of an Independent Labor candidate lessened the Liberal vote. Conservative successes had been common throughout Lancashire, especially among the working class. This working-class Conservatism might have resulted from hostility to the Liberalism of middle-class employers, although the employer class had begun rapidly to shift toward Conservatism. Probably more important as a cause of working-class Conservatism in Lancashire was dislike of the massive Irish immigration, which had made Lancashire the most Catholic county in England.[12] Against these Conservative trends must be noted the important assistance Liberalism in Lancashire had received from Lord Derby's change of party allegiance following his resignation in 1878 from Disraeli's cabinet out of opposition to the pro-Turkish foreign policy. His influence counteracted that of Tory

---

[12] Henry Pelling, *Social Geography of British Elections, 1885–1910* (London: Macmillan, 1967), pp. 241–45, 284–87.

landlords in the region, especially in the boroughs where other forces inhibited landlord predominance.[13]

Belloc benefited from a strong Lancashire belief in free trade, which was regarded as essential to the future of the local cotton and coal industries. He stood firmly for free trade against the specter of imperial preference, or ultimately protection, which had been raised by Chamberlain. The Unionist Colonial Secretary had hoped imperial preference would forge a material bond of imperial unity that would overcome any weakness in imperial loyalty and strength that had resulted from the Boer War or from the isolated diplomatic position in which that war had placed the British Empire.[14] This proposal severely upset the equilibrium of the Unionist cabinet, which had come under the leadership of Arthur Balfour upon the resignation in the previous year of his uncle, Lord Salisbury. Balfour had no doctrinal objections to imperial preference, but he was anxious lest it should endanger Unionist unity and cause a loss of power before the government had properly attended to what he regarded as more essential considerations, the preservation of the union with Ireland and reform of the defense structure of the empire.[15]

---

[13] Trevor Lloyd, *The General Election of 1880* (London: Oxford University Press, 1968), pp. 119–20, 151.

[14] Peter Fraser, *Joseph Chamberlain* (London: Cassell, 1966), pp. 235–36.

[15] R. B. McDowell, *British Conservatism, 1832–1914* (London: Faber & Faber, 1959), p. 171.

He persuaded the opposing factions in the cabinet—Chamberlain and his followers, and the free traders like C. T. Ritchie, the Chancellor of the Exchequer, Lord Balfour of Burleigh, and Lord George Hamilton —temporarily to postpone public discussion of the issue. Then in September 1903, after having received Chamberlain's offer of resignation to free himself to wage in behalf of imperial preference a public campaign that would not be directed against the ministry, Balfour forced the resignations of the above-mentioned free traders. Later the Duke of Devonshire, the most politically powerful free-trade Unionist and Chamberlain's old colleague in the leadership of Liberal Unionism, also resigned.

The free-trade Unionists opposed Chamberlain's ideas not just because of their belief in free trade, but also because they viewed his campaign as an attack on the traditional structure and position of the party comparable to the Liberal-Imperialists' efforts to "clean the slate" of Gladstonian liberalism. This was because the movement of Chamberlain, who himself came from radical, Nonconformist, middle-class stock, was presenting an extraparty, popularly based challenge to a traditional, closed, hierarchical Conservative Party leadership, dominated by landed elements who were often bound closely together by family ties. One of that group, the young MP Winston Churchill, who would eventually secede to the Liberal Party because of the free-trade issue, feared that Chamberlain's dream of imperial preference would lead to an Americanization of British politics, that is, to the replacement of the traditional and hierarchical Conservatism that defended the landed interest and the established church with a new party led by "rich, materialist, and secular" commercial and mercantile elements and influenced by "the touts of protected industry."[16] Churchill's fears proved valid as the tariff-reform movement gradually, under the prodding of journalistic supporters like Alfred Harmsworth and industrial backers like the steel and mining executives Charles Allen, Sir Alfred Hickman, and Sir W. T. Lewis, shifted its appeal from imperial preference to protection for British industry. It also presented itself as the means for financing social reform. This was regarded as the only type of appeal that could attract the masses of the British electorate away from the national orthodoxy of free trade and the hostility, which the Liberals earnestly evoked, to "stomach taxes," or the taxes on food which were involved in imperial preference.[17]

The tariff reformers shared many motives with the Liberal-Imperialists: a commitment to the empire, the strengthening of British society through the positive use of state power, and a rejection of the nineteenth-century distrust of the state. Common to both movements was

---

[16] Alfred M. Gollin, *Balfour's Burden* (London: Anthony Blond, 1965), pp. 57–61.

[17] *Ibid.*, pp. 196–203.

an emphasis upon national efficiency, which stressed
administrative reform and a scientific assault on the
various social and economic problems impeding the
flourishing of an "imperial race." Naturally such scien-
tifically oriented attitudes were completely antithetical
to both elements of Belloc's outlook—his medievalism
and his nineteenth-century radicalism. Appropriately,
both tariff reformers, such as Leopold Maxse, the editor
of the *National Review,* Leopold Amery, the chief cor-
respondent of the *Times* for the Boer War, and W. A. S.
Hewins, the director of the London School of Economics, and Liberal-Imperialists, such as Haldane and
Grey along with the Fabian socialist H. G. Wells, were
members of a small dining club founded by the Webbs
and called the Coefficients. The group was intended as
a potential brain trust for a contemplated new national
party committed to the empire and efficiency. But tariff
reform broke up the Coefficients, and made academic
any visions of such a party.[18] Indeed, the hostility of
many Conservatives to Chamberlain's campaign created for a time a possibility of a Liberal opening to
the right whereby the free-trade Conservatives would
join with the Liberals in a coalition under a Liberal-
Imperialist, ideally, Rosebery. The increasing success
of Liberals in by-elections, however, and the likelihood
of their being able to form a majority by themselves,

---

[18] Bernard Semmel, *Imperialism and Social Reform* (London:
George Allen & Unwin, 1960), pp. 75–82.

as well as the failure of the free-trade movement within the Conservative ranks, brought not a free-trade coalition but a small secession of Conservatives to Liberalism, the most notable seceder being Winston Churchill.[19]

Belloc followed a standard radical approach in his criticism of protection: that the benefits it could bring existed already, whereas the evils it could correct would not have existed except for the power of monopoly privilege to use government for its own purposes and to the detriment of community well-being. He could find in England none of what he regarded as possible justification for a system of protection, such as impediments to internal exchange within a nation or an inability to discover foreign markets. Instead, England's system of internal communications was such as to make it the leader in industrial affairs. England was also "the one nation which has best studied and acquired foreign markets." Furthermore, because of the complex nature of the English economy, he saw no country "better fitted with ready and concentrated floating capital, rapid and frequent information, diversity of machinery or central position to turn at once to the development of a new industry on the failure of an old one."

Admitting that many areas of Great Britain's potential agricultural and industrial energy were undevel-

---

[19] Jenkins, *Asquith*, pp. 154–57.

oped, Belloc insisted this was the consequence of economic evils for which protection was no cure. Instead, an enormous waste of capital existed because of "the laxity of our commercial laws and our modern toleration of speculative scoundrelism." Any weakness of England's dairy, forestry, and agricultural sectors was "simply because our great landlords have ruined the land." In short, the misapplication or unemployment of English resources and manpower could not be corrected by interference with foreign trade because it resulted from "a system of government in which it is our pleasure that the community should never defend the weak, and in which it is our glory that the rich alone should have a voice in government."[20]

Opposed though he was to the protectionist movement, Belloc was forced to admit that it was more than a passing enthusiasm, that it was in fact an enduring challenge to British political orthodoxy because its appeal was based upon certain strong attitudes in British public life. One of these attitudes he called the sense of "the practical," or "the tendency to regard each problem as it arises in the concrete." He insisted that it was mainly this attitude rather than pure economic doctrine which had accounted for the original establishment of free trade; that is, English society had been attracted by the obvious immediate benefits that seemed likely to re-

---

[20] Hilaire Belloc, "The Argument for Protection," *Contemporary Review* 87 (June 1905): 842–43.

sult from it. At the beginning of the twentieth century, however, the same attitude was causing Englishmen to fear free trade, for they noticed the recent prosperity of protected countries like Germany, France, and the United States, the increasing number of foreign-made articles sold in England, the exclusion of British goods from certain foreign markets, and the decline of certain British industries as a result of foreign protection. Appeals based upon pure economic doctrine would be futile to those practical-minded Englishmen, who could not immediately perceive and appreciate what should have been countervailing assurances, namely, the expansion in shipping, the insurance business, and foreign investments. For them, "the phrase 'invisible exports' sounds . . . something like a jest."[21] Yet, these later factors had more than made up what had become an increasing deficit in British overseas trade. In the first few years of this century, furthermore, "visible exports" from Britain began for the first time in fifty years to grow more rapidly than imports.[22]

Belloc noted two other attitudes which, while not as important as the English spirit of practicality, were instrumental in fanning the flames of protectionism. They were "dislike of the foreigner" and what he called the

---

[21] Hilaire Belloc, "The Protectionist Movement in England," *The International Quarterly* 10 (October 1904): 183.

[22] Arthur J. Taylor, "The Economy," *Edwardian England, 1901–1914,* ed. Simon Nowell-Smith (London: Oxford University Press, 1964), pp. 109–10.

"individual development of the gentry." The meaning of the former is obvious. By the latter he meant the determination in any particular era of members of the ruling classes to commit themselves to any new idea or cause, by which they can push "to the uttermost extreme a passion for private experience, private adventure, and the private solutions" to the problems of the generation.[23] This attempt by Belloc to picture protectionism as an upper-class enthusiasm was inaccurate since many of the most outspoken free traders were Conservatives of ancient and prestigious lineage, like Winston Churchill and Lord Hugh Cecil, or Whigs, like the Duke of Devonshire, while the protectionists often came from newer wealth, middle-class, and even radical backgrounds, like Chamberlain himself and L. S. Amery.

Belloc was confident that those for whom traditional radicalism always had great solicitude, the small farmer and the agricultural laborer, would be against protection:

> Mr. Chamberlain's scheme would not only raise the price of the small farmer's implements, building material, feed, etc., in a small but irritating degree, it would harass him by putting an additional tax upon his clothes, his furniture, and his few luxuries. The agricultural laborer is also dead against it. He is against it on the simplest of grounds, the ground of the big loaf.[24]

---

23 Belloc, "Protectionist Movement," p. 185.

24 *Ibid.*, p. 186.

For the short run, he was convinced that the British electorate would remain committed to free trade and suspicious of "food taxes," a conviction massively borne out in the Liberal triumphs in the 1906 election, especially in Lancashire, Belloc's political stalking grounds. But he feared the long-run success of protectionism because it had the support of most of the great London daily papers and would appear attractive as a simplistic solution for any recurrence of bad times to that relatively recently enfranchised electorate, which was "gradually learning that the suffrage is a power which they can translate into legislation." But the force that he believed would cause the greatest demand for protection was the need of the treasury, which, in view of increased government expenses, was finding its traditional sources of indirect revenue all but exhausted.

In addition to the protection issue, there were two controversies occupying the public's attention at the time of Belloc's entry into politics which would have suggested to a contemporary that, contrary to the advocates of a new politics of national efficiency, the new century was simply continuing the controversies of the old. These controversies reflected traditional radical and Liberal hostility to two pieces of legislation of the Balfour government: the Education Act of 1902 and the Licensing Act of 1904.

Radical hostility toward the Education Act was, in the eyes of more pragmatic twentieth-century reformers, the most clear-cut example of the doctrinal irrelevance of nineteenth-century radicalism in the face of social urgency. Hailed by historian R. C. K. Ensor, a member of the Fabian Society, as being "among the two or three greatest constructive measures of the twentieth century,"[25] it was essentially an effort at rationalizing, centralizing, and modernizing the elementary, secondary, and technical schools of England and Wales. In some ways it seemed contradictory for such a measure to be opposed by radicals, who had regarded a universal and free, compulsory national education system as a key requirement for the preparation of the responsible citizenry so central in the radical ideal society. The National Education League had been formed in Birmingham to agitate for universal education. Significantly, one of the central figures in the league was Joseph Chamberlain, and it served as the nucleus around which he helped to organize in 1877 the National Liberal Federation, which sought to advance the cause of popular radicalism against the more conservative, or Whiggish, parliamentary Liberal Party. The radicals were displeased with the 1902 Education Act, however, for much the same reasons their forebears had opposed the 1870 act, the first comprehensive piece of national education legislation: it included denominational schools in the national education sys-

---

[25] R. C. K. Ensor, *England, 1870–1914* (London: Oxford University Press, 1936), p. 355.

tem, and appeared to give an advantage to those of the Church of England.

The 1870 act had called for the creation of school boards, to be elected by the rate payers, for localities in which the Education Department had determined there was a shortage of schools. These boards were then empowered to supplement the existing supply or non-supply of voluntary schools by erecting new ones, which were to be financed out of the rates. The religious instruction in these "board" schools was to be purely nondenominational. However, these rate-financed "board" schools were purely supplementary to the existing voluntary, denominational schools, which were qualified to receive an increased government grant which did not come from the school rates. The government was determined to maintain the denominational voluntary schools because of the view that public funds were insufficient to provide all of the necessary schools for a universal system.[26] Admittedly this act advanced, with governmental assistance, the ideal of universal education, which local boards were permitted to make compulsory, and which, in both "board" and "voluntary" elementary schools, was made free by an act of 1891. Yet it was not the radical ideal of a secular national system. It especially infuriated the Nonconformists because the Church of England schools were the

---

[26] John William Adamson, *English Education, 1789–1902* (Cambridge: At the University Press, 1930), pp. 353–60.

prime denominational beneficiaries and because the church's schools had an educational monopoly in some areas where, despite the presence of many dissenters, the authorities regarded those schools as sufficient for the district's educational needs. The late Victorian radical objective in education was asserted by Belloc's collaborator in the *Essays in Liberalism,* J. L. Hammond, who believed that schools should "be the public instruments of a popular authority, rather than the private weapons of a sectarian party . . . because education is so momentous in its results on character we dare not trust its direction to any but a public and popular authority, least of all to men who can forget the claims of citizenship, even if it be in obedience to the dictates of a church."[27]

The radicals were also dissatisfied with the 1902 act, which sought the expansion of the national government's role in education in matters of supervision as well as financial assistance. The framers of the act, especially its principal author, and Education Department official, Sir Robert Morant, who would become the permanent secretary of the Board of Education in 1903, were concerned less with the radical ideals of nonsectarianism and popular control than with efficiency and modernization, which necessitated centralization and the creation of common national standards.

---

[27] J. L. Hammond, "A Liberal View of Education," *Essays in Liberalism* (London: Cassell, 1897), pp. 216–17.

The act therefore established 318 local education authorities to replace the 2,568 school boards in controlling the board schools. The local authorities, unlike the old boards, were also empowered to provide out of the education rates maintenance expenses and teachers' salaries for the voluntary or denominational schools, which in turn accepted intensive state supervision in their secular curriculum, if not in their religious instruction. The authorities were able, furthermore, to provide secondary and higher education, which contrasted with the contradictory or uncertain mandate and attitude of the old boards as to their mission or the nature of secondary education.[28]

The continued and more direct assistance which the denominational schools received as a result of the act infuriated the traditional radicals. Their Nonconformist allies, whose own voluntary denominational schools had been declining in number, probably because of the satisfaction Nonconformists had with the purely nonsectarian "Bible Christianity" taught in the board schools, were incensed at the substantial public aid being given to the Church of England and Roman Catholic schools. The number of the latter was increasing because of Anglican and Catholic dissatisfaction with the simple Bible Christianity of the board schools, which was insufficient for "sacramental

---

[28] S. J. Curtis, *Education in Britain Since 1900* (London: Andrew Dakers, 1952), pp. 41–43.

Christians."[29] Nonconformist hostility to the bill became quite dramatic, as some followed the suggestion
of the veteran Baptist minister Dr.

John Clifford and
of the National Council of the Free Churches and
refused to pay their education taxes if they were used
to support denominational schools. On the political
side, just as Joseph Chamberlain had helped make his
political name by opposition to the 1870 act, the Welsh
radical David Lloyd George pushed himself forward
from the radical backbench to the front ranks of Liberalism by his parliamentary and platform opposition to
the act. The success of the act's opponents in by-
elections inspired the other leaders of the party, including the Liberal-Imperialists (with the exception of
Haldane), to rally in hostility to the act.

It seems highly probable that the zeal of the Liberal
hierarchy, as well as that of Lloyd George, in this
cause was prompted primarily by the prospects of both
Liberal unity and electoral success that it would augment.[30] The determination of the Liberals to repeal the
act when they returned to power proved to be less than
ardent. This failure was one of the major issues that
came to convince Belloc of the insincerity of party
politics. He, for his part as a Liberal candidate, had

---

[29] Adamson, *English Education,* p. 364.
[30] Curtis, *Education in Britain,* pp. 34–40; Elie Halévy, *Imperialism
and the Rise of Labor, 1895–1905* (New York: Barnes & Noble,
1961), pp. 208–10.

agreed with the party's opposition to the act. This position derived from his traditional radical hostility toward the Anglican establishment and his solicitude for those Nonconformists whose children had to be educated in publicly supported Anglican schools in localities where there were no nonsectarian board schools.[31] His position, however, as we shall see when discussing his parliamentary role in the attempted repeals of the act, was complicated by the fact that his Roman Catholic coreligionists, on this issue, if on nothing else, were cobeneficiaries with the establishment he despised.

The other issue which suggested that the Liberals' return to power in late 1905 and their electoral victory in January 1906 constituted a traditional Nonconformist and radical mandate was the controversy over the Licensing Act of 1904. This act attempted to settle a generation-old controversy over the question of compensating the owners of liquor licenses which had been withdrawn by local magistrates on grounds of their redundancy in particular localities. The magistrates were acting in accordance with legislation introduced during the first Gladstone ministry (1868–74) that sought to end the mid-nineteenth-century policy of free trade in beer by lessening the number of public houses and regulating the conditions of operating them. When

---

[31] Speaight, *Hilaire Belloc,* p. 190.

the House of Lords ruled in *Sharp* v. *Wakefield* in 1891 that licenses were not private property and that their former holders were not entitled to compensation, lower magistrates became reluctant to suspend licenses. The act of 1904 sought to resolve the dilemma by authorizing the compensation of licenses suspended for redundancy, but not misconduct, out of a special tax on the trade itself rather than out of the general revenue. This was regarded by the radicals and the Nonconformists as a sellout to the brewing interests, which had, as part of the general economic tendency toward the consolidation and replacement of private firms by public companies, come to dominate the nation's public houses. This interpretation was a logical conclusion from the frankly partisan political character the struggle for temperance reform had taken in the late nineteenth century, as the brewers sided with the Conservatives while the temperance movement, as befitted its Nonconformist spirit, became identified with the Liberals, especially after the endorsement by the National Liberal Federation at its Newcastle Conference in 1891 of the temperance proposals for popular local option over the renewal and even the issuance of licenses. Local option had been advocated without success for years by the radical MP Wilfrid Lawson.[32]

That the Liberal government of 1906–10 failed to

---

[32] Henry Carter, *The English Temperance Movement: A Study in Objectives,* 2 vols. (London: Epworth Press, 1933), 1:212–18.

change the 1904 act became another example in Belloc's eyes of the fraudulence and insincerity of party politics. In his own electoral campaign, he had taken the standard radical position of wanting to destroy the power of the brewing monopoly. His hostility toward the brewing interests, however, was not based upon the standard temperance motives, but motivated in large part by solicitude for the small publicans, who in former times had managed their own houses, but the vast majority of whom had become "the servants, and probably the debtors also, of a small and very wealthy clique," the brewers.[33]

Several circumstances surrounding and assisting the Liberals' return to power in December 1905 and their subsequent electoral victory the following month suggest other factors as being more responsible than any radical mandate or popular desire for revision of the education and licensing legislation. For one thing, both radicals and Liberal-Imperialists shared in the formation of the government and the electoral victory. The incumbent Conservative prime minister, Balfour, had not expected this Liberal unity when he decided to resign on December 4, 1905, rather than call an election. He hoped that the Liberals, upon being faced with the problems of forming a government, would become torn by dissension and cause the political pendulum

---

[33] Speaight, *Belloc*, p. 191.

to swing back in a Unionist direction. He had good reason to think so following an adamant statement by Rosebery on November 25, 1905, in which he proclaimed his refusal to serve under Campbell-Bannerman because of the latter's indication of his continued support for that other radical Liberal aim, Irish Home Rule.[34] But Campbell-Bannerman managed to placate the other leading Liberal-Imperialists, Asquith, Grey, and Haldane, who ultimately abandoned a private pact, the "Relugas compact," which they had made among themselves, not to serve under Campbell-Bannerman unless he would take a peerage and leave the leadership of the House of Commons to Asquith. They all gave in to the unyielding Campbell-Bannerman, in large part out of fear of creating the very thing the Unionists were hoping for—Liberal disunity—especially before an election in which free trade would be the main issue.[35]

In the Campbell-Bannerman government, the Liberal-Imperialists Asquith, Grey, and Haldane occupied the important positions of Chancellor of the Exchequer, Foreign Secretary, and Secretary of War. But the ministry was balanced by the inclusion of such champions of the Gladstonian tradition as John Morley, the Marquess of Ripon, and James Bryce, who became respectively the Secretary of State for India, the Lord Privy Seal, and the Chief Secretary for Ireland. The

---

[34] James, *Rosebery,* pp. 454–56; Gollin, *Balfour's Burden,* p. 276.
[35] Jenkins, *Asquith,* pp. 167–74.

pro-Boer and Celtic-fringe of radicalism was represented by David Lloyd George, the President of the Board of Trade; and John Burns, a former member of the Social-Democratic Federation and leader in the London dock strike, was President of the Local Government Board, although admission to high office seemed greatly to subdue his early radicalism. Besides the inclusion of Liberal-Imperialists in important positions, another important factor drawing the new Liberal government away from pure Gladstonianism was the secret pact made between the party whip, Herbert Gladstone, and the leaders of the Labor Representation Committee (LRC), Ramsay MacDonald and Keir Hardie. By it the Liberals and the Laborites agreed not to compete in certain elections where a three-cornered race would redound to the favor of the Conservatives. The advantage to the Liberals in this arrangement consisted of its being a means of permitting anti-Conservative votes to be cast by certain Conservative working-class voters who could never bring themselves to vote for the Liberals, the historic party of the capitalists, and of securing to the anti-Conservative cause the funds of the trade unions at a time when much of the traditional Liberal sources of money had been diverted to the Unionists.[36] The labor movement had been stirred to political action, and to a

---

[36] Frank Bealey, "The Electoral Arrangement Between the Labor Representation Committee and the Liberal Party," *Journal of Modern History* 28 (December 1956): 372.

working agreement with one of the major parties by the decision in the *Taff Vale* case (1901), which had made unions and their funds liable to injunctions, as well as to suit for damages done by their agents. In the 1906 election thirty LRC candidates, twenty-four of whom were not opposed by the Liberals, were elected. In the long run the presence of this new political force obviously influenced liberalism, and British political thinking in general, to abandon traditional Gladstonian individualism with its insistence on government retrenchment.

There was another development which inhibited the enactment of a radical legislative program, despite the massive Liberal majority returned to the Commons in January 1906 and the astounding presence of more than 200 Nonconformists in the House. This development was the actual decline in Nonconformist church attendance and enthusiasm, which suggested that the furor against the Education and Licensing Acts was somewhat superficial and not a major concern of the electorate. What had happened to that mainspring of Liberalism, Nonconformity, was that several generations of prosperity as well as the removal of religious barriers to social and educational advancement had lessened the reformist zeal of the Nonconformists and had, in fact, made them Conservative and tempted many to switch to Anglicanism as more suited to their new status. Furthermore, the traditional Nonconformist family enterprises, which had been major agencies for influencing employees and the community at large in favor of Liberal causes, were being replaced by more impersonal public companies. At the same time increasing working-class consciousness was lessening the importance of any paternal role of employers in forming the political opinions of their workers.[37]

The absolute Liberal majority also made the party less dependent on the votes of the Irish nationalists; and immediate attention toward Irish Home Rule, one of the most divisive questions within the ranks of Liberalism, was less necessary. As a result, the traditional radicals, who were enthusiastic over the 1906 victory, were destined for a very rude disappointment as the changing political temper moved the government in the direction of a different kind of radicalism, namely, collectivism. A key figure in promoting this switch was the man who had made his political name as a champion of traditional radicalism and Nonconformity, David Lloyd George. Belloc was a fine example of the disappointed radicals who clung to the old faith.

---

[37] John F. Glaser, "English Nonconformity and the Decline of Liberalism," *American Historical Review* 63 (January 1958): 360–61.

.

Chapter Three

Dissatisfied Radical,
1906–09

Not long after the 1906 election, Belloc began to
play the role of irreconcilable radical that characterized his career in Parliament. The issue on which
he first rebuked the Liberal government for having
disregarded its electoral mandate was one which Campbell-Bannerman himself had successfully exploited during the election, the question of the importation of
Chinese labor to work the goldmines of the Transvaal.
This was an issue, like free trade, in which the old
nineteenth-century radical ideal of a harmonious em-
ployer-employee alliance against the forces of privilege
and monopoly cold be temporarily revived. It combined
the spirit of antiimperialism with working-class solidarity, sentiments very often antagonistic to each other.
The object of criticism was the Conservative government's authorization in 1904 of the recruitment and
mass importation of Chinese laborers for work in the
goldmines of the Rand on the plea of the mine owners

that it would otherwise have been impossible to recruit
enough workers to make the mines profitable. The pro-
Boers, who suspected the mine owners of having sought
the Boer War as a means of removing Boer obstructions
to their opportunities for profiteering, were easily able
to view this labor importation, as Lloyd George did, as
having "brought back slavery to the British Empire."
Naturally the peasant Boer population consistently
feared these foreigners, who were Asiatic and who had
often been recruited from among the less savory sectors
of the population, not only as rivals for employment
but as threats to their property and person as well. The
British working classes automatically rejected the idea
of government-sponsored recruitment of cheap foreign
labor.

In a campaign speech at Albert Hall on December
21, 1905, Campbell-Bannerman announced that his
government had given orders "to stop forthwith the recruitment and embarkation of coolies in China and
their importation into South Africa." The more legally
conscious members of the cabinet, however, particularly
the Liberal-Imperialist Chancellor of the Exchequer,
Asquith, reminded the Prime Minister that licenses for
the importation of 14,000 coolies, which had been
issued the previous November, had not yet been used.
Were the government to revoke these licenses, it might
be legally required to compensate the mine owners. As
a result, the Prime Minister was persuaded in a cabinet

meeting held even before the elections to limit his prohibition to the future issuance of licenses, not to the use of licenses already issued.[1] Belloc was not easily satisfied, however, and demanded in his maiden speech that the government commence deportation of the laborers within three months, set a rate, preferably of 5,000 a month, at which the deportation was to continue, and make the whole cost of the process fall upon the mine owners.[2] He repeated his demand several weeks later, when he insisted that the repatriation of the Chinese had been the mandate of the election. The members of the House "had been returned as the servants of the election and the government existed only to do their will." The shortage of labor which had been used to justify the importation in the first place, he asserted, had been deliberately created by the forced lowering of wages by the mine owners. Since the repatriation of the Chinese at his desired rate would take eighteen months, he believed that this would give the mine owners plenty of time to rehire native labor and avoid economic disaster.[3]

Aside from the question of Chinese labor, which the Liberal government had at least indicated its intention

---

[1] Roy Jenkins, *Asquith* (London: Collins, 1964), pp. 179–80.

[2] *Parliamentary Debates* (Commons), 4th ser., 152 (February 22, 1906): 614.

[3] *Ibid.*, 4th ser., 125 (April 15, 1906): 797–99.

to end, the pro-Boer radicals ought to have been generally satisfied with the government's policy toward the former enemy, since the policy's full effect was to all intents and purposes an abandonment of all that the war had been fought for—British hegemony in South Africa. For one thing, the preliminary constitution that had been granted to the Transvaal in 1905 was replaced with one more amenable to the wishes of the Boers. The 1905 document had annoyed the Boers because of the pro-British bias that resulted from its property qualifications for voting, the veto power it granted the British government over the Transvaal's legislative council, the initiative in financial matters given to the Governor-General, and the linguistic ascendancy assigned to English. The constitution granted by the Liberal government, on the other hand, practically established universal suffrage, placed the English and Dutch languages on an equal legal footing, and established an executive-nominated second chamber that inhibited the popular assembly no more than any similar chamber in any other colony in the empire. The following year a similar grant of self-government was extended to the Orange River Colony, whose population was homogeneously Boer, unlike the Transvaal's which had an English majority, although enough of the British population voted for the Boer nationalist party to give it a majority in the assembly. Then, in 1908 and 1909, a constitution for a politically united South Africa was drafted by representatives of the various governments, and approved by the British Parliament in September 1909.[4] Latter-day British liberals have come to have second thoughts about this Gladstonian generosity of the Liberal government which, in fact, permitted the permanent exclusion of the black population from the government of South Africa.

It was as a result of the grant of self-government to the Transvaal that the Chinese laborers were eventually repatriated. Before being able to order this step, however, the Prime Minister of the Transvaal, General Botha, had to overcome certain governmental financial difficulties that placed his regime at the mercy of the mine owners who were the beneficiaries of the inexpensive Chinese labor. Belloc was particularly solicitous that the British government assist the Transvaal government in counteracting any pressures, such as threats to close the mines, which the owners might put on it. He inquired several times of Winston Churchill, who was Undersecretary for the Colonies, whether the British government was prepared to force the mines, whose owners were threatening to shut them down, to remain open under the threat of taking them over. Churchill replied that such a course of action would be illegal if it was without legislative approval and impractical

---

[4] Elie Halévy, *The Rule of Democracy, 1905–1914* (New York: Barnes & Noble, 1961), pp. 32–36.

since the only mines likely to close would be those that were unprofitable for the government to operate.[5] The difficulty was solved the following spring when, at the Imperial Conference, Botha received from the British cabinet a guarantee of a loan of five million pounds which thereby freed his government from the pressures of the mine owners and permitted him to order the repatriation of the Chinese.

The solicitude of pro-Boer radicals like Belloc for the self-government of the Transvaal and the Orange River Colony was not extended to the English-settled South Africa province of Natal. There the English settlers, whom the radicals regarded as colonists unlike the indigenous Boers of the other provinces, had, in the opening months of the Campbell-Bannerman ministry, forcefully suppressed a native revolt in which 3,000 native lives were lost. The British government first prohibited the execution by the colonial government of twelve natives summarily condemned for their part in the revolt, but later, over the objections of the radicals, yielded to the protests of other colonial governments such as Australia and New Zealand over this interference in internal matters and permitted the Natal government to proceed with the executions. Belloc argued that the presence of British troops in the Natal for the purposes of protecting the white residents ought

[5] *Parliamentary Debates* (Commons), 4th ser., 156 (May 7, 1906): 49–50.

to have given the British government some right of interference in the territory.[6] At other times he was anxious for explanations of reported floggings of Zulus by the Natal government for purposes of obtaining evidence, or of imprisonments under a general warrant. He also wanted private mining companies to be prevented from using Zulu prisoners as forced labor unless they would pay the government a sum equal to the wages they would have had to pay free labor.[7] Eventually the general South African constitution that was accepted in 1909 absorbed Natal into a Boer-dominated central system and left it none of the independence which a federal arrangement might have allowed. Needless to say, the absorption of Natal did not imply that the treatment or condition of the black population would be improved.

While the Liberal government, in spite of its strong Liberal-Imperialist flavor, acted toward South Africa in a manner ultimately satisfactory to the upholders of the Gladstonian heritage of self-government, its policy in the large nonwhite territories of the empire such as Egypt and India was one of opposition to indigenous nationalist movements, and so was bound to irritate radicals like Belloc. This was especially the case in

---

[6] *Ibid.*, 4th ser., 155 (April 2, 1906): 168–69.
[7] *Ibid.*, 4th ser., 166 (December 10, 1906): 1551–52; 184 (February 12, 1908): 1016–17; 187 (May 4, 1908): 1649.

Egypt where Lord Cromer, the last of the three great proconsuls of the Chamberlain era, was still the British Consul General and exercised over the regime of the Egyptian khedive the same benevolent despotism that Lord Curzon had exercised as Viceroy of India and Lord Milner as Governor General of South Africa. Completely unsympathetic to the demands for autonomy by the Egyptian nationalists, Cromer viewed Britain's role there as a tutorial responsibility based, not on self-interest, but on the duty to instill in the subject people, not necessarily feelings of loyalty toward the British Empire, but at least such qualities as "loyalty to good conduct, to high standards, to the moral code of the upright English official" with which in the distant future Egypt could become either part of the empire or autonomous.[8]

An incident occurred on June 13, 1906, which intensified radical hostility to Cromer. There was a riot at the Nile Delta village of Denshawai in which a British officer died. It had been precipitated by some British officers who had gone pigeon shooting against the wishes of the inhabitants. A special tribunal beyond which there was no appeal condemned four villagers to death and imprisoned twelve others. The executions, which were preceded by floggings, had a particular note of harshness in that they were performed before the relatives of the victims. Belloc joined other parliamen-

---

[8] A. P. Thornton, *The Imperial Idea and Its Enemies* (London: Macmillan, 1959), pp. 210, 240–41.

tary radicals in challenging the power of the special tribunal.[9] His Sussex neighbor, Wilfrid Scawen Blunt, the foremost English advocate of the Egyptians, published a pamphlet condemning the atrocities and, after an evening of conversation with Belloc, was convinced that the Denshawai case and the Natal suppression "together ought to shut English mouths forever about Russia and the Congo,"[10] a theme which Belloc would repeat when he later found himself at odds with other radicals who criticized the government of the czar and the Belgian administration in the Congo. Cromer's defense of the trial, which took place during his absence from Egypt, and the support which the Liberal-Imperialist Foreign Secretary, Grey, gave him angered the critics. Belloc was convinced that the sworn evidence of the case had been deliberately destroyed with the cognizance of Cromer and Grey, and feared that a "little more of that sort of thing and all control of external action by Englishmen will become impossible."[11] Cromer resigned the next year and in 1908 the remaining Denshawai prisoners were released. There was, however, no substantial change in the policy of benevolent paternalism toward Egypt.

The government's policy for India was somewhat

---

[9] *Parliamentary Debates* (Commons), 4th ser., 160 (July 12, 1908): 1055.

[10] Wilfrid Scawen Blunt, *My Diaries, 1888–1914* (London: Martin Secker, 1932), p. 565.

[11] Hilaire Belloc to C. H. Norman, September 19, 1907, Berg Collection, New York Public Library, New York, N.Y.

different, although still unsatisfactory to the radicals. There the Viceroy, Lord Curzon, who had ruled with the splendor and autocracy of an Eastern potentate, was succeeded by a Whig, Lord Minto, who approached his mission more as a compliant civil servant than as a proconsul. This made him a more appropriate collaborator with the Liberal Secretary of State for India, John Morley, the elder statesman of the Gladstonian tradition. The general tenor of the Morley-Minto program for India was to move away from the paternalism of the Curzon era toward a gradual extension of legislative and administrative powers to the rising educated and middle classes of India in order to forestall the further rise of extreme Indian nationalism. The two major obstacles to Morley's fulfillment of his policy were "the access of Indian extremists to English radical opinion" and "the influence on conservative opinion at home of the retired Anglo-Indians, accustomed to wield authority and with a practiced pen."[12] The latter were obviously hostile to his reforms, while the former, especially 150 parliamentary radicals, who had formed an Indian committee, were hostile toward Morley's authorizing the enforcement of certain regulations from the days of the East India Company that allowed the prosecution of the authors of seditious articles in India, the prohibition of public meetings, and

---

[12] John Viscount Morley, *Recollections*, 2 vols. (New York: Macmillan, 1917), 2:156.

the deportation without trial of agitators. Morley obviously intended to combine his reforms with a policy of firmness against the nationalists. Belloc was among the dissatisfied radicals who complained of the prosecution and the deportations, particularly the hesitancy of the India office in providing disclosure of the reasons for the prosecutions and deportations.[13]

In all of these criticisms of the government's imperial policy there was much of the traditional radical suspicion of a compact between the professional government services and "the governing class" to keep foreign and imperial affairs free from democratic interference.[14] Such suspicions were intensified when Asquith, the Liberal-Imperialist, succeeded the ailing Campbell-Bannerman as Prime Minister in the spring of 1908. W. S. Blunt believed the new ministry to be "certainly retrograde as far as humanitarian views are concerned, and is now as purely Whig imperialist as it could well be made."[15]

Paradoxically, at about this time, Belloc criticized what was probably the foremost radical antiimperialist cause in a generation—the condemnation of conditions in the Belgian Congo—as he urged the Foreign Secre-

[13] *Parliamentary Debates* (Commons), 4th ser., 177 (July 2, 1907): 523; 5th ser., 2 (March 9, 1909): 174, (March 16): 901–2.

[14] A. J. P. Taylor, *The Troublemakers* (London: Hamish Hamilton, 1957), p. 98.

[15] Blunt, *My Diaries,* p. 613.

tary, Grey, not to heed the demands of the Congo
Reform Association with regard to policy toward
Belgium and the Congo.

In 1884 the great powers of Europe had agreed to
abstain from the Congo basin in their colonization of
Africa and to allow that region to be governed as an
independent and private state of the Belgian king,
Leopold II. He ran it pretty much as his private property and amassed great riches by granting monopolies
in various regions of the territory to entrepreneurs who
were unrestrained in using the most brutal methods for
the purposes of exploiting native labor. British humanitarian opinion was alerted to this atrocious system
primarily by the writings and agitation of E. D. Morel,
a former agent for a shipping company who had turned
his full attention to the cause, and by the reports of
Roger Casement, a British consul in the Congo, also
once an agent for a shipping company. Morel and
Casement formed the Congo Reform Association in
1904 to press the British government to intervene and
force the Congo Free State to comply with the conditions of the Berlin Agreement regarding treatment of
the natives. British opinion was nearly unanimous in
support of their efforts, and ultimately King Leopold
relented and shifted the control of the Congo from his
own hands to the Belgian parliament. The Congo
reformers were unsatisfied, however, and persisted in
demanding that this transfer of responsibility not be
simply a means of covering up the abuses.

Belloc dissented from this particular antiimperialist crusade, partly because he suspected any cause which received such massive support even from some who were ordinarily not reformists. He shared the cynicism of the Continental powers and signatories of the Berlin Convention, France and Germany, who refused to support the British demands on Belgium, about the motives of many of the Congo reformers. This cynicism derived especially from the financing of much of the agitation by Liverpool merchants whose solicitude for the Congo natives was suspected of being secondary to their quest for access to the markets where Leopold had granted monopolistic privileges, and from the membership in the Congo Reform Association of Lord Cromer, the retired Egyptian "proconsul" whose reforming credentials were somewhat tainted by the Denshawai incident. In Belloc's opinion, the reform agitation was "the work of a group of particularly despicable commercial men of the lowest type." He noted "a vague feeling among the merchants in the North of England that there are pickings to be got and that there is money in it."[16] He did not deny the atrocities, although he did not rule out the possibility of exaggeration. But such "acts of cruelty and tyranny" were inevitable whenever Europeans came into contact with primitive races "under our modern system of production"; they happened in the British colonies as well. Like the Roman Catholic

---

[16] Belloc to Norman, February 25, 1908, Berg Collection.

Archbishop of Westminster, Francis Cardinal Bourne, he sensed a certain note of anti-Catholicism in the reform agitation against Belgium, a Catholic nation, and was suspicious because none of the Congo missionaries who protested about atrocities was a Catholic, although the large majority of the missionaries to the Congo was Catholic. Bourne was suspicious as well of the complaints of certain Protestant missionaries that they were denied religious toleration in the Congo, especially since they had, just a few months before, publicly proclaimed their appreciation of the tolerance and assistance extended them by the Belgians.[17]

Belloc's primary reason for urging noninterference in the affair was his sympathy for the efforts of the Foreign Secretary, Lord Grey, to establish as amicable relations as he could with the various European powers in order to neutralize the power of Germany. Such efforts would be undermined by interfering in the internal imperial affairs of another nation especially when Britain had a few skeletons to hide in its own imperial closet. Even if the accounts of the atrocities were true, it was not diplomatically opportune to act as Britain could have done in

> a much better and happier past when we had one rival fleet aways hopelessly inferior to our own, when we were

---

[17] *Parliamentary Debates* (Commons), 5th ser., 8 (July 22, 1909): 636–38, 673; Ernest Oldmeadow, *Francis Cardinal Bourne*, 2 vols. (London: Burns, Oates & Washbourne, 1940, 1944), 2:25–34.

masters of all forms of industrial production, when we had a small infantry of the line which was admirable for its purpose.

. . . That time had passed, however, and it was necessary for us to depend quite as much upon a close system of alliances, and a close calculation of the various national forces around us.[18]

Belloc found himself, therefore, in the curious position for a radical of lamenting the weakness of the Foreign Secretary in the face of pressures from a popular agitation. Convinced that the Foreign Office was hostile to the reform agitation, he believed that its acquiescence to demands that protests be made to Belgium would be "entirely due to the weakness of Sir Edward Grey."[19]

It was this anxiety about the German threat, natural to a part Frenchman, that put Belloc increasingly at odds with many of his old radical allies, who were hostile toward Britain's friendship with France and Russia, who would be doubtful about, if not hostile to, Britain's involvement in World War I, and who became anxious for reconciliation with Germany after the war. Paradoxically, and because of this, the few programs of the Liberal government which Belloc did applaud were the very ones most closely connected with Liberal-Imperialism: Haldane's military reforms and Grey's

---

[18] *Parliamentary Debates* (Commons), 5th ser., 8 (July 22, 1909): 674.

[19] Belloc to Norman, February 27, 1908, Berg Collection.

Entente policy (notwithstanding Belloc's occasional suspicion of Grey's weakness). The two major protagonists of Congo reform had quite a different attitude toward Germany: E. D. Morel met very great hostility and was suspected of pacifism and pro-Germanism during World War I, and Sir Roger Casement was convicted and executed for treasonous collaboration with Germany while working for Irish revolution. Significantly, it was his disillusionment over the unenthusiastic response of the Foreign Office to his reports on the Congo that drove Casement in the direction of revolutionary Irish nationalism.[20]

Belloc's greatest disappointment with the Liberal government was over its failure to obtain those radical domestic objectives for which he and others had campaigned in the 1906 election. On the two central issues of education and licensing legislation, the Liberal government's failure was mainly a result of the Unionists' use of the veto power of the House of Lords. The Lords' action was not so much a flagrant disregard of a democratic electorate's mandate by an hereditary body, as a reflection of the actual temper of the electorate, a reflection missing in the House of Commons' passage of the traditional radical legislation. The Unionist strategists, who called for the use of the veto, shrewdly

---

[20] René MacColl, *Roger Casement* (London: Lonsborough, 1959), p. 48.

perceived that the traditional radical objectives were not the real desires of the electorate. Their hesitancy in using the veto against other bills such as the trade unions dispute bill, which had a more collectivist or social character, indicates that they were not acting with a simple disregard of popular feelings. Belloc's espousal of the radical position on the issues of education and licensing was complicated by certain peculiar personal features; as a Catholic and a part Frenchman, he was inevitably uncomfortable in the company of teetotalers and Nonconformist advocates of Bible-Christian education.

His position on the education legislation which the Liberal government tried to pass, in compliance with the election pledges to undo the work of the 1902 act, related directly to the dilemma in which the leaders of the Roman Catholic church in England found themselves. Their school system, like that of the Church of England, had benefited from the 1902 act which the Conservatives had passed and was likely to suffer from the Liberal policy of ending state assistance to all but nondenominational schools. In addition to the Catholic hierarchy's appreciation of the Conservative Party's position on education, there was among some of the bishops a greater sympathy with conservatism in general. This was the case among those who had close association with the "Old Catholics," that is, the recusant families who had maintained their Catholicism in England despite persecution and other disabilities following the Reformation. Such Catholics, who were largely upper class or aristocratic, like the Duke of Norfolk, were unsympathetic to the more democratic, socially conscious, and Ultramontane Catholicism championed by Cardinal Manning. Manning had been particularly solicitous for both the newer converts to Catholicism (like himself) and the group which was becoming the numerically dominant, although unpopular, section of English Catholicism, the Irish.[21] Belloc, who as a very young man had known and frequently called upon Manning and regarded him as one of the greatest influences on the formation of his thoughts,[22] was unsympathetic to the Old Catholics. For one thing, his English mother had been not only a convert to Catholicism, but a convert from the milieu of Unitarian Nonconformist radicalism that was completely alien to the Old Catholic environment. Belloc's dislike of the Old Catholics also stemmed from his resentful memory of their domination of the Catholic community at Slindon, in Sussex, where he was raised. Arundel Castle, the residence of the Duke of Norfolk, was nearby.[23]

But it was not just these conservative Old Catholics but the hierarchy at large that was disturbed by the fact that the great bulk of the Irish Catholic vote in Eng-

---

[21] Vincent Alan McClelland, *Cardinal Manning* (London: Oxford University Press, 1962), p. 162.

[22] Hilaire Belloc, *The Cruise of the "Nona"* (Westminster, Md.: Newman Press, 1956), pp. 54–55.

[23] Robert Speaight, *The Life of Hilaire Belloc* (New York: Farrar, Straus & Cudahy, 1957), p. 17.

land, because of the Home Rule issue, had gone, as had Belloc's political sympathies, to the Liberal Party, whose position on the education question was contrary to the church's interest.[24] Fearful of the dangers to the Catholic system should the Liberals fulfill their election promises and deny state assistance to all but nonsectarian schools, the bishops, under the leadership of Cardinal Bourne, prepared to enlist mass Catholic support to ward off any Liberal attack on school aid. Bourne issued a Lenten pastoral which stated the justifications for assistance to the Catholic schools. He cited the principle, suggested by Manning, that all Englishmen alike should "have, under reasonable conditions, schools properly built and fully equipped at the public cost—to which all alike contribute—but of a character to which they can send their children without any injury being done to their conscientious religious convictions." Such injury, he claimed, would be inflicted upon Catholics, were public provision for education to be available only in schools which offered nondenominational Bible-Christian religious training. He furthermore insisted that the Catholics, if their appeal for consideration were disregarded, would "be bound in conscience to use to the uttermost every legitimate means of resistance which we possess."[25] The Bishop of Salford, Belloc's own constituency,

---

[24] Henry Pelling, *Social Geography of British Elections, 1885–1910* (London: Macmillan, 1967), p. 431.
[25] Oldmeadow, *Cardinal Bourne*, 1:282–83.

stressed in his pastoral the traditional Catholic position on the primacy of parental authority over that of the state in the matter of the education of the child. Noting the late arrival of the state into the field of education, the bishop viewed the quest for national educational uniformity, which would be "regardless of the consciences of a mixed community," as leading to the strangulation of religious freedom in education whereby "parental right should be practically abolished and the autocracy of the state substituted for them."[26]

In April the President of the Board of Education, Augustine Birrell, introduced an education bill designed to satisfy the Liberal election pledges. It preserved the local education authorities which the 1902 act had created to replace the old local school boards, thereby acknowledging the demands of centralization as opposed to the local rights of which the Nonconformists were so jealous. But the bill went on to state that "a school shall not be recognized as a public elementary school unless it is a school provided by the local education authority." This was a reversal of the trend of previous education legislation to regard the voluntary denominational schools as part of the national education system and eligible for certain state assistance. Instead, the proposed bill denied assistance from either school rates or state grants to all but nonsectarian schools. The voluntary denominational

[26] *Ibid.*, p. 286.

schools, however, could merit public assistance were they to hand themselves over to the local education authority and accept the virtual loss of their denominational character, for sectarian religious instruction would be permitted in them for only two hours a week on a voluntary basis and not during the regular school hours or at public expense.[27]

The Liberal government, however, was as aware as the Catholic bishops of the support the Catholic electorate, especially the Irish community in England, had given to its victory. Accordingly, the Liberals sought to appease the Catholics of England, as well as their allies in Parliament, the Irish Nationalists, who had agreed to collaborate with the English Catholic hierarchy in seeking to protect the position of the Catholic schools.[28] The government's concession was essentially a contradiction of the bill's main purpose of advancing nondenominational education. It consisted of a clause permitting voluntary schools that received public assistance to maintain their denominational character if four-fifths of the parents of the pupils in a school desired it.

In Parliament, Belloc sought to reply to the critics of this concession who argued that Catholics should be forced to pay the expenses themselves if they wanted

---

[27] Bernard M. Allen, *Sir Robert Morant* (London: Macmillan, 1934), p. 228.

[28] Oldmeadow, *Cardinal Bourne,* 1:277, 298–303.

a special kind of educational system. He replied that such a criticism would be valid if there could be devised "a purely neutral and secular system." But the non-sectarian system was, in fact, Protestant, even though a nondenominational kind of Protestantism. Since the religion of the majority was therefore endowed, so also should the Catholic minority be given assistance. As for the argument that making exceptions for minority sects like the Catholics would prompt similar requests by many other groups and result in an unmanageable complexity, Belloc insisted that there were only two sects, the Jews and the Catholics, who were insistent on a peculiar system of education. Most Protestants, he believed, would be satisfied with the simple nondenominational Bible Christianity of the state schools. While there were some Protestant parents who demanded "a highly definite dogmatic teaching," these were not so great in number as to qualify under the four-fifths provision.

Although he was pleased with the effort made to conciliate the Catholics, Belloc indicated his own and official Catholic dissatisfaction that the extension of assistance to denominational schools under the four-fifths clause was left to the option of the local authorities. While he believed that the personnel of the local administrations were "as just as and perhaps more just than the people of any other country," there were "a few exceptions," which were "enough to light a flame which is sure to be felt throughout the whole of our corporate body." Because of this, he insisted, the Catholics should be able to appeal the decisions of local authorities to the Education Department, a central and removed body "which we can trust better than the momentary fads and bigotry of a local body." He was also anxious that the eligibility of new Catholic schools for public assistance be determined according to a standard formula of the number of children enrolled rather than by the arbitrary decision of a local authority, which would be "a going back to the government of stock-jobbing or the form of government which has misgoverned Ireland."[29]

Catholic dissatisfaction intensified when an amendment was made to the four-fifths rule, which made it applicable only to urban communities with a population in excess of five thousand. This was done because of a Nonconformist fear that many Church of England schools in rural districts would remain qualified for state assistance. It had been the monopoly position of these very schools in certain areas that had been the major irritant of dissenters who disliked both the necessity of their children attending such Anglican schools and the use of their tax money to finance them. But this dilution of the four-fifths rule would have had

---

[29] *Parliamentary Debates* (Commons), 4th ser., 156 (May 7, 1906): 1072–75.

a severe effect on Catholic schools as well, as it was estimated that nearly half of them would become ineligible for assistance.[30]

Although he had supported the bill through its second reading with the hope that the features disagreeable to him and the Catholics would be removed, Belloc turned against it when such alterations were not made in the committee stage. The survival of such features as the limitation of the four-fifths provisions to towns exceeding five thousand population he deemed a betrayal by the government of the Catholic voters who had supported the Liberals and of those MPs who had received considerable Catholic support in the election. He urged a mass rally of sixty thousand Catholics in Manchester, saying that there was "a duty incumbent upon us of breaking this measure by resistance both within the Houses of Parliament and without"; for, as the bill then stood, "Protestantism is endowed at the public expense and rightly, for this is a Protestant country, but, while Catholic money goes to endow this Protestant teaching no adequate provision is made that Catholics should receive their share of the general funds."[31]

However, any civil disobedience or withholding of taxes by Catholics similar to the tactics employed by

---

[30] W. F. Brown, "The Education Bill of 1906," *Dublin Review* 140 (January–April 1907): 136.

[31] *Times* (London), October 15, 1908, p. 5a.

the Nonconformists in opposition to the 1902 act was made unnecessary after the House of Lords had finished with the 1906 bill. There the champions of the denominational schools went on the offensive and, by a number of amendments, completely changed the nature of the bill from one aimed at excluding denominational schools from the national system to one positively promoting denominational education and actually prohibiting complete secularism in publicly assisted schools. The demands of the Catholics were more than satisfied as the minimal population requirement of five thousand for districts where denominational schools could receive assistance was removed, and the percentage of parents whose consent was necessary for denominational schooling was reduced from four-fifths to two-thirds. Furthermore, denominational instruction was permitted in the schools that were set up and maintained by the public educational authorities. The fight to save the bill from these amendments was led in the House of Lords by the Marquess of Ripon, the Lord Privy Seal and the Liberal leader in the Lords. He was a Roman Catholic and naturally incurred considerable hostility from his coreligionists for this role.[32] After the bill was returned to the House of Commons, Belloc, like the other major champions of the Catholic demands, the Irish Nationalists, decided to vote with the

---

[32] Lucien Wolfe, *Life of the First Marquess of Ripon,* 2 vols. (London: John Murray, 1921), 2:280–81.

government and to reject the amendments of the House of Lords *en bloc* despite the benefits they extended to Catholic education. Belloc explained that "no consistent radical could be dependent even for a good thing upon the nonelected chamber," which included in its ranks men sitting "simply by hereditary right" and others "who had openly purchased their places in the assembly."[33] But this was not as generous a gesture for the defense of radicalism as it might appear, for, regardless of the vote of the Catholics and the Irish Nationalists, the acceptance by the Commons of the Lords' amendments was as unlikely as the Lords' acceptance of the original bill.

When the Lords reinstated their amendments after the Commons' rejection, Campbell-Bannerman, against his own first instincts, decided to follow the opinion of his cabinet and drop the issue rather than accept the challenge of the Unionist leader, Balfour, to dissolve Parliament and go to the people. It was reckoned that the education bill, despite the oratory of the election campaign, did not have an appeal wide enough to ensure a Liberal victory in another election. Rather than risk the Liberal majority, or incur the financial burden of another election, it was decided to let the Lords "fill the cup": that is, to present numerous pieces of legislation for the Lords' slaughtering block, in the

---

[33] *Paliamentary Debates* (Commons), 4th ser., 166 (December 10, 1906): 1621.

hope that eventually enough of the public would become thoroughly exasperated with the Lords and wholeheartedly sympathetic to the government.[34]

This policy, however, ran the risk of disheartening more of the government's sympathizers than it would attract in additional support. In a sense, the Liberal strength in the nation had reached its peak and had nowhere to go but down. The Liberal majority in the Commons, moreover, was partly a freakish thing, unexpected even by many of those elected, and was not a true indication of popular sentiment. Furthermore, the Unionists were not about to employ their massive majority in the House of Lords blindly and indiscriminately. Indeed, Balfour and the Marquess of Lansdowne, the Unionist leader in the House of Lords, had agreed to collaborate "to secure that the party in the two houses shall not work as two separate armies." Expecting that the Liberal cabinet would "bring in bills in a much more extreme form than the moderate members of their own cabinet probably approve," Balfour thought the House of Lords could not "escape the duty of making serious modifications in important government measures." Rather than feed the flames of radicalism, he was sure that if this was "done with caution and tact," it was quite possible that the House of Lords might "come out of the ordeal strengthened rather than weakened by the inevitable difficulties of the next few

---

[34] Jenkins, *Asquith,* p. 191.

years."[35] The very selective employment of the Lords' veto was demonstrated by their care not to use it against highly popular measures such as the trades dispute bill, introduced by a Labor MP to overcome the *Taff Vale* decision and to exempt trade union funds from damage suits. The veto power of the Lords was instead used primarily against the traditional radical causes—like the education bill and the bill to end plural voting. Despite the oratory of radicals like Belloc about the arbitrary disregard of the public by the Lords, the vetoing of these measures reflected the actual decline in popular interest in and support for the causes of traditional radicalism.

Another attempt to deal with the religious controversy in education was made in 1908 when Reginald McKenna, who had succeeded Birrell as President of the Board of Education, introduced an education bill which called for a single category of state elementary school in which only nondenominational Bible instruction would be given. The special provision in the 1906 bill for the benefit of the Catholics was not included in the later bill. Belloc spoke sympathetically of the general purpose of the bill, unification of elementary education. He thought there was "no one who cared for the results of elementary education in the modern state

---

[35] Memorandum, quoted in Lord Lansdowne, *A Biography,* p. 353; Roy Jenkins, *Mr. Balfour's Poodle* (London: William Heinemann, 1954), pp. 21–22.

who would not wish to see a simple and a united system." He knew such a system would anger the "territorial squires" and "a certain number of archaeological ecclesiastics," the prime villains in the sight of traditional radicals, and he was delighted by that fact. But the bill had another group of avid opponents, his fellow Catholics. He suggested as proof of their determined insistence on a separate school system the enormous sacrifice made by Catholics, for the most part from the poorer classes, to finance it. To satisfy this unique insistence of the Catholics, he urged the inclusion in the bill of the four-fifths provision of the 1906 measure. He repeated the earlier justification he had given for the Catholic claim for special treatment, namely, the actually Protestant character of the nondenominational schools, for "no matter how much they attempted to make the system purely secular, it would certainly remain in tone and atmosphere a Protestant, and an English Protestant, system."[36]

Before the second reading of the bill, however, and after Asquith's assumption of the premiership, new efforts at compromise between church and chapel were made by yet another President of the Board of Education, Walter Runciman. After a summer of negotiations with leading Anglican bishops, including the Archbishop of Canterbury, and leading Nonconformists like

---

[36] *Parliamentary Debates* (Commons), 4th ser., 189 (May 19, 1908): 199–202; (May 20): 311–14.

Dr. Clifford, a bill was drawn up under which the Church of England would hand over to the local education authorities its denominational schools in those areas where they were the only schools. In return for this concession, the Church of England would be allowed to give voluntary religious instruction three mornings each week in those schools as well as in the other schools of the education authorities in rural and urban areas. The only benefits for which those Church of England, Catholic, and other denominational schools that wished to preserve their sectarian identity would be eligible were some state grants; they would be regarded as having "contracted out" of the national system.[37]

Despite the approval given by the Anglican hierarchy, the Church of England supporters in the House of Lords were unsatisfied; so, naturally, were the Roman Catholics, and this measure also failed. Although the religious question in education remained unsolved (or, more likely, was solved in the sense that most people lost interest in it), the Liberal government did secure the passage in 1907 of legislation of a more technical and administrative than doctrinal nature, which was in keeping with the emphasis that had been urged by the Liberal-Imperialists and the Coefficients. These measures concerned themselves with the medical inspection and treatment of schoolchildren, the provi-

---

[37] Allen, *Sir Robert Morant,* pp. 240–42.

sion of new secondary schools, scholarships for higher elementary education, and the unification of teacher standards.

A major concern of the House of Commons in 1908 was that other traditional Liberal Nonconformist cause, a licensing bill, which also met the Lords' veto. The failure of the bill convinced Belloc of the vileness of the party system, although the grounds for his own sympathy for such legislation were different from those of his Nonconformist temperance allies. The bill sought to advance temperance by closing 32,000 public houses, about a third of the total of England and Wales, over a period of fourteen years, with compensation to be provided out of a special tax on the trade itself. While the temperance enthusiasts were hostile to compensation, the facts that it was not taken from the general taxation and that a large number of houses were to be closed were very satisfactory to them. But, for Belloc, the justification for the bill, which "deserved the support of every radical worthy of the name," was that, by it, for the first time "in our industrial generation," an attempt was being made "to tackle one of the great monopolies." That monopoly was the brewing industry, which, by means of the tied-house system, controlled most of the public houses in the land. He believed that "if the tied-house system had not arisen, and if the independent over the tied or brewery-controlled houses. He also the difficulty would not have arisen." His attitude, therefore, was quite different from that of the temperance advocates, like the United Kingdom Alliance, which saw the solution to the drink problem in the closing of public houses rather than in changing the type of ownership, although they also recognized the financial power of the brewers as a major obstacle to attaining their ends.

Because of the different ends he hoped for in any licensing bill, Belloc thought that a number of amendments were necessary to overcome the bill's weaknesses. Mainly, he was concerned because it did not deal adequately with the specific question of the tied houses, which should be attacked "not at the end of fourteen years but at once." One step toward that end which he suggested was to treat the individually owned public houses with preference in licensing and taxation over the tied or brewery-controlled houses. He also believed that too much power was given to the magistrates and not enough to popular sentiment in issuing licenses. Another complaint, which contradicted a major goal of the temperance enthusiasts who advocated the power of local option to close completely the public houses in an area, was that in the bill no power was given to the people of a locality "to augment as well as to diminish the number of licenses." He was thinking of those "areas in England where the fanaticism of the great landed proprietor, or more often of his wife, forbids the people to have that common meeting place, that village club, which a well-conducted public house is." He was also disappointed in the bill's failure to "provide sufficiently for compensation to the tenant or manager and the employees of the closed houses."[38] He further distinguished himself from the temperance advocates by opposing an amendment which called for their pet project of local option to impose complete prohibition. Such an amendment had nothing to do with what he thought was the main purpose of the bill—"that the state should resume control . . . over the liquor traffic"—but was, instead, based on "a totally different principle, the principle that fermented liquor was a bad thing for the individual or for the state and in some way to be legislated against." This was something, he insisted, the English people were resolved "to have nothing whatever to do with." Indeed, he went so far as to speak favorably of an amendment extending the drinking hours on Sunday.[39]

The licensing bill, like the education bill, was overwhelmingly rejected by the House of Lords, despite the support given to it by the Anglican bishops. But by this time Belloc had become convinced that the villain blocking radical legislation was not so much the House of Lords as the Liberal government itself. Instead of introducing a short bill aiming at the destruction of the tied-house system, which "would have been as popular

---

[38] *Parliamentary Debates* (Commons), 4th ser., 186 (May 4, 1908): 1748–50.

[39] *Ibid.*, 194 (October 20, 1908): 970–71; (November 13): 797.

a measure as the government could have brought forward," it sponsored an "intensely and deservedly unpopular" measure aimed at the restriction of the use of fermented liquors. The only explanation he could find for the government's having put forward such a bill was its anxiety to cater to what he came to regard as "the principal force in politics"—the desires of the contributors to the secret party funds.[40] Belloc saw this disregard of popular wishes for the sake of secret contributors as common to both parties, with the Conservatives rallying to the defense of the monopoly brewing industry, an evil complex he desired corrected, and the Liberals serving the wishes of wealthy temperance enthusiasts and the soft-drink interests, who advocated the restrictive legislation he abhorred. He sought to demonstrate his independence of another source of Liberal support, the grocery interests, by supporting a Conservative amendment to the bill which would extend the restrictive powers of the licensing authorities over groceries as well as public houses.[41]

The cumulative effect of these various disappointments in attaining what he regarded as the radical mandate of the 1906 election, ranging from the question of Chinese laborers in South Africa through education to

---

[40] Hilaire Belloc, "On Licensing," *The English Review* 2 (June 1909): 600.

[41] *Parliamentary Debates* (Commons), 4th ser., 192 (July 21, 1908): 1828.

licensing, prompted Belloc to turn his attention toward what he saw as the cause of this betrayal of popular wishes, the party system itself. A newer privileged class, the plutocracy which financed the parties, had replaced in his eyes the older aristrocracy and landed class that had been the bane of the nineteenth-century radicals. It did not occur to him that the very democratic masses whose wishes he desired to see implemented had actually lost interest in the radical causes, that it may have been more the Liberal government's awareness of what was on the electorate's mind than any dependence upon secret financial backers that accounted for its reluctance to force the issues. Instead, his disillusionment with the party system intensified in the next two sessions of Parliament as a result of the controversy arising from the 1909 budget and the efforts to deal with the recalcitrant House of Lords.

Chapter Four

Break with
the Party System,
1909-10

The worst evils of the party system, as Belloc saw it, were made clear in the controversy surrounding the House of Lord's rejection of the 1909 budget. The major protagonist of the budget was the new Chancellor of the Exchequer, David Lloyd George, who succeeded Asquith when the latter had replaced Campbell-Bannerman as Prime Minister. Lloyd George had made his name in politics as a radical pro-Boer, who promoted such Welsh particularist and Nonconformist causes as disestablishment in Wales, disobedience to the 1902 Education Act, and temperance legislation. He had been made President of the Board of Trade in Campbell-Bannerman's cabinet partly to balance the strong Liberal-Imperialist character of many other members. But from this more traditional radical background, he eventually emerged as a major proponent of a changed and newer liberalism, with a collectivist or statist inclination far exceeding the "clean slate" aims of the Roseberyites earlier in the decade. Furthermore, he demonstrated much better than they an ability to play the relatively new game of mass democratic politics, as he could both read and influence the moods of the electorate. It was for both of these roles, the master politician and the champion of the new liberalism, that Lloyd George incurred the wrath of Belloc who adhered to the cause of traditional radicalism. Belloc saw the new style of mass politics and the collectivist new liberalism as closely intertwined, and subservient to the interests and needs of the newer privileged class, the capitalist plutocrats, who had come to replace the landed aristocracy. His animus toward the plutocrats had even prompted a certain mellowing in Belloc's nineteenth-century radical disdain for the landed establishment.

In this chapter we will study his distaste for the prevailing political system, and in the following chapters examine his antipathy to the new liberalism, which he believed would lead to the "servile state."

The 1909 budget was not really a venture in new liberalism, except in the sense that any increase in government revenue would facilitate an increase in government power. It consisted mainly in proposals for expanding revenue returns from existing sources, such as increases of twopence on the pound in the income tax, as well as a supertax on very high incomes, a one-third increase in death duties, an increase of halfpenny an ounce in the tobacco duty, and an increase of sixpence a bottle in the whiskey duty. The major innovation was the land tax, which consisted of a capital gains tax of twenty percent on the unearned increment of land value whenever that land changed hands, as well as a duty of a halfpenny on the pound on the capital value of undeveloped lands and minerals. This land tax was entirely in accord with the decades-old radical agitation, in which Belloc himself had taken part, against the privileged landed interests whose riches, being derived from rents, were regarded as largely "unearned" since the value of rent was viewed as the result of action by the community rather than by the owner. Land taxation was the rallying point for that coalition of such varied groups as the Henry Georgeite single-taxers, land nationalizers, Nonconformist moralists, financial reformers, members of the influential middle-class Land Law Reform Association, Fabians, trade unionists, and Laborites, whose support the Liberals had gradually been enlisting since the 1890s. The party's leadership had been paying lip service to the concept since the beginning of the century.[1] This tax required an assessment of all the lands in the country, and would, therefore, expose them to further increments in taxation. Here was a major source of the vehement hostility toward the

---

[1] Ping-Ti Ho, "Land and State in Great Britain, 1873–1910" (Ph.D. diss., Columbia University, 1952), p. 240.

budget. Yet, when actually put into operation, the land tax yielded less revenue than the cost of its administration and consequently was dropped in a few years.

The budget had become necessary partly because of the increased expenditure by the Admiralty for the construction of Dreadnoughts. These ships were regarded as essential to maintain British naval superiority in view of the German naval expansion. Significantly, Lloyd George and the man who had replaced him as President of the Board of Trade, Winston Churchill, had been the most outspoken opponents of the naval program in the cabinet. Another expense that prompted the budget was the noncontributory old age pension plan, which commenced on January 1, 1909. This program, which gave five shillings a week to people over seventy who had less than ten shillings a week income, was another of those socially oriented pieces of legislation of the Liberal government which the Lords had not opposed. Lastly, the budget provided means whereby the government could meet increased expenses without having recourse to protection as was championed by many Unionists.

Belloc reacted favorably to the proposed budget which, he believed, contrasted with so many of the less popular measures introduced by the government. It was based, he believed, upon "the very principle" for which "the majority on this side of the House were sent here by the electors," being "in every sense, in every detail, and in all its extent . . . a radical budget."[2] He regarded the surtax on income exceeding £ 5,000 a year as legitimate since "the distribution of wealth in this country as between the rich and the poor bears no relation to that of any other modern society." That the tax on beer was not as severe as he had first feared, and that the duty on tea was not increased pleased him, for both taxes would have fallen upon "those who can ill afford to pay [them]." Similar anxiety over the retrogressive nature of sales taxes on popular commodities prompted him to wonder if there was any possibility for the tax on tobacco being graduated. He regarded the land taxes as a most gentle manner of dealing with "an anomaly of the grossest kind," whereby "9,000 men own the better half of a country in which some 30,000,-000 people live."[3]

A grievance with the budget that he held in common with the Irish Nationalists was the belief that the whiskey tax constituted an unjust burden upon Ireland where distilling was an important industry. While the tax itself was not oppressive, he thought that its effect on Ireland, where whiskey was the national drink, would be disproportionate since he regarded Ireland as

---

[2] *Parliamentary Debates* (Commons), 5th ser., 5 (May 4, 1909): 968–69.
[3] *Ibid.*, pp. 969–72.

already overtaxed. Solicitude for the Irish distillers was a not insignificant motive of the Irish Nationalists.[4]

The only other matter that drew Belloc's attention during the debates on the budget was the suggestion of including in the budget an increase in the licensing fees for public houses. He saw in this a means whereby the "tied-house" system, that is, the brewing interests, that had been spared by the veto of the licensing bill in the previous session, could be attacked. However, to achieve such a result, he suggested that "the high license might be made to apply only to premises whose tenants or managers suffer from a restriction of their trade to one firm"—that is, only to public houses that were part of the tied-house system and controlled by the breweries—while the cost of the license for the free house, unconnected with the breweries, "might be left as it is." An alternative serving the same ends would be to have the cost of the licenses "graduated in proportion to the number of licenses controlled directly or indirectly by any one brewery or distillery."[5] He was ultimately dissatisfied, however, with the tax on liquor licenses that was actually proposed, for it failed, in his view, to assault directly the tied-house monopoly. Instead, it was based upon a mixture of motives, but

---

[4] F. S. L. Lyons, *The Irish Parliamentary Party, 1890–1910* (London: Faber & Faber, 1951), p. 125. *Parliamentary Debates* (Commons), 5th ser., 4 (May 4, 1909): 970; 11 (October 4, 1909): 1686–87, 1731–32.

[5] *Times* (London), February 10, 1909 (1), pp. 4f.

essentially on the same principle behind the 1908 licensing bill: "that it is immoral to consume fermented liquors." This opinion was held by only "a tiny minority in the state, . . . whose vitality is augmented exceedingly by wealthy faddists." This would be proven, he believed, by an audit of the secret party funds which would show that among the contributors to the Liberal Party, the vast majority were "men who hold that the consumption of fermented liquor is immoral."[6] This was another instance in which he saw the solution desired by the electorate frustrated by the private interests of the subscribers to the secret funds, in this case wealthy teetotaler, Nonconformist supporters of the Liberal Party, and the brewers who gave financial backing to the Conservatives.

But these points aside, he remained sympathetic to the budget, especially in view of the alternative proposal for a system of import duties that was being put forward by many of the Unionists and the Tariff Reform League. He regarded protection as so dangerous for a commercial nation like Great Britain, that even were he to differ from every other thing in the budget, he would still "support it as a free-trade budget" rather than accept protection.[7] What was given as a justification for protection by the tariff

---

[6] *Parliamentary Debates* (Commons), 5th ser., 11 (October 5, 1909): 1857–58.

[7] *Ibid.*, 5th ser., 12 (November 2, 1909): 1709–10.

reformers, that the revenue would thereby be drawn
from a broader basis in the population than would be
the case with the budget, was also a major reason why
the working classes and Labor opposed it and.sym-
pathized with the free-trade budget, for they were
anxious that the costs of government, especially of
social reform, be borne on a progressive basis.[8] The
Conservative leaders argued that the 1909 budget ex-
ceeded the ordinary limits of a finance bill and, instead,
was virtually a revolutionary act, particularly because
of its land assessment features. These fears had naturally been intensified by the demagogic campaign of
Lloyd George in his quest for public support for the
budget, as he pictured the struggle as a crusade against
the aristocracy, the landlords, and the privileged
classes. Some suggest that he was deliberately seeking
to provoke the Lords into rejecting the budget, in the
belief that this was the type of popular issue, unlike
the vetoed education and licensing bills, on which the
government could successfully go to the country and
receive an anti-Lords mandate from the electorate.[9]
But more likely, the government leaders, especially
Asquith, had hoped that the peers would not reject
the budget, for they were neither anxious for an elec-

---

[8] Bernard Semmel, *Imperialism and Social Reform* (London:
George Allen & Unwin, 1960), pp. 164–65.

[9] George Dangerfield, *The Strange Death of Liberal England, 1910–
14* (New York: Capricorn Books, 1935), pp. 22–25.

tion nor confident of Liberal success in it.[10] However, the Lords did veto the budget, forcing an election in January 1910, and its results fulfilled Asquith's fears, as the albatross which the Liberal-Imperialists had always wanted to discard from the party, and which had been removed by the massive 1906 majority, now returned. Because the Liberal and Unionist MPs elected were almost equal in number, the government was forced to rely upon the eighty-two Irish Nationalists and the forty Labor members to maintain its position. Furthermore, the Irish, who were still annoyed with the whiskey tax, threatened to withhold their support for the budget unless resolutions were introduced in the Commons for reform of the House of Lords, after which a Home Rule bill could be brought forward with hope of success.

While the government was making up its mind as to the approach to follow with regard to the recalcitrant House of Lords, as well as trying to come to terms with the Irish, radicals like Belloc were suspicious that nothing really would be done to curb the Lords' veto. He had already established his independence from the government by running for reelection from Salford as an independent without the endorsement of the national Liberal Party. In a letter to the *Times,* Belloc indicated his suspicions that the question of the reform of the House of Lords would go the same way as the licensing

---

[10] Roy Jenkins, *Asquith* (London: Collins, 1964), pp. 222–23.

and education bills, that is, legislation would be allowed to become hopelessly complicated by amendments and lengthy debates so as to lose sight of the original purpose and to confuse and disinterest the public. He feared the much altered legislation would then be rejected by the House of Lords and another general election would ensue which would not be fought on the clear-cut issue of reform of the House of Lords. If this were the case, he insisted, it would mean "a deliberate intention to shelve the whole question of the House of Lords . . . the determination of the professional politicians to keep up the worst unrealities of an outworn system." They aimed at "preventing the democratic reform upon which the great majority of this people are certainly determined."[11] When Asquith announced to the House of Commons that he had neither asked for nor received, as a consequence of the January election returns, guarantees from the King for the creation of many additional peers to ensure the passage in the House of Lords of any Lords' reform legislation, Belloc suggested that the proper course for the Liberal cabinet would be to resign. The cabinet "had an immensely strong strategical position," because with there being, if not a Liberal majority, at least an anti-Unionist majority of 124, the Conservatives would be very hard put to try and govern. But he did not think that such a "straightforward course"

---

[11] *Times* (London), February 14, 1910, p. 8b.

would be taken because there was "no intention of destroying—as it should be destroyed—the power of the other House," for he knew the party leaders were "playing a game."[12]

There were alternative methods by which the House of Lords might be reformed: either its composition could be changed to make it more responsive to the popular will or its veto power could be eliminated. Campbell-Bannerman had suggested the latter course in 1907 with his proposal to leave the Lords only a suspensory veto with which they could delay but not permanently block legislation. That course was preferred by the radicals to any change in the composition of the House of Lords such as, for instance, the appointment of life peers, or in other areas, like joint sessions of both houses when they differed on legislation. They feared that while such reform might make the House of Lords less of an anomaly in a democratic age, at the same time they might invigorate it and not work to ensure the supremacy of the House of Commons. Some in the cabinet, led by Asquith's Liberal-Imperialist colleague Sir Edward Grey, were unsympathtic to any reform which would move toward single-chamber government or Commons' supremacy and even gave intimations of resigning should such be pursued. But ultimately the cabinet agreed to seek to suspend the

---

[12] *Parliamentary Debates* (Commons), 5th ser., 14 (February 22, 1910): 122–23.

Lords' veto power, as Grey's fears of a single-chamber system were satisfied by including in the reform bill a preamble stating an intention to change the composition of the second chamber from a hereditary to a popular basis. Such action has never been taken, however. Basically the proposed bill stated that the Lords could only postpone legislation for a period of three successive sessions of Parliament, and could neither veto nor amend money bills. The Speaker of the House would determine what was a money bill. Last, the bill reduced the maximum duration of Parliaments from seven to five years. Therefore, the effect was in the direction of single-chamber government.

The strategy the cabinet decided upon in the case of a Lords' veto of the reform bill was to go on the offensive. Should there be a veto, Asquith suggested two alternatives for King Edward: either to agree to a dissolution and another election in which a possible Liberal victory would be followed by the creation of enough new peers to guarantee passage of the reform bill (after which Home Rule would be introduced), or to ask the Conservatives to try to rule as a minority government.[13] In the meantime the controversial budget finally passed both houses, and lines were being drawn for the confrontation on the reform bill. Belloc was delighted that the government had decided to bring the House of Lords question to the front and would

[13] Jenkins, *Asquith,* pp. 232–33.

press for ending the veto power in preference to the other reforms. He believed that it had been the pressure of the small band of parliamentary radicals that had prevented the issue from being shelved. There was still another objective, however, which he thought should be fought for before another general election, and that was the reform of the electoral law.[14]

The particular democratizing steps he desired were a wider suffrage (although not for women), shorter residence requirements for voting, and an alternative vote whereby the second choice of voters would be considered in order to prevent in an election with more than two contestants a victory by a candidate receiving less than a majority of votes. He was convinced, with the faith of a nineteenth-century radical, that a broadened electorate would overwhelmingly support the Liberals. Two years later, after the controversy over the reform of the Lords had been settled, Asquith's government did introduce a franchise and registration bill that sought to broaden the male franchise, end plural voting and the university constituencies, and reduce the residence requirements for voting. It was estimated that the bill would have increased the number of electors by more than two million. But the bill was withdrawn after the Speaker of the House ruled that

---

[14] Hilaire Belloc to Charles Goodwin, April 6, 1910, Robert Speaight, ed., *Letters from Hilaire Belloc* (London: Hollis & Carter, 1958), pp. 26–27.

female suffrage amendments that had been introduced had so changed the character of the bill that a new one would have to be put forward. Rather than combine franchise extension with female suffrage, the government dropped the bill entirely,[15] and it was not until the Representation of the People Act was passed in 1918 that virtually universal male suffrage was attained. Significantly, the first election held under these conditions was won by the coalition led by Lloyd George in which the Unionists were dominant.

The expected struggle over the House of Lords was postponed by the sudden death on May 7, 1910, of the worldly and politically experienced, if not politically sophisticated or interested, King Edward VII, and the succession of his politically innocent, domestic, and unsophisticated son, George V. The cabinet was of a mind not to force the new sovereign to have to consent at the outset of his reign to the unpleasant decision of packing the House of Lords to ensure passage of the reform bill, a cause of whose popular mandate the new king was uncertain.[16] Instead the cabinet consented to a constitutional conference with the opposition leaders in the hope of arriving at a compromise solution to the issue. The conference, at which Asquith, Lloyd George,

---

[15] Homer Lawrence Morris, "Parliamentary Franchise Reform in England from 1885 to 1918" (Ph.D. diss., Columbia University, 1921), pp. 86–87, 95–96.

[16] Harold Nicolson, *King George the Fifth: His Life and Reign* (London: Constable, 1952), p. 130.

the Earl of Crewe (Colonial Secretary), and Augustine Birrell (Chief Secretary for Ireland) represented the cabinet, and Balfour, the Marquess of Lansdowne, Austen Chamberlain, and the Earl of Cawdor represented the Unionists, held twenty-one sittings over a period of five months. Ultimately it had to announce on November 10, 1910, its failure to arrive at a settlement. Information as to the proceedings was deliberately withheld until much later when biographies of the participants appeared.

The very existence of the conference was all that was needed to convince Belloc of the insincerity of the Liberal cabinet's intentions to curb the House of Lords and of the validity of his theory that no real differences separated the parties. Actually, Asquith desired the conference not only because of his concern over forcing the King to take a controversial stand, but also because of his doubts (legitimate as events proved) of Liberal success in another election.[17] Even when the conference failed and it was decided to call another general election, Belloc remained convinced that it was simply a means of further postponing the issue. He insisted that the will of the majority that the House of Lords be curbed was already manifest, and, he asked, "Does anyone in his senses expect more than twenty or thirty seats to change at this election?" Instead, an unnecessary election "on which the two front benches are determined, in conference and by agreement . . . is

---

[17] Jenkins, *Asquith,* p. 240.

being fought on no issue, and is being imposed merely to save what is left of vitality in the party system."

Since the leaders of the parties, who controlled, rather than were subject to, the elected House of Commons, were unsympathetic to popular wishes and responsive only to the desires of the plutocratic governing class, he could see no consequence emerging from the election other than the formation of a coalition government. The appropriate action for the Liberal prime minister, according to Belloc, should have been either to get guarantees from the king of additional creations should the Lords veto reform, or, failing that, to resign and dare the opposition to try and govern without a majority. Since the unreality of the party struggle prevented this from being done, he could not see how any man, other than those "represented by the Socialist Labor party or . . . the Irish party . . . [could] put himself forward under any general party program whatsoever." For his own part, unless he could "come forward in complete independence of the system" and "stand as an Independent to represent my constituency," and not "play the party game," or "talk about the wicked leader of the opposition and the good prime minister—angels here and demons there," he would not stand for reelection.[18]

In point of fact, Asquith had secured the guarantees Belloc desired from the new King, but they would be

---

[18] *Parliamentary Debates* (Commons), 5th ser., 20 (November 18, 1910): 98–104.

given only after another election had returned a Liberal majority.[19] However, there was some legitimacy in Belloc's suspicion of the constitutional conference, for both sides had considered a compromise which was directed more to constitutional reform of the House of Lords than to establishing the clear-cut ascendancy of the House of Commons which the radicals desired and which would have been attained by ending the absolute veto power of the Lords. The conference had considered proposals that the Lords not be allowed to reject a finance bill unless a joint committee of both houses ruled that such a bill contained other than financial matters, and that other rejected legislation which had passed the Commons in two successive years be dealt with by a joint session of both houses, in which session the power of the Lords would be diminished so as to permit a substantial majority in the Commons to have supremacy. All of this indicated the soundness of the radical fears that the Lords would not be tamed by the deliberations of the conference, because most modern financial legislation has social and political motives other than merely the raising of revenue and such could easily be regarded as not exempt from the Lords' veto. Furthermore, ministries very often do not have the substantial majorities to overcome the numerically reduced but probably qualitatively invigorated House of Lords that they would confront in a joint session.

Ultimately the conference broke down on the ques-

---

[19] Nicolson, *King George the Fifth,* p. 138.

tion of what would be included in a third category of "constitutional" or "organic" legislation, which would, in the case of a Lords' veto, be permanently killed. The specific question on which no agreement could be reached was the Unionists' sympathy for, and the Liberals' opposition to, the inclusion of Home Rule in this category.[20] Significantly, the Unionists waged the election campaign not on the unpopular defense of the House of Lords, or even on tariff reform, which Balfour said he would submit to a referendum only in the event of a Unionist victory, but on opposition to Home Rule. The willingness of the Unionist leadership to acept some changes in the Lords and their reluctance to push protection indicated to Belloc their complicity with the Liberal leadership in the unreal political game. Because of this he believed the Tory followers would be disappointed even should they win the election. He believed that "what is left of Tory feelings in my own country would have voted for keeping the House of Lords as it is," yet a Conservative victory would not work toward that end, just as a vote for the Conservatives would not really be a vote for protection.[21]

Belloc's decision not to seek reelection in the December 1910 election was not, however, one suddenly ar-

[20] Jenkins, *Asquith*, pp. 238–40.
[21] *Parliamentary Debates* (Commons), 5th ser., 20 (November 18, 1910): 101.

rived at. There were, moreover, other motives behind it besides his disenchantment with the party system. As early as June he had written:

> Every day that passes makes me more determined to chuck Westminster; it is too low for words. The position is ridiculous and the expense is damnable. More than that, it cuts into my life, interferes with my earnings, and separates me from my home—all three irritating.[22]

For one thing, in his very first year as a member of Parliament, Belloc and his family had moved away from their London home to what became his home for the rest of his life, King's Land, in the village of Shipley, seven miles south of Horsham in Sussex. This meant lengthy separations from his family during the parliamentary session and on his visits to his constituency in Salford, in addition to his already extensive travels while lecturing and writing. These separations were very unpleasant for a man so closely attached to his family.

His political career also conflicted with his literary efforts. He, nevertheless, continued his prolific literary output; in the less than five years that he served in Parliament he managed to have published twenty-one works in addition to numerous articles ranging from contributions to such serious journals as the *Fortnightly Review* and the *Dublin Review* to essays for newspapers. Some of his publications were short political and

---

[22] Hilaire Belloc to J. S. Phillimore, June 12, 1910, *Letters,* p. 27.

religious pamphlets, but there were also three satirical novels (*Mr. Clutterbuck's Election, A Change in the Cabinet,* and *Pongo and the Bull*), two volumes of verse, four volumes of newspaper essays (*On Nothing On Everything, On Anything,* and *On Something*), three books of travel and topography (*The Historic Thames, The Pyrenees,* and *Sussex*), and a biography (*Marie Antoinette*). As has already been indicated, Belloc's continual financial difficulties accounted for much of his literary output. The pressure in the era before MPs were paid must have been intense, and makes apparent how important to him financially was a post he obtained in 1905 as a weekly columnist for a Conservative paper, the *Morning Post.* Unfortunately he clashed too frequently with its editor, Fabian Ware. He sought a more regular and remunerative position with the paper, in which he offered to write a number of leaders on nonpolitical subjects, book reviews, and articles on military subjects, but Ware gave him no definite reply. When he issued a virtual ultimatum, Ware remained unmoved, and Belloc broke with the paper in September 1910.[23] The loss of this income and the necessity to devote more time to recoup the loss may have had no small part in influencing his decision to abandon his time-consuming and unremunerative political position.

---

[23] Robert Speaight, *The Life of Hilaire Belloc* (New York: Farrar, Straus & Cudahy, 1957), pp. 257–59.

Another factor that prompted his hesitancy about seeking reelection was the opposition that had developed within the Liberal organization in his constituency because of his independence of strict party ties. In January 1909 he had written to Charles Goodwin, the Liberal agent for South Salford, that he would have "no complaint whatsoever to make" should "those who have stood behind the Liberal organization with their wealth find it necessary to support someone more moderate or more attached to the party system than myself.[24] Prior to the election in January 1910 he was pessimistic about his chances of being returned, and had resigned himself to defeat with the thought that "the House of Commons is hypocritical and dull beyond words, and membership of it is a tremendous price to pay for the little advantage of being able (very rarely) to expose a scandal or to emphasize a point of public interest."[25] He was reelected, but not without the vigorous opposition of the advocates of women's suffrage, who picketed the South Salford polling booths to indicate their disapproval.

Belloc was hostile toward the suffrage cause even though his own mother had been a pioneer feminist. She had been both a close friend of and a collaborator with Barbara Bodichon in the *Englishwoman's Journal,*

---

[24] Belloc to Goodwin, January 1, 1909, *Letters,* p. 19.
[25] Hilaire Belloc to Maurice Baring, December 18, 1909, *Letters,* pp. 23–24.

a publication of the 1860s that concerned itself with opening careers for women rather than with suffrage.[26] His opposition to female suffrage was not lessened by the increasing militancy of the suffrage movement, particularly of the organization dominated by Mrs. Emmeline Pankhurst, the Women's Social and Political Union, whose tactics tended to alienate a potentially wider following. The WSPU had advanced from disrupting and heckling the speeches of Liberal spokesmen to physically assaulting the property and person of ministers. In the summer of 1909 imprisoned suffragettes had begun hunger strikes to secure their release. In September the government decided to retaliate by forcibly feeding such inmates (as was done in lunatic asylums) rather than release them. Humanitarian opinion was outraged. Keir Hardie, a champion of the suffragettes in the House of Commons, several times questioned the Home Secretary, Herbert Gladstone, about the procedure. Belloc often followed Hardie's questions with rebuttal questions that sought to mitigate the outrage over forced feeding by indicating that it had been used against male hunger strikers in the past without any protests from Parliament.[27] Later, Hardie complained about the treatment received by

---

[26] Roger Fulford, *Votes for Women* (London: Faber & Faber, 1957), p. 41.

[27] *Parliamentary Debates* (Commons), 5th ser., 11 (September 28, 1909): 1094; (October 4): 1653; (October 5): 1849.

Miss Emily Wilding-Davison, a suffragette held prisoner in Strangeways Gaol in Manchester, on whom a hose was turned in order to force her out of her cell in which she had barricaded herself rather than submit to forced feeding. When Gladstone admitted that in so doing the authorities had committed a grave error of judgment, Belloc unsympathetically wondered what other measure could have been used that would have been more merciful.[28]

He was associated with the Women's National Anti-Suffrage League, in which he had such unusual allies as Lord Cromer and Lord Curzon. Other prominent members included the writers Mrs. Humphry Ward and Miss Violet Markham, as well as Ivor Guest, Nicholas Kay-Shuttleworth, and John St. Loe Strachey, the editor of the *Spectator*. When a private female suffrage bill, introduced by David Shackleton, a Labor member for Clitheroe, and sponsored by a multipartisan Conciliation Committee, was debated in Parliament, Belloc again made unusual allies, as he and his old Oxford Union antagonist, F. E. Smith, were among the bill's opponents. He disliked the bill partly because only a limited portion of the female population, "the educated women, the wealthy women, the middle-class women, who have property," would benefit by it. In his opposition, however, he dissociated himself from the arguments of other opponents of suffrage, for instance,

---

[28] *Ibid.*, 12 (November 1, 1909): 1433.

that "women are excluded from public action . . . by a lack of intelligence." He believed the only category of men who regarded women as inferior in intelligence could "be found amongst the very young unmarried men," whose experience of life will cause their opinion of women to pass "from reverence to stupor, and from stupor to terror." He similarly discounted the argument that there should be only male suffrage on the grounds of male superiority in physical force, since he deemed the "idea that a state ultimately reposes in physical force . . . the uttermost nonsense." Indeed, even if it did he was not at all certain that among the modern urban population "the males would rule or come out always best."

What particularly turned him against the bill was that it would not enfranchise that kind of woman "who molds the state, and to whom we who know anything at all of human life would very gladly give some of its governance." These were "the mothers of families and the wives, not the disappointed women, not the women who have not borne or cannot or will not bear children." He insisted that

> under this bill you will bring in every woman who has quarreled with her husband and is keeping a separate establishment; every woman who wishes to live her own life, whatever that may mean; every one of that sex who has a grievance against her Creator; and you will bring in a large body of that other class who number many thousands in every large city, to whom without the

slightest doubt no civic influence whatever should be given, while these others whom, if any, we would gladly admit, are excluded.[29]

In point of fact, the addition of women to the electorate has probably been a boon to those socially conservative causes, like family unity and orthodox sexual codes, that Belloc feared would be endangered by the more radical enthusiasts for female suffrage. This has been because of the votes of those more domestic women whom Belloc would have admitted to suffrage. The conciliation bill in question secured a majority when a division was taken on it, but the cabinet opposed it, and it met the same fate as most private bills by being smothered when sent to a committee of the whole House.

Belloc boasted that opposition to female suffrage was the popular sentiment and that his reelection had been not impeded but indeed assisted by the hostility of the suffragettes. The secretary of the North of England Society for Women's Suffrage insisted, however, that it was the suffrage society's opposition to Belloc, specifically its sponsorship and announcement on November 21, 1910, of a third candidate, the radical journalist H. N. Brailsford, to contest the South Salford seat, that forced the Liberals to obtain Belloc's withdrawal and his replacement as candidate by Charles

[29] *Ibid.*, 19 (July 11, 1910): 96–99.

Russell, whose views on suffrage were satisfactory enough to prompt Brailsford's withdrawal.[30] Belloc challenged this acount and claimed that the South Salford Liberal executive expected his continued candicacy, but he, of his own intent, refused to accept because of his dislike of the party system. As for the suffrage question, it was his opposition to the suffrage society that "was regarded as the most popular part of my declarations in the constituency."[31] In the election the Conservative candidate was returned to succeed Belloc, probably because of the confusion in Liberal ranks following his precipitate resignation.[32]

Although it would have been more common, and probably more suitable to do otherwise, the disillusioned Belloc did not turn his attention away from politics and back to purely literary matters. Instead, he commenced a personal journalistic crusade against the prevailing party system. His major collaborator in this

---

[30] *Times* (London), November 28, 1910, p. 8c. Brailsford, significantly, was more typical of radical opinion on foreign policy than Belloc, as his pro-German and anti-French articles in the *Nation* indicated that journal's difference in tone from the days when it was known as the *Speaker*. This was characteristic of the widening gulf on foreign affairs that Belloc came to experience between himself and his old pro-Boer allies. A. J. P. Taylor, *The Troublemakers* (London: Hamish Hamilton, 1957), p. 112.

[31] *Times* (London), November 30, 1910, p. 10c (1).

[32] Henry Pelling, *Social Geography of British Elections, 1885-1910* (London: Macmillan, 1967), p. 245.

campaign was Cecil Chesterton, the younger brother
of G. K. Chesterton. The latter had always maintained
in his essays and debates a good-natured spirit toward
his antagonists or opponents, but brother Cecil was
much more combative and pugnacious. This made him
a logical, if not prudent, partner for the argumentative
Belloc. Unlike Belloc, whose views sprang from a long-
range philosophical and historical position, the younger
Chesterton had more of a journalistic approach to
matters, involving himself in immediate day-by-day
issues without concern for overall conceptual consistency. His earlier sentiments and connections were very
antithetical to Belloc's. G. K. Chesterton, whose views
were more akin to Belloc's, remembered that during
the Boer War his brother "gravitated to a sort of
practical Tory democracy, which was more and more
permeated by the socialism of Sidney Webb and Bernard Shaw."[33] He was a member of the Fabian Society
and in a book he published in 1905[34] had adhered to
the very theme for which the Webbs praised Lord Rosebery, that liberalism should abandon its traditional
Gladstonian principles and adapt itself to the more
scientific liberalism appropriate to the twentieth century—the very kind of pollution of liberal principles

---

[33] G. K. Chesterton, *Autobiography* (New York: Sheed & Ward,
1936), p. 201.
[34] Cecil Chesterton, *Gladstonian Ghosts* (London: S. C. Brown,
Langham, 1905).

that so offended Belloc. In Belloc's eyes, the new liberalism was not so much an intellectual theory as a smokescreen to cover the new forms of privileged wealth in society.

But despite this difference in outlook, Cecil Chesterton, atypical of a Fabian socialist, was able as early as 1906 openly to appreciate the basically romantic or traditionalist social reformism of Belloc, whom he saw as being "at one with other reformers in that he finds the present condition of the civilized world intolerable." According to Chesterton, however, Belloc did not share the view "of the world as always moving slowly toward a dimly discerned utopia," but regarded it "as continually slipping back from the simplicity and sanity at which men are always aiming." While Chesterton believed that Belloc, "like other men whose ideas form a system," had a tendency sometimes to push them to extremes, he nonetheless thought that "socialists would be well advised if they accepted his primary contention and preached socialism as the only way in which modern civilization can get back to human simplicity." Furthermore, as a Tory democrat, Chesterton believed that in Belloc "the French influence has been the stronger, and that his temper and point of view are more French than English." While this foreignness had permitted Belloc to see certain things about England that most natives would not, at the same time there were "things in the English temper that he does not understand," one of which was "the peculiar character of English patriotism, that it attaches itself to the flag and not to soil." This explained for him Belloc's "grossly, though quite unconsciously, unjust" attitude toward "that great English movement which we call imperialism."[35]

These reservations about Belloc's foreignness and his inability to appreciate certain British institutions did not inhibit Chesterton from joining forces with him in a campaign assailing the very character of British politics. They jointly published, shortly after Belloc's withdrawal from politics, a critique entitled *The Party System*. Their central thesis was that the rivalry between the two major parties was a sham game played by the two front benches for the purpose of determining which one would control the government at any particular moment. In reality there were no substantial differences between them, and both were equally irresponsible to their followings. Politics had become concerned with "a number of unreal issues, defined neither by the people nor by the Parliament, but by the politicians themselves, . . . to give a semblance of reality to their empty competition."[36] This criticism had many elements in common with the conclusions of other commentators on Edwardian politics, who noted the

---

[35] Cecil Chesterton, "Hilaire Belloc," *Living Age* 251 (December 15, 1906): 691–93.

[36] Hilaire Belloc and Cecil Chesterton, *The Party System* (London: Stephen Swift, 1911), pp. 33–34.

increasing control over the House of Commons by the ministry and the declining independence of private members in relation to the party leadership. As we shall see, however, Belloc and Chesterton differed in their emphasis upon a conspiratorial character for these developments, which were to be explained by "a united plutocracy, a homogeneous mass of the rich, commercial and territorial, into whose hands practically all power, political as well as economic, has now passed."[37]

Their criticism was grounded on a theory of representative government that was much more democratic than was common in the British political tradition. Belloc held that there should be "absolute freedom in the selection of representatives" to Parliament, who "must be strictly responsible to their constituents and to no one else" and "must deliberate in perfect freedom, and especially must be absolutely independent of the executive." In such a system, "from the people would come the impulse and the initiative. They would make certain demands; it would be the duty of their representatives to give expression to these demands and of the executive to carry them out."[38] But historically this theory of an independent private membership of the House of Commons, not subject to the control of the executive or the party leadership, was really more anti-

---

[37] *Ibid.*, p. 29.
[38] *Ibid.*, pp. 18–19.

democratic, as it pictured the MPs as members of the grand jury of the nation whose private judgment and considerations would also prevail over the wishes of their respective constituencies. The undemocratic implications of a highly independent private membership became especially obvious when the emphasis of liberalism began to shift away from the nineteenth-century concern with dismantling privilege and monopoly, especially that promoted by government, to the modern conception of the positive state, with powers that could be granted only by broad legislative acts immune from the impediments of recalcitrant private MPs. In short, the ends that the democratic electorate sought could be achieved only if the legislatures were under control of the executive. But Belloc and Chesterton could not see this connection between executive dominance and the development of democracy. Instead, they viewed the growth of executive power as a deliberate means of circumventing the power of the newly enfranchised electorate, and believed it could have been prevented only if the democratic enfranchisement had taken place at one stroke rather than by stages.[39]

Belloc's analysis of the servility of the members of Parliament and the impotence of the House against the wishes of the cabinet was accurate and in accord

---

[39] *Ibid.,* pp. 29–30.

with other contemporary estimates. For example, in *The Governance of England* Sidney Low noted that "if by some silent and miraculous revolution the House of Commons were swept out of existence, while other parts of our Constitution were left standing, the progress of events in all essentials would have been little different from what it was"[40] This was because of certain procedural developments whereby most of the House's time became preempted for discussion and action on the ministry's legislative program, while the time allotted for private members' business declined as did the likelihood for successful private action. For one thing, the opportunity to initiate private business was limited to one afternoon in the week, which meant that most private bills could never be brought forward. Those that were introduced could easily be smothered by shelving amendments or by "blocking motions." A blocking motion was a notice given by a member of the government of his intention to introduce a motion on a subject. This prevented any other motions on the same subject from being raised. The ministry's control over the amount of time allotted for any particular measure was another means of tightening its control over procedure. The situation was best summarized by the comment of A. Lawrence Lowell, in *The Gov-*

---

[40] Sidney Low, *The Governance of England* (New York: G. P. Putnam's Sons, 1913), p. 74.

ernment of England, that the Commons had solved the problem of apportioning time "by giving most of it to the government to use as it pleases, and leaving the private members to scramble for the rest."[41]

This strengthening of ministerial control over Parliament had a long history and was the consequence more of impersonal developments connected with the changing role and functions of government than of any conspiratorial effort of a ruling elite. It began about the time of the first reform bill in 1832, when it became an accepted rule that "all measures of importance and general concern should be prepared in the government departments" because of the superior competence of professionals acquainted with administration over the cruder legislative drafts of private members.[42] This was necessary because of the desire of many interested groups "to use the state for collectivist ends," for despite the prevailing laissez-faire rhetoric, the reform era was characterized by an increase of state intervention by way of factory acts, trade union acts, railway company acts, and other similar efforts at promoting health, safety, and legality in matters like water supply, sanitation, bankruptcy, and so on. Concurrent with these

---

[41] A. Lawrence Lowell, *The Government of England,* 2 vols. (New York: Macmillan, 1916–17), 1:311.

[42] Peter Fraser, "The Growth of Ministerial Control in the Nineteenth-Century House of Commons," *The English Historical Review* 75 (July 1960): 454–55.

efforts were "the reform and expansion of the civil service," beginning about 1800 and intensifying under Robert Peel between 1841 and 1846.[43]

The weakness of party ties during midcentury, however, did manage to delay until at least the 1880s the general acceptance of "the idea that the prime purpose of the House of Commons was to pass legislation," that is, to pass programs presented to it by the ministry or the leaders of the majority. This view was furthered by general impatience with the obstructionist tactics of the minority Irish Party, as well as the impatience of many radical Liberals "with the curbs the old procedures of Parliament placed upon the will of the majority." Procedural reforms were made in 1894 and 1902 to curb these impediments to majority will. For instance, debate on supply was fixed to a number of days, after which votes would be passed by cloture; the right of moving amendments to supply was extinguished; and the opportunities for private action were circumscribed. Joseph Chamberlain was foremost in advocating strengthening the power of the majority in the legislature; he insisted that the representative system would be a farce "if with one hand you pretend that the majority elects a government; and then with the other

---

[43] J. Bartlett Brebner, "Laissez-Faire and State Intervention in Nineteenth-Century Britain," *The Journal of Economic History,* supp. 8 (1948): 59–73; reprinted in *The Making of English History,* ed. R. L. Schuyler and Herman Ausubel (New York: Dryden Press, 1952), p. 508.

you prevent that government from doing its proper work." More traditional Liberals, like James Bryce and Henry Campbell-Bannerman, remained solicitous for the minorities in the House, since the nation can often "find a voice through the minority," and the House of Commons was "not a mere factory of statutes, not a mere countinghouse." After 1900 the ministerial control of the House of Commons was strengthened as much by "the refinement of the two-party system and the greater self-discipline and decorum of the major parties" as by further reforms in parliamentary procedure.[44]

The procedural changes inhibiting the private member were more the consequence than the cause of the development of the machinery of the party system. That machinery had become more sophisticated and powerful with the introduction of the democratic franchise and was ostensibly formulated to advance the wishes of the democracy. But in fact the reverse seems to have occurred; the machinery became rather the instrument for securing mass adherence to the leadership of the parties than the means of making the leadership responsive to popular wishes. In his classic analysis of the modern popular party organizations, the National Union of Conservative Associations and the National Liberal Federation, that had developed in the late

---

[44] Fraser, "Growth of Ministerial Control," pp. 461–63.

1860s, the 1870s, and the 1880s, M. Ostrogorski concluded that the caucus, that is, the popular organization, "has not been able to provide the parties with a
really democratic government; it has created the forms
of it, but not the essence." The popular organizations
displaced the old politics, that is, Whiggism and old-
fashioned Toryism, which had an aristocratic and proprietary character. It also displaced classic radicalism,
which was hostile to any strict central organization. The
caucus, however, failed to create a really democratic
situation; it succeeded only "in bringing into glaring
prominence the contradiction between the capacity and
the power of the masses." The supposed "ex-ruling
class, the middle class," which was allegedly dethroned
by the mass organizations, had "by dint of adroitness,"
preserved "in the management of parties the reality of
power." The ruling class, in "pretending to bow down
before the masses . . . let them say what they liked,
allowed them the satisfaction of holding forth and of
voting extravagant resolutions in the caucuses, provided
that it was permitted to manage everything; and to
cover its designs it developed the practice of wire
pulling." Or in what Ostrogorski admitted might be too
sweeping a conclusion, "The monopoly of the leadership which was held by the representatives of the old
ruling classes tends to give place to a monopoly of wire
pullers backed by plutocrats."[45]

---

[45] M. Ostrogorski, *Democracy and the Organization of Political
Parties* (New York: Macmillan, 1902), 1:580–81, 592.

This was essentially the theme stressed by Belloc and Chesterton, who insisted that none of the resolutions and policies proclaimed by the National Liberal Federation and the National Union of Conservative Associations "has the smallest effect on practical politics until it has been ratified by the central office . . . the hinge upon which everything else depends." They insisted that the central offices of the parties kept control over the local parties and dominated the selection of candidates as well as the issues to be raised in an election, in complete disregard of the representative principle. The reason the central office had this power was its control over the party funds necessary to wage elections. Hence, Belloc and Chesterton contended, it was possible for three types of men to be selected as candidates for Parliament: the richest man in a particular locality, who "subscribes largely to the funds of the local organization, sometimes paying all its expenses out of his own purse," who, naturally, if he wished, would be chosen as a candidate; a rich man "with no special local connections," who solicited a candidacy directly from the central office by putting down a subscription to "the secret treasury of the party," in return for which a seat would be found for him varying "in security with the amount of the said subscription"; and, last, a talented but relatively poor man who would in some way "connect himself with the governing group," and who as one of "the most serviceable tools of the party bosses" would find his poverty no obstacle to his success, so long as he was submissive to the machine," with "the sacrifice of his freedom (and honor)" as "the condition of his securing these advantages."[46]

Belloc, perhaps more effectively, but at least more humorously, depicted these aspects of the political scene in a series of satirical novels, written either while he was still in Parliament or immediately thereafter. The first of these, *Mr. Clutterbuck's Election*,[47] dealt with the adventures or misadventures of a wealthy businessman, Clutterbuck, whose fortune was largely attributable to questionable government contracts for materials and ventures that under ordinary circumstances would never have been sold or undertaken. His and his wife's ambitions to enter more important circles gradually prompted political aspirations in him, aspirations that were satisfied only after displaying his generosity to the governing party's secret treasury. Upon his electoral success, the still politically innocent Clutterbuck became more ambitious and desired a peerage, which he learned was purchasable. His political secretary, however, was incapable of satisfying his ambition on such short notice, despite Clutterbuck's imprudent publicizing of his expectation. Clutterbuck's disappointment led him to consult with William Bailey, a high-society maverick whose radical views were quite untypical (and, incidentally, very much like Belloc's).

---

[46] Belloc and Chesterton, *Party System,* pp. 119–23.

[47] Hilaire Belloc, *Mr. Clutterbuck's Election* (London: Eveleigh Nash, 1908).

He suggested that Clutterbuck make public reference to a highly irregular overseas venture about which Clutterbuck himself knew nothing but which involved very important behind-the-scenes figures in society, including the Duke of Battersea. The duke was Mr. I. Z. Barnett, the international Jewish financier of Belloc's earlier novel *Emmanuel Burden*, who had by the time of this book been elevated to a peerage. The political powers took the counteroffensive against Clutterbuck's embarrassing remarks, and were able to have his recent election to Parliament declared void on the very technical charge of corrupting the electorate because his election agent had purchased some glasses of whiskey for a handful of voters. Clutterbuck ultimately abandoned his crusade against the overseas venture, was restored to the good graces of the establishment, and was given his desired peerage.

In addition to the manner in which candidates were selected, the novel dwelt upon several other aspects of the political scene which incensed Belloc, particularly the role of secret party funds, the sale of peerages, and the inadequacy of the then existing provisions against electoral corruption which were often actually used to serve corrupt purposes. It has been noted that although the extension of the franchise and the appearance of popular party organizations had ended the older style of political leadership, it had not created a system of true democratic control. A similar point must be noted about the elimination of the grosser forms of bribery and treating of the electors that had characterized British politics prior to the democratic era. The decline of corruption was not so much a result of corrective legislation like the Secret Ballot Act of 1872 or the Corrupt and Illegal Practices Act of 1883, as a result of a "mental transformation" of the masses, whereby the voter regarded his suffrage "as a lever of political power rather than as a privilege for picking the candidate's pocket," and "corruption became outmoded and gave way to demagogy." The individual voter was thus no longer subject to crude bribery, and candidates were spared the considerable expenses involved.

The expenses and effort needed for a parliamentary campaign and career remained, however, causing another kind of corruption in which candidates of limited means were dependent upon the central party organization and the local associations for funds, and the ancillary party organizations for services.[48] Paradoxically, the limiting of local election expenditure by the Corrupt and Illegal Practices Act of 1883 and the creation of new constituencies without local patrons by the 1885 redistribution actually worked to increase expenditure by the parties at the national level. This

---

[48] William B. Gwyn, *Democracy and the Cost of Politics in Britain* (London: University of London, Athlone Press, 1962), pp. 92–93, 100–101.

expenditure grew from £30,000–50,000 in 1880 to £80,000–120,000 in 1906.[49] These great expenses and a candidate's dependency for monetary and organizational assistance were important persuasive reminders with which a ministry could "often subdue rebellion in its own ranks, and to a certain extent keep its antagonists from going to extremities, by allowing it to be known that if certain things are done, or not done, there will be a general election." An election would be particularly unpleasant for an independent-minded MP, who would find himself cut off from assistance.[50]

The existence of the party funds naturally raised questions about the contributors and about their expecting something in return. Belloc and Chesterton tended to regard the role of the "secret funds" and the efforts to satisfy the contributors to them as "the most important fact about English politics." They regarded as particularly onerous the fact that "the ordinary method of replenishing the party funds is by the sale of peerages, baronetcies, and other honors in return for subscriptions," but "much more insidious" was the fact that many wealthy men contributed to the funds in order to get "a measure of control over the machine

---

[49] H. J. Hanham, "The Sale of Honors in Late Victorian England," *Victorian Studies* 3 (March 1960): 282.

[50] Low, *Governance of England*, p. 111.

which governs the country." This was done "sometimes to promote some private fad of their own, but more often simply to promote their commercial interests."[51]

As early as February 18, 1908, Belloc had moved in Parliament a private resolution condemning the secrecy of political funds. He believed at the time that the secrecy of these funds was still just a threat to political life, but that it was developing into "an imminent peril." The dangerous aspect of these funds was that great political weight was given "to the few men who are large subscribers," while insufficient weight was given to those who should be the real source of authority over Parliament, the voters. The influence of these funds also violated what the democratic radical Belloc deemed the central convention or rule of British government, namely, that the initiative in legislation should proceed from the electorate through the Commons and finally to the ministry, "the spokesman of the majority." Instead, the initiative was transferred to the ministry acting in response to the contributors. If the names of the contributors to these funds had been made publicly known, it would "become impossible in the near future that the discipline of any party should be only made effective by a payment in secret to a fund, and a payment in secret out of that fund to a private individual."[52]

---

[51] Belloc and Chesterton, *Party System,* pp. 101–4, 110.

[52] *Parliamentary Debates* (Commons), 4th ser., 184 (February 19, 1908): 899–905.

The struggle over the licensing bill of that year had been for Belloc a very clear indication of the sinister influence of the secret funds. He viewed the positions of both sides of the House as having been influenced by them; the Unionists had opposed any reform of the drink trade because of the support they received from the brewers, and the Liberals had aimed at inhibiting the use of liquor rather than reforming the industry because, as "an audit of the secret parliamentary funds would show," behind their government was a body of contributors, the vast majority of which were men "who hold that the consumption of fermented liquor is immoral."[53]

G. K. Chesterton, Belloc's close asociate, had in the previous year, 1907, questioned the raising of party funds by the sale of honors in a letter to the *Daily News*. This issue aroused the ire not only of radicals like Belloc and Chesterton, but also of the spokesmen of the right, like Lord Robert Cecil, who resented the pollution of the hereditary aristocracy.[54] Belloc insisted that any analysis of the peers created in the previous twenty years would show that very few possessed the theoretical qualifications of a peer, that is, "a man called to the Council of the Nations because he is in some way especially fitted to advise on some matters of public

---

[53] *Ibid.*, 5th ser., 11 (October 1909): 1858.

[54] Elie Halévy, *The Rule of Democracy, 1905–14* (New York: Barnes & Noble, 1961), p. 314.

policy." In examining the peers created in the Birthday Honors List for 1910, he found most sadly lacking any criterion for the honor other than great wealth, especially of a mercantile or commercial character, and services to the party in one form or another.[55]

Such umbrage at the less than outstanding appointments to the House of Lords was hardly warranted, for peerages had traditionally been awarded for other than idealistic reasons. The younger William Pitt bestowed titles freely on borough patrons for the purpose of securing for himself a majority in both houses of Parliament. Subsequently, restraint in the use of political honors substantially declined for "once this example had been set, Pitt's successors in office were not slow to follow it."[56] Robert Peel was almost alone in his belief that honors ought be awarded on the basis of merit rather than as a means to secure support or because they were solicited, and as a result very few peers were created during his ministry. But, for the most part, under other prime ministers peerages were awarded to satisfy partisan supporters and to secure majorities in the House of Lords.

A difference which did take place in the later part of the nineteenth century was the gradual abandonment of the one qualification that had been adhered to even

[55] Belloc and Chesterton, *Party System,* pp. 104–10.
[56] Gerald Macmillan, *Honors for Sale* (London: Richards Press, 1954), pp. 234–35.

when appointments were made for political purposes. That qualification had been that peerages be awarded only to the landed classes. After 1868 a few business-men began to get peerages, and after 1886 it was no longer exceptional, so that the House of Lords took on an increasing commercial and industrial flavor. This was not because honors were purchased, but because of changing social and economic conditions. And with their greater economic power, the leaders of industry and commerce were becoming better able to afford the expenses of social leadership than the landed classes, whose economic position at the time was deteriorating. Furthermore, while businessmen were entering the House of Lords, an increasing number of the landed aristocracy were turning toward business to maintain their position.[57] The presence of many industrial or commercial figures in the House of Lords cannot, therefore, be interpreted as primarily the result of the purchase of peerages.

In the 1890s, however, the standards of appointment began to slacken, as the party whips, who were the originators of most nominations to the peerage as well as the real controllers of the national party funds, per-mitted expectations of honors to develop in the minds of men whose financial help they needed. The Conserva-

---

[57] Ralph E. Pumphrey, "The Introduction of Industrialists into the British Peerage: A Study in Adaption of a Social Institution," *American Historical Review* 65 (October 1959): 1–16.

tives were better able to resist this abandonment of
standards than were the Liberals, who had become
financially hard pressed after the Liberal-Unionist
secession in 1886 when many of their wealthier supporters left them. Certain honors were awarded in
1895 to contributors by the Rosebery ministry, but only
because W. E. Gladstone had approved their being
promised in 1891 by Arnold Morley, the chief whip,
and Francis Schnadhorst, the secretary of both the Liberal Central Association and the National Liberal
Federation. But this action "established the principle
that peerages and baronetcies might be had at a price."
Afterward, Lord Salisbury continued to oppose the
use of the practice by the Unionists, but did allow funds
to be accepted by the party from men who believed the
donations would get them the prize. After 1902, under
the Balfour, Campbell-Bannerman, and Asquith ministries, the sale of honors became an accepted practice
by both sides.[58]

Belloc's and Chesterton's criticisms of the sale of
honors continued a line of radical attack beginning
with the proposal made in 1894 by the radical MP
Wilfrid Lawson, that a statement be issued at the time
honors were bestowed explaining the services for which
they were granted. In 1914 the issue was raised in the
House of Lords itself by a Conservative peer, Lord
Selbourne, who moved a resolution to the effect that

---

[58] Hanham, "Sale of Honors," pp. 277–89.

contributions to party funds not be a reason for the awarding of an honor. He was supported by a Liberal peer, Lord Charnwood, who believed, like Belloc, that the sale of honors could be only completely done away if the contributors to party funds were publicized. Otherwise the purchase of peerages could be camouflaged by ostensible services to the nation. Finally, in 1917 the Lords passed resolutions which insisted that the reasons for an honor be publicized and that the prime minister satisfy himself that the award was not connected with contributions to party funds. The coalition government of Lloyd George flagrantly disregarded the principle and the increase of peers continued at an even higher rate, primarily to amass party funds that remained under Lloyd George's control.[59]

In their accusations that policies as well as honors were sold to raise party funds, Belloc and Cecil Chesterton alluded to a posthumous controversy surrounding Francis Schnadhorst, who, as we have seen, was instrumental in breaking the inhibitions against the sale of peerages. The *Spectator* in 1901 charged that Schnadhorst had, a decade earlier, received funds from Cecil Rhodes, the empire builder, for the benefit of the Liberal Party in return for a guarantee that the Liberals not evacuate Egypt should they come to power.[60] While there was no doubt that the funds were received and

---

[59] Macmillan, *Honors for Sale,* pp. 16–21, 241–42.

[60] Belloc and Chesterton, *Party System,* pp. 110–11.

that the Liberals did not evacuate Egypt, this accusation, like much of Belloc's case, drew from a single instance a generalization about the whole political situation. Even with regard to this particular case, the Liberal leaders who formulated the Egyptian policy, with the possible exception of Gladstone, were unaware of Rhodes' contribution or of how Schnadhorst employed it. Furthermore, the British position in Egypt would have been maintained at any rate since the Foreign Minister was the Liberal-Imperialist Lord Rosebery.[61]

We have seen how Belloc's suspicion that the contributors to party funds were the determining influence in the licensing controversy had been a decisive factor in causing his disillusionment with the party system. He thought the only alternatives that had been presented to the nation were Balfour's licensing bill, "which meant in effect the endowment of brewing and distilling firms out of public funds," and Asquith's bill, "which meant a system of irritating restrictions upon the drinking habits of the people, restrictions leading logically to prohibition." But neither bill made an effort to break the drink monopoly, which was the real evil. The reason, according to Belloc, was that both parties

> need the money of rich men to conduct the sham fight upon which their own prestige and salaries depend. . . .

---

[61] Gwyn, *Democracy and the Cost of Politics,* pp. 115–20.

> The Conservative Party relies largely upon the subscriptions of wealthy brewers and distillers. . . . [The Liberal Party relies on] men who live by manufacturing non-alcoholic drinks. Their interest in the suspension of alcoholic drink is obvious.

Wealthy temperance advocates also contributed to the Liberal Party. As a result, the public was left a very limited alternative: "Their decision is only between the brewer and the cocoa manufacturer" (the latter probably referring to Nonconformist chocolate manufacturer George Cadbury, a supporter of the Liberals as well as proprietor of the Liberal *Daily News*).[62]

Belloc's comments on such features of the Edwardian political scene as the role of the secret funds and the sale of honors and policies had some legitimacy, although he probably overdrew the picture. His noting of the decline of the private member of Parliament and the dominance of the ministry in legislative matters was valid, although it is debatable whether such developments either should be lamented or could have been avoided in the age of the positive state. Where his criticisms seem to have become decidedly exaggerated was in his discussion of the actual governing elite, the rival front benches. He regarded them as different branches of the same closed oligarchical corporation

---

[62] Belloc and Chesterton, *Party System,* pp. 113–14.

that employed unreal political issues to determine
which branch should have office. He insisted that

> it is necessary . . . for the understanding of modern British
> politics to realize that the two front benches are not two
> but one. They are united not only by the close bonds of
> relationship, intermarriage, and personal friendship which
> exist between them, but also by a common interest. It is
> to the interest of both to keep the game going, and it is
> also to the interest of both to prevent the game from be-
> coming too real. It is, of course, quite true that, within
> these limits, each side genuinely wants to win. Apart from
> the sporting interest of the conflict, there are very material
> prizes to be gained by the winning side. To many politi-
> cians it makes a considerable pecuniary difference whether
> they are in office or in opposition. . . . This, however,
> remains a secondary object, subordinate to the essential
> aims of both front benches, the maintenance of the party
> system.[63]

To substantiate his case, he emphasized the methods
whereby the front benches were selected, the process
of co-option, that is, they recruited themselves rather
than be selected by the party at large. He also stressed
the fact that so many of the members of both front
benches came from the same upper-class social circles
and often were directly related or at least intermarried.
He thought that this "tendency to govern by clique,"
which "could not possibly arise in a genuinely democratic society," was increasing even though aristocracy

---

[63] *Ibid.*, pp. 59–60.

or oligarchy was no longer the professed form of government.

There was no doubt, as Sidney Low remarked, that the political system of Edwardian England had "preserved much of its oligarchical character" as effective power continued "to be retained in the hands of a comparatively small body of persons, many of them born to politics and brought into it young"; that there was a "relatively rather small governing class, consisting of the few thousand representatives of the nobility, landowners, capitalists, and leading professional men, who make up London society"; and that social situation was an important determining factor in the selection of officials.[64] But it does not seem warranted to conclude from this any conspiratorial corruption for the purpose of maintaining power. Rather, the explanation would be that such was a characteristic of English society which a radical and a French republican like Belloc would fail to recognize, or if he did notice, would despise. That was a characteristic noted forty years earlier by Walter Bagehot: England was and continued to be, even after the democratic extension of the franchise, a deferential country, where

> the numerical majority . . . is ready, is eager to delegate its power of choosing its ruler to a certain select minority. It abdicates in favor of its *elite,* and consents to obey whomever that *elite* may confide it. It acknowledges as its sec-

---

[64] Low, *Governance of England,* pp. 185–89.

ondary electors—as the choosers of its government—an educated minority, at once competent and unrestricted; it has a kind of loyalty to some superior persons who are fit to choose a good government, and whom no other class opposes.[65]

Belloc believed, however, that the oligarchic front benches maintained their power and control over the members of Parliament primarily through the disciplinary mechanisms already discussed, especially the threat of forcing the membership to confront the expenses of an election. Another way was through the support of the large numbers of "placemen" or MP's who entered "politics as a profession with the object of obtaining one of the well-paid offices in the gift of the ministry." Their votes could always be counted upon by the ruling group.[66]

Belloc continued to attack the system in his novel *A Change in the Cabinet,* which dealt with finding a sinecure cabinet position for a bankrupt and dull-witted young socialite, George Mulross Demaine, so that he might maintain his social position. The negotiations for the appointment were conducted by his relative Mary Smith, a central personality in the governing social circles and "the friend, the confidante, the cousin, the sister-in-law, or the aunt of at least three quarters of

---

[65] Walter Bagehot, *The English Constitution* (Garden City, N.Y.: Doubleday, Dolphin Books, n.d.), pp. 286–87.

[66] Belloc and Chesterton, *Party System,* p. 48.

what counts in England." It went without saying that while the leader of the opposition was her close friend, "much closer and dearer to her was her other cousin, the young and popular Prime Minister."[67] A fictional post, warden of the Court of Dowry, was secured for the aspirant by arranging that its occupant, Charles Repton, be elevated to the peerage. Repton was, besides a member of the cabinet, a director of a company involved in overseas development. This was an exception to the rule that cabinet members not hold public directorship while in office, and it was made in his case because of the company being "so great an imperial business." Before Repton was elevated or Demaine appointed, however, the director suffered attacks of the head ailment *veracititis,* which caused him imprudently to tell the truth at a shareholders' meeting of his company as well as on the floor of Parliament. His message to the shareholders was that a project in which the company was engaged was entirely fictitious and was being publicized solely to increase the price of shares. His comments in Parliament, and later to the Prime Minister, echo Belloc's theme that the moving force in politics was the income that could be derived from a public position itself or from the influence such a position gave. (This would contradict the very justification given for the deferential character

---

[67] Hilaire Belloc, *A Change in the Cabinet* (London: Methuen, 1909), pp. 17–18.

of British politics, for it was assumed that a wealthy ruling elite would be spared the temptation of corruption because of their wealth.) Ultimately, Repton was cured of his malady, and the elevation and appointment came about without further discomfort for the establishment.

Belloc's appraisal of British politics seemed most outlandish in his insistence that the oligarchical leaders of the two parties had no real political differences other than their rivalry for office, and that they were in fact in collusion to preserve the appearances of the party struggle in order to maintain control over their respective followers. One instance of front-bench collaboration that he cited was the failure of the Liberal government elected in January 1906 to end immediately the importation, and to commence the repatriation, of the Chinese laborers admitted into South Africa by the Unionists at the behest of certain "South African Jews" who employed them.[68] Another was the failure of a special commission of the House of Commons that investigated the Jameson raid to discover any collusion in or foreknowledge of the raid by the Colonial Secretary, Joseph Chamberlain, despite the presence on the commission of such Liberal critics of imperialism as Sir William Harcourt and Henry Campbell-Bannerman.

We have remarked the Liberal government's insist-

---

[68] Belloc and Chesterton, *Party System*, pp. 55–56.

ence that legal considerations inhibited its rescinding the licenses for importing coolie laborers which had already been issued by the Unionist government. Furthermore, it had refused to issue any more such licenses. As for the Jameson inquiry, some recent historians insist that "the available evidence has already put beyond doubt—that the Colonial Secretary [Chamberlain] and the High Commissioner [Cecil Rhodes] were deeply implicated in the conspiracy that caused the raid." Although neither one knew anything of the specific raid itself, both were involved in the preparations for an eventual armed intervention into the Transvaal.[69] The commission, which could have destroyed Chamberlain politically with an adverse report, was very mild and docile in its treatment of him; it tolerated rudeness by witnesses, failed to pursue points, and limited its condemnation to Rhodes while exonerating the colonial secretary. What remained of the effectiveness of the commission's findings was destroyed completely when the exonerated Chamberlain, during the parliamentary debate on the commission's report, stated his belief that Rhodes had done nothing dishonorable. For some time afterward there were radical suspicions that the antiimperialist Harcourt had made a deal with Chamberlain. There also were suspicions of complicity by former Liberal ministers, including

---

[69] Jean van der Pod, *The Jameson Raid* (Cape Town: Oxford University Press, 1951), p. 259.

Lord Rosebery, in the preparations for the raid. But if this was true, why would Harcourt have been hesitant about attacking imperialist opponents within his own party?[70]

Another example of alleged front-bench complicity that Belloc cited was quite clear-cut. It occurred during the conference held after Edward VII's death in an effort to resolve the dispute over reform of the House of Lords. Belloc and Cecil Chesterton inaccurately assumed that a deal had been made at the conference. Its alleged terms were that legislative measures agreed on both front benches would be introduced earlier in the parliamentary term and, with the Lords' veto power being changed to a suspensive nature, be certain of eventual passage. On the other hand, popular and private measures, which both front benches opposed, would deliberately be delayed until the end of a parliamentary term in order to make them incapable of surmounting even the suspensive veto.[71]

The conference, in fact, failed but not before consideration was given to the formation of a coalition government. Had a coalition resulted, it would have confirmed in Belloc's mind the solidarity of the front benches against the independent members of both

---

[70] Peter Stansky, *Ambitions and Strategies* (Oxford: Oxford University Press, 1964), pp. 235–52; Ethel Drus, "The Question of Imperial Complicity in the Jameson Raid," *English Historical Review* 68 (1953): 590–92.

[71] Belloc and Chesterton, *Party System,* pp. 57–58.

parties. The proposal for a coalition had been put
forward, surprisingly, by David Lloyd George, the very
member of the Liberal government who was most
vehemently denounced for his radicalism in the rhetoric
of the Unionists. The proposals were discussed outside
the conference. The Liberal ministers informed of them
were Asquith, Grey, Haldane, Churchill, and Lord
Crewe. The Unionist members of the conference—
Balfour, the Marquess of Lansdowne, Austen Chamberlain, and the Earl of Cawdor, and other prominent
Unionists, such as F. E. Smith and J. L. Garvin, the
editor of the *Observer* (the editorial pacemaker of the
Northcliffe press), Lord Curzon, Walter Long, and
Andrew Bonar Law—were also aware of them. The
proposals called for a coalition government which
would be able to deal with certain vital questions that
either party would be unable to deal with by itself
because of the inevitable political strife they would
raise, especially among the more partisan or die-hard
members of both parties. The particular questions with
which Lloyd George believed that "the party and parliamentary system was unequal to coping" were the
"shadow of unemployment," the jeopardizing by international rivals of "our hold on the markets of the
world," "an arrest in that expansion of our foreign
trade," the lack of social insurance for the victims of
"ill health or trade fluctuations," the dependence "on
overseas supplies for our food," the declining cultiva-
tion of the soil, the decline of the countryside, danger-

ous overindustrialization, an "excessive indulgence in alcohol drinks" that "was undermining the health and efficiency" of much of the population, the poisoned relations with the United States because of the Irish controversy, the threatened domestic revolution because of the struggle over the House of Lords, the "threatened civil war at our doors in Ireland," and a possible great war "into which we might be drawn by some visible or invisible ties, interests, or sympathies."[72] The original agenda for the coalition ministry included the further strengthening of the navy, compulsory military service, reform of the Poor Law, social insurance, and "imperial preference to the British dominions on existing duties" and an inquiry to see what further preference and protection devices could be devised. All of these were satisfactory to the Unionists, in that they combined domestic social reform with the strengthening of the military and tariff reform. They would certainly outrage ardent free-trade, retrenchment, and antimilitarist Liberals, but were matched by Liberal projects on the agenda which would irritate many Unionists. These included Welsh disestablishment and a form of Home Rule.

The distribution of positions in the coalition governing was even considered. Asquith was to serve as Prime Minister but after having been raised to the peerage,

---

[72] David Lloyd George, *War Memoirs* (London: Toor Nicholsen & Watson, 1933), 1:34–37.

Balfour would be leader in Commons and president of a committee of national defense; Lansdowne was to be Foreign Secretary; Churchill, the War Minister; and Austen Chamberlain, the First Lord of the Admiralty. Lloyd George indicated his willingness to relinquish office if it was felt that his presence in the government would be too offensive to the Unionists.[73] Naturally, a prerequisite to the whole agreement as to programs and positions would have to be a solution to the question of the House of Lords.

The proposals were very seriously considered by both sides, but were ultimately rejected by the Unionists, especially after Balfour had consulted with the former Unionist chief whip Aretas Akers-Douglas Viscount Chilworth, who believed the rank and file of the party would never tolerate such a deal. Balfour could not bring himself to yield on the question of Irish Home Rule. But there was great enthusiasm for the coalition by younger Unionists, like F. E. Smith and J. L. Garvin. Garvin used his post as editor of the *Observer* to create favorable response to the idea. He was especially attracted by the opportunities the coalition posed for military reform, tariff reform, and imperial preference. He believed that in return the Unionists should be willing to concede to a compromise federal Home Rule solution that would meet both the Liberal

---

[73] Austen Chamberlain, *Politics from Inside* (New Haven: Yale University Press, 1937), pp. 292–93.

demands that something be done for Ireland and the Unionist demands that the unity of the empire be considered. But Balfour wrote to him that he was convinced that any concession on Home Rule, even in a federal scheme, would prompt more the distintegration than the unity of Great Britain.[74]

Garvin's and the *Observer's* hostility to compromise in Ireland prior to the talk of a coalition, and its resumption of the editorial leadership of the more extreme Tory press soon after the breakdown of both the conference and the private discussions regarding the formation of a coalition, tended very much to confirm Belloc's suspicions of the role of the press in the party game and its artificial or sham exploitation of issues. He was convinced that the press was more devoted to the party system "than is any part of the state except the professional politicians themselves." He did not believe, however, that this was the result of corrupt control of the press. He thought it would be difficult "to point to a single case" in which a newspaper's support for a professional politician "could be connected with any money reward of the kind." Rather, the momentum of custom or the force of inertia had preserved the ritualistic party loyalties of the press "long after they have ceased to have reality in the minds of its readers."

---

[74] Alfred M. Gollin, *The Observer and J. L. Garvin, 1908–14* (London: Oxford University Press, 1960), pp. 208–10, 215–18.

This was partly because the readers "expect this ritual to be performed."[75]

The proposed coalition did not come off, but it did foreshadow the coalition government that was actually formed during World War I and continued for a few years afterward under Lloyd George. It included some, like F. E. Smith and, for a while, Winston Churchill, who were most enthusiastic about the idea of coalition in 1910. Furthermore, in contrast to Belloc's view of these individuals and their efforts as the logical development of a fradulent party system in which there were no real differences between the parties, the attempts at coalition were really motivated by a desire to surmount the partisan differences that impeded effective government. In a sense, the coalitionists were like Belloc and Chesterton in their contempt for the existing party system, although for different reasons. One coalitionist in particular, Alfred Viscount Milner, who served in the later coalition governments (who also had been the great proconsul for South Africa during the Chamberlain era at the Colonial Office, and who was a particular object of radical and antiimperialist detestation), was very pronounced in his disdain for parliamentary politics, which he regarded as hopeless and incapable of producing the statesmanship required to

---

[75] Belloc and Chesterton, *Party System*, pp. 218, 222–23.

rule the empire. He was fearful that democracy and the British Empire were going to fall "unless we can emancipate ourselves . . . from machine-made caucus-ridden politics, and give men of independence and character more of a chance or, to put it better, encourage the development of independence and character instead of encouraging nothing except sophistry and skillful manipulation." He was "perfectly indifferent" about democracy, although he regarded it as the inevitable form of government for his country at the time. Therefore, he accepted it "without enthusiasm, but with absolute loyalty," and would "make the best of it."[76]

The common detestation for the party system by the like of Milner and Belloc and Chesterton was not, however, identical. Milner was critical of the very idea of partisanship, which had prevented national problems from being solved by the most competent leaders. Belloc and Chesterton, on the other hand, criticized the party system because it was not sufficiently partisan, but simply a fradulent game played between two branches of the same plutocracy. The coalitionists, like Milner, distrusted democracy and the necessity that political parties cater to its whims, while Belloc and Chesterton despised a party system which they thought

[76] Alfred M. Gollin, *Proconsul in Politics* (London: Anthony Blond, 1964), pp. 46, 314.

neither democratic nor partisan. Yet, as we shall see subsequently, Belloc's dissatisfaction with the party system of Great Britain gradually drove him more in the direction of the other critics and made him more sympathetic to authoritarianism.

Chapter Five

The *Eye-Witness* Against the New Liberalism, 1911–12

Belloc's indictment of parliamentary politics coincided with a widespread inclination, across the political spectrum from left to right, toward extraparliamentary, extralegal, "direct" action. So serious was the situation that some regard the turmoil of the four years preceding World War I as the nearest Great Britain had come since the seventeenth century to civil war or revolution. This quasi-revolutionary atmosphere resulted both from Conservative opposition to the programs of an uncertain Liberal government with a confused mandate (for example, the Unionist approbation of the illegal preparation for violent resistance to Irish Home Rule), and from radical dissatisfaction with the insufficiency or insincerity, or both, of the government's attempts to adapt its policies to meet the problems and crises of a changed economic and social structure (for instance, the syndicalist tone of industrywide dock, railway, and mine strikes). It was with the latter group that the radical Belloc was more in sympathy, for he interpreted the so-called new liberal departure from the nineteenth-century themes of parliamentary supremacy and a limited state simply as camouflage for preserving the ascendancy of the newer privileged establishment, the plutocracy, that controlled the party system. This was despite the fact that many of the theoreticians of the new liberalism were his pre-1906, pro-Boer, radical allies. Admittedly his hostile analysis of the new liberal positive state was from the perspective of a nineteenth-century radical who idealized an economy of small holders, peasant proprietors, and family enterprises. Yet his ideas had much in common with the thinking of almost revolutionary progressives, like the guild socialists, who shared his distrust for parliamentary politics and ameliorative welfare legislation that tended to postpone the drive for worker control of the means of production. Belloc's distrust of the new liberal positive state was motivated more by a fear of what that state would do to the poorer classes, which he believed would be relegated to a permanent servile status, than by any Manchesterian laissez-faire solicitude for the property rights of capitalists, who he thought were using the new liberalism to perpetuate their plutocratic position. But before examining Belloc's criticism, let us review the factors that prompted the development of the new liberalism in the first place.

The new liberalism was a manifestation of the heightened social consciousness that appeared in the Edwardian era. That consciousness had been stimulated by several things, not the least of which was the startling indication of national ill health suggested by the high percentage of Boer War military recruits drawn from the lower classes of urban industrial Britain that had to be rejected because of physical disability. This record prompted a somewhat disingenuous concern for the poor by the advocates of imperialism, not so much for the sake of the poor themselves as for the elimination of poverty as an ailment weakening the strength of the nation and the empire. Examples of this "social imperialism" ranged from the Liberal-Imperialist rejection of Gladstonianism through the advocacy by the Webbs and others of a new party of national efficiency to the protectionist campaign of Joseph Chamberlain. A more flagrant manifestation of the social Darwinian implications of this social consciousness was the lively interest at the time in eugenics, conscription, and physical fitness programs.[1] Not all of the social consciousness of the period stemmed from social imperialist roots, however. Much of the outrage at the social problem was prompted less by jingoist fears of national military weakness than by a series of detailed scientific

---

[1] Bentley B. Gilbert, *The Evolution of National Insurance in Great Britain* (London: Michael Joseph, 1966), pp. 81–87; see also Bernard Semmel, *Imperialism and Social Reform* (London: George Allen & Unwin, 1960).

inquiries into the actual conditions of the British urban masses.

Two classic examples were Charles Booth's multi-volume study of the living conditions of London and B. Seebohm Rowntree's survey of the conditions in York. Booth, a Liverpool shipowner and statistician, combined personal observation with the scientific use of census returns, school attendance records, and various other information that had become available because of the increasing number of state agencies with record-keeping responsibilities. His conclusion was that about one-third of the London population lived just at or below the poverty line, according to his definition of poverty. In addition, a similar portion of Londoners lived in conditions of overcrowding, and the death-rate statistics varied in proportion to the incidence of poverty. Obvious from his study was the close relationship between poverty and casual employment and old age.

The examination of conditions in York in 1899 by B. Seebohm Rowntree, the son of a cocoa manufacturer, revealed similar conclusions. Rowntree's statistics as to the weight and height of children from different income levels reinforced the suggestion derived from army recruitment figures about the correlation of poverty and physical unfitness.[2] Such findings naturally

[2] *Charles Booth's London,* ed. Albert Fried and Richard Elman (New York: Random House, Pantheon Books, 1967); B. Seebohm

must be balanced with more recent historical analysis which holds that "the half-century preceding the First World War had brought remarkable improvements for the wage-earning classes as a whole," and that "it is improbable that there had ever been a time when, materially, things had been so good for most of the population." But despite this, and despite certain inadequacies in Booth's and Rowntree's devices for determining poverty, as well as the probably unrepresentative character of London and York, which were short of factories and large workshops, the same historian admits there still was no doubt that a significant portion of the population in the late Victorian-Edwardian era, while possibly smaller than had been the case earlier in history, was living in miserable straits and possibly had even "undergone some decline in their average material standards."[3]

The Booth and Rowntree statistics influenced many advocates of social reform, particularly the writers connected with pro-Boer publications like the *Daily News* and the *Speaker* who upheld the radical Liberal tradition against the spirit of imperialism. In one collection of their essays, *The Heart of Empire,* it was

---

Rowntree, *Poverty: A Study of Town Life* (London: Macmillan, 1901); M. B. Simey and T. S. Simey, *Charles Booth, Social Scientist* (London: Oxford University Press, 1960); Asa Briggs, *Social Thought and Social Action* (London: Longmans, 1961).

[3] William Ashworth, *An Economic History of England, 1870–1939* (London: Methuen, 1960), pp. 249–52.

regretted that the attention of the populace had been distracted from social reform by "other and noisier enthusiasms—the lust of domination, the stir of battle, the pride in magnitude of empire." Political figures no longer alluded to the "condition of the people" lest they "should distract attention from the acquisition of vast territories on the confines of the world." These essayists, who included Charles F. G. Masterman, the literary editor of the *Speaker* and the *Daily News,* and the historians G. P. Gooch and G. M. Trevelyan, hoped that their examination of the various social problems, such as housing, the condition of children, the distribution of industry, drinking, and charitable activities, would remove some of the indifference to reform at a time when foreign policy had "for some years occupied the time, expended the money, and absorbed the energies of the country."[4] These reformers viewed themselves as carrying on in the liberal tradition of Bright, Cobden, and Gladstone with its emphasis upon democracy, international morality, and humanitarianism. Their general concern was to combat "reaction," which was what they called the prevailing temper of British and European politics during the previous generation when "the ideal of peace had given way to that of extended domination. . . . The conceptions of personal freedom, of national rights, of international peace, had been relegated by practical men to the lumber room of

---

[4] Charles F. G. Masterman, ed., *The Heart of Empire* (London: T. Fisher Unwin, 1902), pp. xi, 3–4.

disused ideas."[5] Basically, they sought to reestablish the
notion that "the political order must conform to the
ethical ideal of what is just" in contrast to the late
nineteenth-century doctrines of imperial destiny, social
Darwinism, and simple *Realpolitik*. A somewhat similar
note had been expressed in the early *Essays in Liberalism* by Belloc, who was associated with this group of
radicals; he called for liberalism to combat with "clear
and abstract principles clearly understood" the pragmatic arguments of actual success and realism used by
its opponents.[6] Appropriately, Masterman applauded
Belloc and G. K. Chesterton for being the most vigorous of the new group of authors coming to replace the
prevailing reactionary literary temper as represented
by the like of G. A. Henty and Rudyard Kipling.[7]

These radical writers could employ the logic of nineteenth-century humanitarian liberalism in their struggle
against "reaction," and could appeal to it especially on
the issues of free trade, Chinese labor in South Africa,
antiimperialism, and religious disestablishment in education during the 1905 electoral triumph of the Liberal
Party (in which not a few of these same writers, like

[5] L. T. Hobhouse, *Democracy and Reaction,* 2d ed. (London:
T. Fisher, Unwin, 1909), p. 4. Hobhouse had been a Fellow at
Merton College, Oxford, who left the academic world in 1897 to
become an editorial writer for the *Manchester Guardian.*

[6] Hilaire Belloc, *et al., Essays in Liberalism* (London: Cassell,
1897), pp. 5–7.

[7] C. F. G. Masterman, "After the Reaction," *Living Age* 244 (January 28, 1905): 202–4.

Belloc and Masterman, were elected to Parliament). With the establishment of a Liberal government, however, they were confronted with the task of reconciling the fundamentally antistate bias of their political creed with the actual implementation of social and economic reform. At this point their dissatisfaction with the slow pace of Liberal social reform became similar in many ways to Belloc's criticism of party politics. J. A. Hobson, the celebrated economist-theoretician of anti-imperialism, for instance, appealed to the commentaries of Ostrogorski and Lowell to demonstrate "how feebly and irregularly the real spirit of democracy pulses through" the British party system and how domination over Parliament by cabinets "marks a domination of representative government and a failure of democracy."[8] But other than just advocating constitutional reforms designed to facilitate the implementation of the democratic mandate, Hobson was concerned that liberalism develop "the intellectual and moral ability to accept and execute a positive progressive policy which involves a new conception of the functions of the state."

In a sense, the seeds of the new liberalism were planted in the writings of John Stuart Mill. The individualist utilitarian, who saw social creativity and progress resulting from individual liberty, acknowl-

---

[8] J. A. Hobson, *The Crisis of Liberalism: New Issues of Democracy* (London: P. S. King & Son, 1909), pp. 6–9.

edged such things as the lack of freedom in the relationship of lowly paid and poorly educated workmen with their employers and challenged the orthodox assumption of political economists by insisting on a distinction "between the laws of the production of wealth, which are real laws of nature, dependent on the properties of objects," and the modes of the distribution of wealth, "which, subject to certain conditions, depend on human will." He regarded as likely to bring society "nearer to some ideal standard" the proclamation of the goal, if not the method, of the St. Simonians in which "the labor and capital of society would be managed for the general account of the community."[9] But more decisive than Mill in reconstructing the philosophical foundations of English liberalism away from its anti-state, individualist tone was the English idealist Thomas Hill Green. While Green's position on tangible issues had not departed greatly from the standard Victorian liberal posture, that is, a bias toward private action and a concern for the individual moral betterment of the members of the lower classes, the central theme of his political philosophy was decidedly new. Instead of emphasizing individual freedom or liberty for its own sake, and conceiving of the state as a reluctantly accepted inhibitor of freedom, Green interpreted freedom as the means whereby the individual fulfills a moral

---

[9] John Stuart Mill, *Autobiography* (Garden City, N.Y.: Doubleday, Dolphin Books, n.d.), pp. 128, 185.

duty or obligation to attain the good, and viewed the state as "a society in which the rights of men are defined and harmonized," that is, where free men pursue the common good.[10] This more positive conception of liberty and of the state prompted the conclusion that men must be provided the opportunity to pursue the good. There would necessarily have to be state programs to enhance the position or status of most men, whether through the removal of impediments to human development or the provision of the means of its assistance. In short, state power would be increased not to lessen human freedom but to extend it.

One of the major theoreticians of the Edwardian new liberalism who drew upon the philosophical foundations of Green was L. T. Hobhouse. Significantly, at the time when the liberals were still seeking to overturn the reaction and were campaigning on the more negative and traditional causes of free trade and retrenchment, he sought to stress the consistency between the old school and the new requirements. He pictured "socialistic legislation" like factory and workmen's compensation acts "not as an infringement of the two distinctive ideals of the older liberalism, 'liberty and equality,' " but "as a necessary means to their fulfillment." He sought to demonstrate this consistency by

---

[10] Melvin Richter, *The Politics of Conscience* (London: Weidenfeld & Nicolson, 1951), pp. 225, 248.

alluding to Cobden's willingness to acknowledge the absence of the conditions of real freedom of contract and the necessity for state intervention in the case of child labor, and to Gladstone's similar posture with regard to Irish land reform.[11] In a later work he indicated a much more decided evolution from the older liberalism as he regarded "liberty as primarily a matter of social interest." In the spirit of Green he stressed the organic character of society, whereby the individual realizes his own good as part of the common good, and held that the social ideal consisted in the possible ethical harmony of men, a situation which was not natural (like Adam Smith's harmony of private interests) but which could be attained "partly by discipline, partly by the improvement of the conditions of life."[12]

Another of the pre-1906 pro-Boer radicals who proclaimed the creed of the new liberalism, J. A. Hobson, asserted that liberalism no longer needed "relics of that positive hostility to public methods of cooperation which crippled the old radicalism." He justified the enlargement of the authority and the functions of the state as "an enlargement of personal liberty." Personal liberty was to be gained by state action in the sense

---

[11] Hobhouse, *Democracy and Reaction*, pp. 216–19.

[12] L. T. Hobhouse, *Liberalism* (New York: Oxford University Press, 1964; first published 1911), pp. 67–71.

that it would seek to provide the individual citizen with "equality of opportunity" of access "to all material and moral means of personal development and work as shall contribute to his own welfare and that of his society." The means by which these goals could be obtained were the gradual replacement of the private ownership of urban and large portions of rural land by public ownership, which would permit access to land by those desirous of working it and keeping it "on terms regulated by a public authority and not a private owner"; a national public transportation system whereby cheap and frequent service would be available to all regions without discrimination in behalf of richer individuals and localities; "the public ownership and operation of industrial power for sale on equal terms to all who want it"; equal access to credit on reasonable terms, if necessary, through "a public system of loan banks"; state insurance for "security of employment and of livelihood"; public financing and provision of the costs of justice to relieve "private litigants from all expenses in the preparation and conduct of criminal or civil cases, and the removal of all such work from a private to a public profession"; and "free education . . . the first and most urgent issue of our time," by which he meant an education open to all, with poverty no impediment, "from the primary school to the university, disinterested in its aims and management."[13]

---

[13] Hobson, *Crisis of Liberalism,* pp. 91–113.

For the implementation and financing of such goals the new liberalism required fundamental alterations in traditional liberal concepts of property and the sources of wealth, both of which had to be acknowledged to have a social as well as a personal basis. Such alteration was done not by robbing the rich for the benefit of the poor, but "by distinguishing the social from the individual factors in wealth, by bringing the elements of social wealth into the public coffers, and by holding it at the disposal of society to administer to the prime needs of its members."[14] Property and wealth were seen as dependent on society not just because of the protection it gave them, but because of the owners' dependence in production on labor, talent, and machinery, which are "the gift of acquired civilization" and for whose use society provides the conditions and opportunities. These considerations should inspire tax policies whereby wealth, which was the consequence of society as a whole, could be made available for public purposes, while that which derived from individual enterprise would be preserved by its producer. Examples of the former would be taxation of publicly created monopolies, like the liquor traffic, and of "unearned" private wealth, such as speculative income from shares and inherited wealth, especially if it was evident that the existence of these forms of wealth did not stimulate the productive energies of society. The next step would

---

[14] Hobhouse, *Liberalism,* p. 98.

be a supertax on very high "earned incomes," which tax would be valid on the grounds that it would not be likely "to discourage any services of genuine social value by a rapidly increasing surtax" on such large incomes.[15] The notion that property and wealth have a social aspect, therefore, evolved in new liberal thinking beyond the view that society deserved some of the credit for their production to the view that property and wealth should be distributed according to the social value of the producer's services.

The theoreticians of the new liberalism naturally had to confront the criticism made by Conservatives that their position was ultimately no different from outright socialism. In reply, they immediately sought to distinguish their views from that doctrinaire, revolutionary socialism more typical of the Continent with its materialistic interpretation of history, its attribution of all value to labor, its denial of the legitimacy of rent, interest, and profit, and its preaching of class warfare. Similarly they dissociated their position from that type of undemocratic socialism which would completely centralize power in the hands of administrative experts without heeding the masses. The new liberals indicated their anxiety lest any program of social reconstruction should create an unendurable bureaucracy, dwarf individuality, or impair motives of productivity. But, once the notions of individual rights and personal

---

[15] *Ibid.,* p. 104.

independence were respected, they admitted the increasing similarity of their views to much that went by the label of socialism or collectivism—for example, their acceptance of the view that "the state is vested with a certain overlordship over property in general and a supervisory power over industry in general."[16]

Although Hilaire Belloc had always made quite clear his hostility to socialism, he had not by 1910 challenged those of his old pro-Boer radical allies who were formulating the theories of the new liberalism. Indeed, he was sympathetic with much of their zeal for social reconstruction and with their impatience at the vulgarity and the inequity of the Edwardian social structure. What is more, he had been in accord with their dissatisfaction over the Liberal government's relative legislative impotence prior to 1910, especially on the question of confronting the Unionist-dominated House of Lords. However, as we have seen, his interests in Parliament were primarily in the more traditional radical causes such as education, licensing, and antiimperialism. He did not involve himself in, although he did not oppose, the legislative struggle for programs of social reform that were of a new liberal character.

These programs were sponsored by such significant

---

[16] Hobson, *Crisis of Liberalism,* pp. 137–38; Hobhouse, *Liberalism,* pp. 88–90, 108–9.

ministers and undersecretaries as David Lloyd George, Winston Churchill, Herbert Samuel, Reginald Mc-Kenna, and Walter Runciman. The main push toward this new liberal legislative program of social reform came after the Liberal-Imperialist Asquith had succeeded the more traditional Liberal Campbell-Bannerman as Prime Minister in 1908. The ministerial leadership in these programs, however, was assumed for the most part by the pro-Boer radical section of that ministry (with the exception of Churchill), typified by Lloyd George, while the Liberal-Imperialists, especially Grey and Haldane, concentrated on foreign affairs and military reform. Paradoxically, the framers of the new liberalism were not the Roseberyites, who had called for such almost a decade before, but the very inheritors of the Gladstonian tradition and the "fly-blown phylacteries." Lloyd George, for instance, had indicated that British liberalism did not intend to meet the fate of Continental liberalism and be swept aside "before it had begun its work, because it refused to adapt itself to new conditions." Instead, while not abandoning its traditional goals of "freedom and equality," he said that the Liberal Party would seek to promote "measures for ameliorating the conditions of life for the multitude." The new liberalism, as he labeled it, would not just use "the national discontent of the people with poverty and precariousness of the means of subsistence" as a motive force for seeking civil rights, but also work for "the removing of the immediate causes of discontent."[17] The direction in which the government would move had been indicated by the former Tory free trader who had entered his radical phase, Winston Churchill, Undersecretary for the Colonies under Campbell-Bannerman, who became President of the Board of Trade under Asquith. He expressed a wish for such things as the public ownership of monopolies, the interception of the unearned increase in the speculative value of land, and more municipal enterprise. But he also desired "to see the state embark on various novel and adventurous experiments" such as its becoming "the reserve employer of labor"; the nationalization of the means of transportation, and the means of "the care of the sick and the aged, and, above all, of the children"; and "the universal establishment of minimum standards of life and labor."[18]

The first major pieces of new liberal legislation passed prior to the struggle with the House of Lords were the Old Age Pension Act of 1908, introduced that April by Lloyd George shortly after he had become Chancellor of the Exchequer in the Asquith cabinet, and the Labor Exchange Act of 1909, which was introduced that summer by Churchill as President of the Board of Trade. Both were attempts to get at the

---

[17] David Lloyd George, *Better Times* (London: Hodder & Stoughton, 1910), pp. 49–54.

[18] Winston Churchill, *Liberalism and the Social Problem* (New York: Hodder & Stoughton, 1909), p. 81.

problem of poverty from premises different from the Poor Law's tendency to identify poverty with immorality or personal unworth. Old-age pensions, for instance, were made available as a matter of right to all over seventy years of age whose income did not surpass £31 a year. There was no test of destitution imposed on the applicants and the funds came from national revenues rather than from local rates. The considerably greater number of pensioners than had been expected indicated both how sizable was the number of aged poor and how the stigma of destitution as well as the harsh deterrence principle attached to the Poor Law relief had inhibited the really deserving aged poor from seeking assistance.[19] That the system was to be administered by the post office was an interesting commentary on the unpreparedness of the government for such a national service.

The Labor Exchange Act was another great step in the national government's assumption of the role of service to the citizenry. It was the brainchild of William Beveridge, a young social investigator whose examinations of the problem of unemployment had prompted Churchill's drawing him into the Board of Trade. Beveridge, the son of a member of the Indian civil service, was typical of that group of Oxford graduates whose sensitivity to the urgency of that

---

[19] Maurice Bruce, *The Coming of the Welfare State,* 3d ed. (London: B. T. Batsford, 1966), p. 155.

problem had prompted them to serve in the various university settlements established within poor areas to get a greater understanding of the poor and their plight in order better to develop programs of reform and guidance. Beveridge, whose college was Balliol, appropriately served from 1903 to 1905 as the subwarden at Toynbee Hall in London's East End. Toynbee Hall was the most celebrated of the settlement houses and had been formed in the winter of 1883–84 by a committee at Balliol that had been inspired by the call of the famous Canon Samuel Barnett, a man who had attracted to his circle such diverse but socially conscious Oxford scholars, especially Balliol men, as Alfred Milner and Arnold Toynbee. The hall had been named after that young historian following his premature death in April 1883.

Beveridge's experience and social investigation prompted certain conclusions which he publicized in a book and in the columns he wrote for the *Morning Post,* at the time Belloc was its literary editor, in 1906–08. The central conclusion was the distinction between unemployment and underemployment. The former was the status into which regularly employed workers occasionally fell because of trade fluctuations or seasonal variations in industry. These men for the most part could be adequately assisted by their unions or their friendly societies during times of distress, and could, although they were unlikely to, seek assistance from the very inadequate system created by the Unemployed

Workmen's Act of 1905. But a much more serious problem was underemployment, that is, the situation of those who were permanently without work or at least only occasionally employed as casual workers. Such people needed assistance of a more permanent nature because their plight could not be met by a system designed to deal only with periodic employment crises. In their case a period of trade depression meant only "the gradual and barely perceptible worsening, for three or four years, of conditions of life which are always bad." In Beveridge's eyes, any solution to their problem would be inadequate which would "leave industrial disorganization untouched and deal only with resultant human suffering."[20]

The Labor Exchange Act sought to take the first step toward such a national industrial organization by creating a national system of labor exchanges in order to bring positions and workers together. Naturally, the sponsor of the act, Winston Churchill, viewed them as only a first step in his desire to "thrust a big slice of Bismarckianism over the whole underside of our industrial system." The exchanges were partly inspired by the German experience, as were further steps he desired, such as unemployment insurance, national infirmity insurance, state industries, and state control

---

[20] William H. Beveridge, *Unemployment, a Problem of Industry* (London: Longmans, Green, 1909), pp. 190–91.

of an amalgamated railway system.[21] But before these further steps could be taken, the confrontation with the Lords over the 1909 budget had to be met.

In some ways the struggle over the 1909 budget could be looked upon as the first major struggle for the new liberalism, since one of the reasons for the requested tax increase was the expense connected with such government social services as pensions and labor exchanges, as well as other projected programs. In the struggle over the budget, there was no indication of Belloc's eventual hostility toward the new liberalism. In fact, he enthusiastically approved the budget, particularly the graduated character of the taxes and the attack on landed privilege. During the debates on the budget, as we saw, he limited himself to general statements of approval, demands that the Lords be more directly challenged, and criticism of certain more detailed points in the budget, such as the whiskey tax, especially as it applied to Ireland.[22] Almost simultaneously with the legislative appearance of new liberal programs and the budget, however, he published several articles on such fundamental questions as whether or

---

[21] Winston Churchill to H. H. Asquith, December 29, 1908, quoted in Gilbert, *National Insurance in Great Britain,* p. 253.

[22] *Parliamentary Debates* (Commons), 5th ser., 4 (May 4, 1909): 967–74.

not direct taxation had reached a limiting point, the difficulties of equitable and accurate assessment for taxation purposes, the inadequacy of many customary means of measuring national wealth especially for purposes of calculating feasible tax burdens, and the danger of relying on either the taxation of rent or death duties as major sources of revenue. In all of these there is a hint of that suspicion of the efforts and the competence of state power that would characterize Belloc's subsequent fears of the servile state.

Although he preferred direct taxation on the wealth of individuals to indirect taxation on commodities or products because it was "the most just, the most immediate, the most simple, and the most easily calculated," he believed that these qualities existed only when the direct taxation was very low and where the social conditions under which it was levied were very simple. But when that direct tax went above a certain level, it would tend to break down and be incapable of returning the projected revenue. Furthermore, he believed that point had been arrived at in modern England when there would be difficulty in raising directly even quite small percentage increments upon the apparent total income of the citizenry, and, "above all, that for the large social experiments of the future, direct taxation will prove completely inadequate."[23]

---

[23] Hilaire Belloc, "The Limits of Direct Taxation," *Contemporary Review* 93 (February 1908): 191.

More recent levels of governmental expenditure and
taxation might make Belloc's concern seem unwar-
ranted, but it must be recalled that, viewed from his
perspective, the late Victorian and Edwardian periods
can scarcely be noted for "Gladstonian retrenchment."
Instead, total annual public outlay, including central
and local government expenditure, has tripled from
1870 to 1914, a growth rate much faster than that of
population and faster than the growth rate in national
income, while the proportion of all governmental revenue that came from direct taxation on income and
capital had climbed from thirteen percent to thirty
percent between 1880 and 1905.[24]

Belloc saw three major reasons why direct taxation
would tend to lose its productivity. The first was the
psychological resistance of the individual taxpayer,
who would evaluate the tax increment he must pay as
an absolute sum in itself rather than as a small portion
of his total income. Furthermore, he would view it not
as a burden covering the period of a whole year, but
only as one pertaining to the day on which it was paid.
In addition, Belloc noted the reluctance of the middle
classes to accept direct taxation beyond that limit
which would impose some lessening of the customary
expenses for their status in life. Before they accepted
such, he believed they "would employ every subterfuge
and every evasion." From a modern perspective, the

---

[24] Ashworth, *Economic History of England*, pp. 230–35.

former danger seems to have been overcome by the system of withholding taxation, although in the present day the latter difficulty is a serious obstacle in the raising of taxes.

A second and more substantial ground for regarding direct taxation as limited in effectiveness was the very serious danger of inequality of assessment, that is, inequity in distributing the taxpaying burden among the citizenry. (For Belloc progressive taxation was not inconsistent with equity.) This inequity resulted from such things as the innumerable opportunities for evasion that would increase with the increasing number of irregular incomes, especially those based on financial speculation. As a result, "such incomes as are permanent, regular, and, as it were, publicly ascertainable, necessarily pay for the evasion of the rest." Another similar problem that increased correspondingly with the tax levy was the difficulty of determining which expenses should be exempted from taxation, or what allowances from taxation should be made for earnings of a more temporary or transitory nature. In short, he stated that the difficulties of equitable assessment are such that the limit at which a community can bear direct taxes would unfortunately be reached when the bearing point of taxation has been reached "for the smaller or more burdened man."[25] This problem of the inequity of assessment was one in which Belloc was

---

[25] Belloc, "Limits of Direct Taxation," pp. 198–201.

definitely prophetic, as modern commentators from all political quarters have noted the elements of retrogression in ostensibly progressive direct taxation because of evasion and exemptions.[26]

A factor which Belloc believed of far greater importance than taxpayer resistance in limiting the ability of direct taxation to provide revenue was what he called "inflation of assessment," that is, the tendency of the state "to exaggerate the total amount of wealth present for taxation." This tendency was inevitable in a complex commercial economy because of what he called the "assessment of imaginaries," that is, the assumption of the existence of wealth "which is, in fact, nonexistent." Regarding the "modern commercial world" as dealing in these imaginaries rather than real wealth, he regarded it as "one vast system of credits reliant each upon all the others, perpetually exchanging investment against investment and living, as by a circulation of the blood, upon a perpetual circulation of acknowledgments of credit mutually received and given." To estimate a nation's real wealth for taxation purposes on these imaginaries, which could "be indefinitely expanded" beyond a basis of real wealth, was certain to result in disappointment and fiscal havoc.[27]

---

[26] Philip M. Stern, *The Great Treasury Raid* (New York: Random House, 1964).

[27] Hilaire Belloc, "The Inflation of Assessment," *Dublin Review* 142 (April 1908): 362.

From the danger of overestimating the possible amount of return from direct taxation, Belloc turned his attention to the similarly perilous central controversy in the Lloyd George budget—land taxation, and the theory behind it of taxing rent, that is, the income which accrues to the owner of a site for its use after the labor and capital expended on it have been compensated.[28] He noted three justifications for the taxation and perhaps the appropriation of rent by the state: rent was not the result of the owner's skill or industry; it was to a degree a product of the community; and, last, it increased in direct proportion to the wealth of the community. He agreed with the first, although he was not certain that "no man can morally own that which he has not called into being." As for the second, he insisted it "is not absolutely or universally true" that the economic rent of a site was a product of the community, as often the community has nothing to do with it.

But it was primarily the third argument for taxing rent that he challenged. His objections were similar to his fears about the exaggeration of a community's wealth in making any direct tax assessments, as he doubted that there was necessarily a correspondence between the increase or decrease of economic rent and the increase or decrease of the total wealth in a community. He argued that "to rely upon economic rent as

---

[28] *Supra,* chap. 4, p. 139.

an index of prosperity; to tax it as a principal source of revenue, still more to tax it as the only source of revenue, would leave the fiscal system out of touch with the true wealth of the community." He insisted that if a large opportunity for the exploitation of natural resources on a very narrow margin of productivity would be opened up, it might result in an increase of the total wealth of the community far out of proportion to the increase in economic rent. Similarly, a sudden decline in the value of certain favored sites with previously high rents might be accompanied by the exploitation of an increased number of less favored sites with lower rents. This would mean that "the total economic rent will fall though the total wealth of the community will rise." Conversely, he challenged more traditional economic doctrine when he stated that a fall in wages and the resultant fall in the margin of production could increase rent while not necessarily increasing wealth. This was because he regarded "fortuitous" the presupposition that "just below the old margin of production, there must be a large number of sites almost good enough to use."[29]

Besides his concern over the tendency of the framers of direct taxation to overestimate the real wealth of a nation, he was solicitous about another aspect of taxation: the potential dissipation by taxation of the na-

---

[29] Hilaire Belloc, "The Taxation of Rent," *Dublin Review* 145 (October 1909): 281–82.

tion's capital, or its source of wealth. Such dissipation, he said, history suggests has been "the most easily avoidable, the most involuntary, the most seductive, the most elusive, and, at the same time, the most fatal of all" the diseases which nearly every great civilization has suffered in its old age. The dissipation of capital, he argued, would not occur were only that wealth taxed which was used for consumption, or were taxed capital to be continued to be used for productive purposes, this time by the state in place of the original private owners. But capital would be dissipated and the community's wealth endangered when the state "takes what was intended by the former owner to be used reproductively and, having taken it, consumes in direct enjoyment." He acknowledged that his analysis of the 1908–09 budget found only a small portion of the revenue coming from capital, but he also noted that only a small part of the government's expenditure was capitalized, while most was used up. Furthermore, most of the new experiments of the government in spending, "from the establishment of old-age pensions, which is almost universally applauded," to the latest sinecure for a "party hack," tended to be forms of consumption alone. To the extent that the state increased its taxation demands on capital, it was essential that a proportionate amount of government expenditure be directed toward reproductive use.[30]

---

[30] Hilaire Belloc, "Death Duties and Capital," *Fortnightly Review* 94 (August 1910): 214–15, 222–23.

In summary, Belloc's suspicions about such things as the limits to which direct taxation could go in securing a return comparable to the real wealth of the community, the taxing authority's inclination to overestimate the real wealth, the tendency for those on permanent, fixed, and not necessarily high income to be forced to bear the heaviest burden in direct taxation, and the danger of the nation's capital being dissipated by taxation utilized in a nonreproductive manner, suggest certain reservations in his mind about the competence of the positive state of the new liberals. Regardless of Belloc's radical sympathy with the desires of the new liberals to alleviate the lot of the poor in society, these reservations were certain ultimately to turn him against "statism" or collectivism and to prompt him to seek elsewhere a solution to the social problems resulting from industrial capitalism.

Belloc's formal break with the new liberalism came on the issue of social insurance, specifically the National Insurance Act of 1911 with its provisions of unemployment and health insurance. From his opposition to it he began to develop his analysis of the impending "servile state." But it is necessary to emphasize the close chronological connection between his break with the new liberalism, with whose earlier measures, like the Old Age Pension Act, he had sympathized, and his break with the party system in general and the Liberal Party specifically. Much of his hostility to the Insurance Act seems to have derived from his hostility to the Liberal front bench. Since the measure in question was not strictly opposed by the Unionist front bench as a party issue, it confirmed his suspicions of collusion between the front benches. It must also be remembered that social insurance was one of those causes which the contemplated coalition government, which was suggested at the time of the 1910 constitutional conference, would have forwarded.[31]

His suspicions found a ready vehicle of expression with the appearance on June 22, 1911, of the *Eye-Witness,* a weekly journal which Belloc edited with the assistance of Cecil Chesterton. It had been founded to continue the campaign, launched by Belloc's resignation from party politics and proclaimed in their tract *The Party System,* to expose the fraudulence of the contemporary political system. Beginning with the premise of front-bench collusion in serving the interests of the ruling plutocracy, the *Eye-Witness*'s opinion of various governmental programs and legislation was bound to reflect these suspicions regardless of their ostensibly socially benevolent character. When these suspicions were coupled with Belloc's bias toward a "small-holding" economy, as opposed to collectivism or centralized expert control, the *Eye-Witness* assumed a decidedly anti-middle-of-the-road tone enabling it to sympathize with the "direct-action" trade unionists of a syndicalist temperament as well as to empathize with

---

[31] *Supra,* chap. 4, pp. 192–94.

the "Ditcher" peers and the Orange Unionists, despite the weekly's democratic and pro–Home Rule position.

For example, on the issue of reform of the House of Lords, which by this time had still not been resolved, the *Eye-Witness* admired the Ditcher Lords' refusal to assent to the Parliament bill. These men were the large number of "backwoods" peers, that is, aristocrats, who had scarcely visited the House of Lords and whose "country" social world had been left behind by the new Edwardian oligarchy of commerce and industry, whom Lord Willoughby de Broke, a traditional landed aristocrat, and the Earl of Halsbury, the septuagenarian former Conservative Lord Chancellor, had gathered together to fight the bill to the end. They were joined by such Unionist notables as Lord Salisbury, Robert and Hugh Cecil, F. E. Smith, the dying Joseph Chamberlain and his son Austen, and Lord Milner. The Unionist leaders, Balfour and the Marquess of Lansdowne, however, had become resigned to its passage when informed by Lloyd George and Asquith that the Liberals had received guarantees from King George V that the Liberal electoral victory of December 1910 would be followed, if necessary, by the creation of a sufficient number of new peers to ensure the bill's passage in the House of Lords. The *Eye-Witness* doubted the existence of the guarantees and suggested the government's "bluff" could have been successfully called if the Conservative leaders had not been playing their part in the party game. Once the Conservative leadership acquiesced, the back of the opposition to the reform was broken, and the government would have only to appoint a minimal number, if any, of new peers to overcome the "backwoodsman" resistance, rather than the unprecedented hundreds suggested in the guarantees. As for the bill itself, the *Eye-Witness* denied that it was a democratic measure, but held that it was instead "framed . . . in the interests of the professional politicians of both sides." This was because it did nothing to curb such central abuses of the political system as the sale of peerages, nor did it approach "so democratic and real a policy as ending the institution [the House of Lords] altogether." Instead, the worst features of the House of Lords "were to be retained" and "its functions as a servant of the two front benches were to be increased." All the bill would really do was destroy the ability of the House of Lords to act independently. Thereby the passage of whatever legislation the front benches had decided upon would be assured.

Since the popularly elected House of Commons did not really reflect general national demands, but was under the control of the front benches, the radical *Eye-Witness* paradoxically called upon that "still largely traditional and English" institution, the House of Lords (which in theory it regarded as "intolerable"), to resist the caucus and thereby permit "some measure of interest and truth . . . to trickle again in the barren public life of England."[32] The Ditchers failed, however,

---

[32] *Eye-Witness,* July 20, August 3, 1911, pp. 129–30, 193–94.

as enough peers voted for the Parliament bill to make
the question of the King fulfilling the guarantees academic, although in fact the guarantees had been made,
even to the point of the government's drawing up a
list of several hundred potential new peers.[33]

Given their premises about the inherent plutocratic
domination of the parties and the collusion of the respective leaders, it was inevitable that Belloc and Cecil
Chesterton would respond suspiciously to that other
great legislative question of 1911, the insurance bill.
Rather than view it as an example of new liberal
socially ameliorative legislation, they interpreted it as
a "disguised tax on the poor" that aimed at the "destruction of the economic power of the great trade
unions," with the ultimate motive of establishing a
legally stratified society of capitalists and workers in
which the latter would be subjected to conscript labor.
The inevitability of such suspicions can be better appreciated if the history of the formation of the bill, as
well as its provisions, is examined. For instance, the
bill, of necessity, had to include numerous concessions
to such varied vested interests as the insurance companies, the friendly societies, and the labor unions if a
national insurance system was to be successfully established. In addition, the theory behind the bill of coercive insurance was entirely alien to Britain, having

---

[33] Roy Jenkins, *Asquith* (London: Collins, 1964), pp. 252–54,
606–9.

been inspired in large part by the German system of
social insurance developed under Bismarck. Yet, it is
doubtful if any system administering such benefits
could have been enacted minus the conservative character of being financed by the potential recipients, nor
would it have been actuarially sound without being
compulsory.

The ministerial interest in the program had developed from a visit to Germany in August 1908 by the
Chancellor of the Exchequer, Lloyd George, who subsequently consulted with the President of the Board of
Trade, Winston Churchill, on the possibility of introducing social insurance similar to Germany's in Great
Britain.[34] The responsibility for preparing the necessary
legislation was divided between their respective departments, with the Board of Trade preparing what
became part two, the unemployment insurance section
of the 1911 act, and the treasury preparing part one,
the national health insurance section. Legislative action
was delayed, however, by the controversy over the
1909 budget and the Parliament bill. Furthermore,
while it was not intended to be such, the Insurance Act
became in fact the culminating measure of the new
liberalism because of the obvious distraction of the
government's attention by the Irish Home Rule question and World War I. Still, it must be distinguished
from the earlier new liberal measures, like the Old

---

[34] Gilbert, *National Insurance in Great Britain,* pp. 266–67, 291.

Age Pension Act, for it was financed not from general revenues but from a compulsory insurance fund.

The unemployment insurance section, which was in large part the work of William Beveridge and H. Llewellyn Smith, the permanent secretary of the Board of Trade, was, because of its experimental nature, limited in its coverage to a small group of relatively low-paying trades that were "subject to temporary, predictable unemployment," such as building, shipbuilding, and mechanical engineering, a total of about two and a quarter million men. Not included were declining trades, trades where casual labor was customary—like dock work—trades employing many women, and trades where workers were more likely to be put on short time than to be laid off, like coal mining and cotton spinning. Membership in the scheme by the selected trades was to be compulsory, with the worker, the employer, and the state each contributing two and a half pence weekly to the insurance fund. In return, an unemployed workman could qualify for seven shillings a week in benefits for every five weeks he had contributed, up to a maximum of fifteen weeks of benefits. The trade unions were included in the administration of the scheme as union members were entitled to draw their benefits through their union rather than at the government labor exchange. It was hoped that this would supplement rather than replace the existing private unemployment benefit systems of some unions. To discourage "malingering" the bill called for a denial of benefits to

workers who lost employment through their own misconduct. This was against the wishes of Churchill, who
believed "there is no reason to suppose that a mitiga-
tion of the extreme severities will tend in any way to a
diminution of personal responsibility." Also, the bill
did not extend benefits to striking workers, although
unemployed workers would not be denied benefits if
they refused work offered by a struck firm.[35]

The *Eye-Witness* was critical not so much of the
concept of unemployment benefits as of the conditions
imposed for receiving them. For one thing, the scheme's
lack of universal coverage was disappointing, but the
paper was more disturbed by the denial of benefits to
strikers, to workers discharged for their own misconduct, and to workers who would refuse employment
similar to what they were used to, and it regarded these
requirements as a step toward the coercion of conscription of labor. These provisions were seen as a denial of
the liberty of the employee since the determination of
eligibility would be made by a "court of referees,
upon which the nominees of the employers plus the
nominees of the politician at the Board of Trade must
always be in the majority." But more disturbing were
the requirements governing the union administration
of benefits. These were viewed less as a boon to the
unions than as a fetter upon them. For instance, the
fact that they could not use funds designated for un-

---

[35] *Ibid.*, pp. 269–71.

employment benefits for militant purposes was seen as designed for "the destruction of the economic power of the great trade unions," which destruction was held to be "probably the motive of the bill."[36] However, despite similar suspicions and reservations by certain labor unions, the unemployment insurance section of the bill encountered a minimum of opposition.

This was in contrast to the violent opposition met by the health insurance provisions in part one. The drafting of this part, which was an excellent example of the increasingly important role of professional governmental administrators, was the combined work of political figures like Lloyd George and Charles F. G. Masterman (one of the radical intellectual journalists elected in 1906, who had been a major theoretician of the new liberalism and who advanced into the ministry itself as undersecretary for the Home Office in 1909) and career treasury officials like William Braithwaite and John S. Bradbury.[37] Unlike the limited coverage of part two, the health insurance scheme was compulsory for all workers or employees, and open on a voluntary basis to the self-employed who earned less than £160 a year. Contributions were uniform and were paid in part by the employer, the employee, and the state, with

---

[36] *Eye-Witness,* June 20, 1911, pp. 14–15.

[37] The story of the origins of the national health service is recounted in the memoirs of William J. Braithwaite, *Lloyd George's Ambulance Wagon,* ed. Sir Henry N. Bunbury (London: Methuen, 1957), particularly the summary by the editor, pp. 17–42.

the worker's contribution being collected by the employer in return for a stamp receipt. The system offered twenty-six weeks of sickness benefits, to be followed, if necessary, by smaller disability benefits for as long as necessary. In addition, the medical services of a general practitioner, maternity benefits, and sanatorium benefits for tubercular cases were offered. Like unemployment insurance, the national health insurance would, it was hoped, supplement rather than weaken existing private agencies which provided health benefits. These included trade unions and the friendly societies, those fraternal organizations which had been a major source of protection against economic and health adversity for a large portion of the Victorian population. According to the bill, the various benefits would be administered through "approved friendly societies."

It was this selfsame fact which prompted the highly effective opposition to the bill by two powerful interests whose dissatisfaction would have ultimately to be appeased by that master politician Lloyd George before the bill's passage would be certain. These were the national doctors' organization, the British Medical Association, and the profit-making industrial insurance companies. The doctors disliked both the small remuneration of four shillings annually afforded for each patient, and the administration of the benefits by the friendly societies. The relationship of the medical profession to these societies had never been pleasant, as the doctors disliked both the workload and the small compensation that often accompanied any contracts to service the members of such societies. The profit-making insurance companies naturally looked with foreboding on the role of their nonprofit competitors in administering the national health insurance. Admittedly, the insurance companies specialized primarily in death benefits, which were not offered by the bill, but the very access the friendly societies would have to almost all the working class put them in a better position to encourage subscription to their own life insurance plans. Most persuasive in changing the bill on this matter was the fact that the agents of the industrial insurance companies were mainly Liberal and a not insignificant force in getting the Liberal Party's message across to the working classes; indeed, they were too valuable to alienate from the party. By way of appeasement, the profit-making insurance companies were permitted to qualify, like the friendly societies, as participants in the plan, and the fears of the doctors were reassured by the decision not to allow the friendly societies to be involved in the administration of medical benefits.[38]

The *Eye-Witness* was hostile to the insurance bill for reasons quite different from those of the elements whom the government had sought to appease, the doctors and the insurance companies. It lamented

---

[38] Gilbert, *National Insurance in Great Britain,* pp. 309–11, 325–26, 358–71.

that the bill was not aimed at giving primary attention to the most needy, "the mass of the casual and ill-paid labor," and that it did not, out of deference to the insurance companies, provide death benefits for widows and orphans. Instead, the bill applied to the "organized proletariat," who could care for themselves through unions and friendly societies, not for their benefit, but that they might be better controlled by the employer class, with the ultimate motive of the "conscription of organized labor to the advantage of organized capital." The tax-gathering and record-keeping functions of employers in the compulsory scheme were believed to give that class "an accurate and automatically accessible record of the employed class and further subject the latter to the former." Last, the compulsory insurance contribution of the workers was regarded as a "high poll tax," higher than any previous tax burden of that class, and "carefully designed to avoid throwing upon the rich the relief of the poor." In short, the really needy would not be assisted, those workers who could assist themselves were compelled to join a system aimed at reducing their status to conscript labor, and the major cost was to be avoided by the ultimate beneficiaries, the capitalists.[39]

Belloc not merely opposed the insurance bill, but suggested a different type of plan which would avoid what he believed were dangers to the liberty of both

---

[39] *Eye-Witness,* July 13, October 19, 1911, pp. 97–98, 545–46.

trade unions and workers and whose cost would be
borne by the wealthy. In fact, his proposed system was
the very opposite of an insurance plan, being more in
the nature of direct state welfare. Under it, the funds
would be derived solely from a tax on employers determined according to the number of their employees.
Priority for benefits for sickness and unemployment
would be given to the lowest-income families in the
nation, "who have perpetually recurrent experiences of
grievous poverty" and whom he estimated to number
three million. He accepted as inevitable the "necessary"
but "humiliating" and "inhuman condition" of requir-
ing proof of poverty to qualify for relief. Whatever
funds might then be left over in his scheme, after the
poorest had been cared for, could then be distributed,
in proportion to their membership, to the various trade
unions and friendly societies to supplement their insurance plans, which served the middle-income wage-
earning families, whose numbers he estimated to be
about six million. Membership in these plans was naturally voluntary, and the trade unions need not be
inhibited from using their funds, other than those the
government gave them, for militant purposes. The advantages, he believed, of this system were that there was
no compulsion, the neediest would be assisted first, the
public expenses of management would be limited only
to assisting the poor, the freedom of the trade unions
would be respected, there would be no opportunity to
regiment the workers for the advantage of the cap-

italists, and, in accord with an elementary principle, the financing would "come from those best able to afford it, that is, the million of the well-to-do who are above the income tax limits."[40]

The legislative history of the bill was not a clear-cut party struggle (which would confirm for Belloc his suspicions about front-bench collusion); the Unionist leadership under Balfour did not directly challenge it, although growing extraparliamentary opposition prompted many rank-and-file Conservatives to question it. The *Eye-Witness* looked to that popular opposition not so much to block the passage of the bill as to prevent its enforcement. A major motive, which the journal saw as likely to cause such opposition, was popular "force of habit and instinct," whereby the Englishman would not be a Prussian and "lick stamps for Lloyd George" or have any part in such a regulatory and coercive scheme. The editors also looked to "the determined resistance of certain great sections of the workers to the dockings of their wages," and were hopeful that even the official press would begin "to find that those who buy it will not much longer tolerate a mechanical defense of so grossly unpopular a measure."[41] This last expectation, especially, was fulfilled

---

[40] Hilaire Belloc, "Honest and Dishonest Insurance," *Eye-Witness,* June 6, 1912, pp. 784–86.

[41] *Eye-Witness,* October 19, 1911, pp. 545–46.

as the *Eye-Witness* found an unusual ally in the North-cliffe press, which ran a vehement campaign against the measure, exploiting the popular distrust of its novelty. In addition, the trade unions, while ultimately accepting the plan, had wondered why the workers should have to contribute anything to it, instead of placing the burden of financing on the state and the employers. There also appeared the opposition of many categories of citizens, like nonworking married women, who were ineligible for the benefits (other than maternity), and others, like agricultural laborers and domestic servants, who regarded their payments as burdensome or unnecessary because either their medical needs were cared for by their employers or their wages were given even during sickness.

The hostility of the last group in particular was viewed as decisive by the *Eye-Witness,* which thought that the point where the bill would "most easily and certainly break down" was "the organized robbery of the domestic servant." The contributions of that portion of the working force, it stated, would account for the successful financing of the scheme.[42] One of the most flamboyant displays of hostility to the insurance bill was a mass protest rally of 20,000 servant girls at Albert Hall. Many titled ladies sat on the platform at which speakers repeated the theme that insurance was

---

[42] *Ibid.*, November 9, 1911, pp. 641–42.

superfluous and a burden for domestic servants as well as for their middle-class employers, who, unlike the very wealthy or the large companies, could not afford the required employer contribution and would be forced either to lessen wages or to dismiss employees. Miss Grace Neal, the secretary of the Domestic Workers' Union, was particularly annoyed at Lloyd George's not having seen her or other representatives of the domestic servants, and was intent on demonstrating that the agitation was an authentic display of the domestics' feelings. Finally, the meeting ratified a motion by Belloc which called for a nationwide organized resistance to the taxation of servants even if the bill was passed as legislation. Maintaining that "the introduction of this bill has been engineered by the great capitalist interests in order to destroy the trade unions," he insisted that "the servant tax was put on to finance the measure." A national organization was needed to counteract what he believed would be the probable government attempt to frighten individual servants or domestics by prosecution for noncompliance.[43]

Despite these threats of noncompliance, the Insurance Act was passed shortly thereafter with the payment of contributions scheduled to commence on July 15, 1912, and benefits available six months later. There remained both the danger of mass disobedience and the

---

[43] *Times* (London), November 30, 1911, p. 8.

necessity for extensive preparations for the administration of the system. Major responsibility for the latter task was given to Sir Robert Morant, the permanent secretary to the Board of Education who became the first chairman of the National Insurance Commission. He and his staff were asked to complete in six months a scheme "far more complicated and comprehensive" than the model German system which "had taken twenty-five years to complete,"[44] and, in large part, they succeeded. Despite all the threats of disobedience by various groups, the only serious danger of noncompliance was the threat made by the British Medical Association that its 32,000 members would refuse to give medical service to the beneficiaries of the act unless the association's demands were met, particularly with regard to remuneration for services. However, the BMA's bluff was called, for the government knew that the fee paid by the national insurance system was actually higher than the average fee paid to doctors under contract to friendly societies. Suspecting, therefore, that the views of the association were not totally representative of the profession and that for many of the less affluent doctors the national insurance system would bring an improvement in their position, Morant began to recruit the pledges of a sufficient number of doctors to

---

[44] Lucy Masterman, *C. F. G. Masterman* (London: Nicholson & Watson, 1939), p. 223.

disregard the BMA and thereby make possible the implementation of the medical benefits. Consequently the BMA yielded.[45]

Simultaneous with the struggle over the insurance bill was an outbreak of near revolutionary feelings by large segments of the working class, as manifested by the paralyzing industrywide strikes of 1910, 1911, and 1912 by the dock workers, the railway men, and the coal miners. The *Eye-Witness* was wholeheartedly sympathetic to the strikes, which were seen as suitable alternatives to ostensibly socially ameliorative legislation, like the insurance bill, that would only lead to a servile status for workers. The journal held that it should be the goal

> of those who would strengthen the dispossessed and proletarian man and save his citizenship, if it can be saved, to demand the further extension of organized labor until from an exception it shall have become the rule, and until the unfortunately small minority of owners, who are now in a clear understanding one with another, shall have to deal with every form of labor as a consciously combined force with cooperative responsibilities.[46]

The strikes were a feature of the second great expansion of the "general labor unions," that is, those unions

---

[45] Bernard M. Allen, *Sir Robert Morant* (London: Macmillan, 1934), pp. 279–82.

[46] *Eye-Witness*, July 6, 1911, pp. 65–66.

"enrolling all classes of labor irrespective of skill or occupation," which had remained stagnant ever since their original development during the labor unrest of the late 1880s.[47] The unrest especially involved two sectors of the working class, the "unskilled and low-paid labor generally, and all grades of wage earners in two industries, coal mining and the railways." Older craft unions, like engineering, shipbuilding, construction, and printing, were spared serious encounters. A general economic cause was the failure of wages to keep pace with the rising cost of living, especially from 1909 to 1913. While the well-organized skilled workers were in a better position to cope with this situation, the general, unskilled workers, for whose services there was limited demand, keenly felt the squeeze. Furthermore, the coal-mining and railway industries, confronted with declining productivity, increased costs, and insufficiently rising prices, responded with greater anxiety and intransigence to union demands than the other industries, which could offset any wage increases with improved equipment that caused greater productivity per man.[48]

The novelty of the industrywide strike and its paralyzing effect on the economy, plus the inevitable out-

---

[47] Eric J. Hobsbawm, "General Labor Unions in Britain, 1889–1914," *Economic History Review,* 2d ser. 1 (August 1948): 123–25.

[48] E. H. Phelps Brown, *The Growth of British Industrial Relations* (London: Macmillan, 1959), pp. 334–37.

breaks of violence by the strikers when nonunion or blackleg workers were employed during the strikes, created a widespread hostility toward the strikers. This partly resulted from the fear of actual revolution. These fears were fanned by the appearance at this time in England of that primarily Latin phenomenon, syndicalism, with its view that the solution to the social problem could come not from political action or legislation, but only from "direct action," specifically strikes, by the working class, which action would eventually lead to worker control of the means of production and the elimination of "wage slavery."

The central figure in this movement was Tom Mann, a leader in the 1889 dock strike, who had returned from Australia where he had come into contact with ideological currents that had originated in America. The sources of these currents were the American Marxist Daniel DeLeon and the Industrial Workers of the World, a labor organization which called for industrial rather than craft unionism and militant class warfare between the workers and the employers. Mann also journeyed to France in 1910 to reinforce his views with the more sophisticated and philosophical concepts of Continental syndicalism, as proclaimed by Georges Sorel, as well as to learn from the evidence of organizational success, as represented by the nationwide syndicalist union, the Confédération Générale du Travail. Mann formed the Industrial Syndicalist Educational

League and propagated his views in a series of monthly booklets entitled the *Industrial Syndicalist,* the most celebrated of which was the *Miners' Next Step.*[49] But although syndicalist flysheets and special periodicals were distributed to the striking workers, and the spirit of syndicalism influenced a certain number of the strike leaders, especially in the London dock strike, it is questionable whether the strikes of the era can really be interpreted as syndicalist actions with ultimate revolutionary aims. More than likely they were simply very heated disputes occasioned by immediate grievances over working conditions, pay, the employment of blacklegs, and union recognition, regardless of the agitators' oratory about class warfare and worker control of industry.

Faced with the problem of industrywide strikes in vital sections of the economy, the government responded primarily with the instruments of conciliation, in which the major role was played by G. R. Askwith, the government's chief industrial commissioner. For instance, the 1911 London dock strike was settled with the shipping federation being induced to recognize the union. Also, in August of the same year, the national railway strike, which had been partly prompted by the Prime Minister's indiscreet criticism of the union, was

---

[49] M. Beer, *A History of British Socialism,* 2 vols. (London: George Allen & Unwin, 1919), 2:357–59.

settled within two days by an appeal made by the more adept and conciliatory Lloyd George for common concern for the national interest at a time of international crisis with Germany (the Agadir affair). The owners agreed to recognize the unions indirectly by abandoning their objections to. the presence of union officials as the workers' representatives on conciliation boards. But in the case of the miners' strike, which began in February 1912 over the issue of a national minimum wage for all miners, conciliation failed and the government resorted to legislation that called for arbitration councils and a minimum wage that would be not nationwide but determined locally by local boards.[50]

The *Eye-Witness* responded to the government's role in settling these crises with the same suspicion it had for the Insurance Act, that is, the government was automatically assumed to be acting for the benefit of the capitalist plutocracy with the ultimate motive of reducing the workers to servile status. For instance, the acquiescence of the union leaders as well as the parliamentary Labor Party to Lloyd George's proposal of conciliation boards with union representatives on them to settle the railway strike was seen as a betrayal of the workers in their "most considerable attack upon the governing classes of this country." It was feared

---

[50] Henry Pelling, *A History of British Trade Unionism* (Baltimore: Penguin Books, 1963), pp. 136–37; Phelps Brown, *British Industrial Relations,* pp. 338–43.

that the boards, on which the workers would be out-
voted by the combined forces of the capitalists and
their allies, the ostensibly neutral government representatives, would result in compulsory settlements of
disputes, whereby the workers would "work not by
their own free will as a matter of contract or bargain,
but according to the will of men richer than themselves."[51] The government's solution for the miners'
strike, which the union leaders accepted—legislation
establishing voluntary arbitration boards and a minimum wage to be determined by local boards—was condemned by the *Eye-Witness* on similar grounds. It was
felt that the boards would be under the control of the
capitalists and that the minimum wage would be determined to suit their interests. They would tend to become compulsory, which would mean "the first great
definite step . . . toward that servile state of society"
would have been taken. It was feared that if the miners
accepted "the principle that they are to be eternally
bound at a wage for the benefit of a handful of owners,
particularly if they admit the ultimate right of government to fix wages, their original status is lost, and they
have passed the boundary that divides the servile condition from the free."[52]

The temperament of the *Eye-Witness* was closely
akin to that of the syndicalists, who distrusted govern-

[51] *Eye-Witness,* August 24, October 14, 1911, pp. 289–90, 391.
[52] *Ibid.,* March 3, 14, 21, 1912, pp. 353–54, 385–86, 417–18.

mental arbitration boards, Parliament, and even the union leaders as agents for the strikers:

> It is imperatively necessary to the proletariat that they should allow no settlement to a dispute to be arranged for them by "leaders" or whatever the betrayers call themselves. That they should not touch a politician nor go near him in such matters they already know: but more than that caution is needed. No matter who speaks and signs for the men the men *themselves* should ratify or refuse to ratify a settlement by a ballot.[53]

From these sentiments it follows that Belloc's *Eye-Witness* was sympathetic with those elements in the Labor Party who were dissatisfied with the moderate leadership of the parliamentary Labor Party, especially that of Ramsay MacDonald, who had negotiated the original electoral arrangement with the Liberals for the 1905 election, an arrangement which had brought so many victories to the Laborites but which inhibited their independence of action in the House of Commons. The basic complaint was that the parliamentary Labor Party had failed to express working-class discontent and had become absorbed in the caucus-dominated parliamentary system, as evidenced most recently by its support of the Insurance Act. This failure was attributable to its membership being "a thoroughly middle-class set of men . . . thoroughly divorced from the populace," who, even if they wished "to express

---

[53] *Ibid.,* August 24, 1911, p. 290.

working-class discontent . . . would inevitably have offended persons from whom places and salaries were to be expected."[54]

Similar dissatisfaction within the Labor Party inspired a left-wing assault on the parliamentary Labor Party. This assault had probably begun with the victory of Victor Grayson in a 1907 by-election in which he ran in a three-cornered race as a pure socialist unconnected with the Liberal Party or without the endorsement of the more conservative local labor unions. In 1910 followers of his spirit sought within the Council of the Independent Labor Party to reassert that organization's original position of fighting "for socialism" and "against BOTH the captalist parties IMPARTIALLY." In the following year the separate British Socialist Party was formed out of an alliance of disgruntled ILP members, the members of the purist Marxist Social-Democratic Federation of H. M. Hyndman, and the Clarion Fellowship, the movement inspired by Robert Blatchford, an ex-sergeant and a journalist who was perhaps the greatest British popularizer of socialism, but whose socialism included a curious mixture of populism and jingoism.[55] Probably the most enduring of these left-wing developments was the launching of a daily newspaper, the *Daily Herald,*

---

[54] *Ibid.,* January 25, 1912, pp. 168–69.

[55] Henry Pelling, *A Short History of the Labor Party* (London: Macmillan, 1965), pp. 24–26.

which originally appeared as a printers' strike sheet. In 1913 George Lansbury, one of the signatories of the minority report of the Poor Law Commission who had served as an MP from 1910 to 1912 and who had appealed in the *Eye-Witness* in 1911 for the creation of "such a public opinion as will destroy what we understand as the party system,"[56] became its editor, and attracted even greater fame for the paper with his policy of no editorial censorship. As a result a variety of radical opponents of the establishment contributed to its columns, ranging from the syndicalists to the suffragists to the pacifists. Needless to say, Belloc and Gilbert K. Chesterton, who for all of their anticapitalism were decidedly antisocialist, became regular contributors to the paper, despite their aversion to the suffragists and the pacifists, and did not break with the *Daily Herald* until World War I, when they opposed the paper's pacifism.[57] Chesterton, for example, could pour his scorn on the leadership of the parliamentary Labor Party in the paper by suggesting that

> Mr. MacDonald has no position, high or low, in any of the three dimensions of the universe. It would not have made the slightest difference for good or ill, to the future of anything or anybody, if the tiger had eaten him. There would have been a Liberal member for Leicester instead,

[56] *Eye-Witness,* November 23, 1911, p. 721.

[57] Raymond W. Postgate, *The Life of George Lansbury* (London: Longmans, Green, 1951), pp. 135–38, 155.

who would have made the same speeches, given exactly the same votes, and, if he were the usual successful soap-boiler, would have eclipsed Mr. MacDonald in everything except good looks.[58]

The *Daily Herald* was temporarily and unsuccessfully rivaled by an official Labor Party paper, the *Daily Citizen,* which was very short-lived.

All of this radical criticism of the parliamentary Labor Party and its leadership has to be weighed against other considerations. For one thing, would there have been anything more than a fraction of the small labor representation that there was in Parliament if MacDonald and Keir Hardie had not made with the Liberal Party prior to 1905 their electoral arrangement whereby the two parties agreed not to challenge each other in certain constituencies? Second, most of the Labor MPs were sponsored by, and most of the party's funds were derived from, the older and more conservative trade unions and their political instrument, the Labor Representation Committee. Consequently, even though its men, Hardie, MacDonald, and Snowden, were the leaders of the parliamentary party, the more radical Independent Labor Party would have found it rather difficult to be the tail wagging the whole Labor Party dog. Last, independent parliamentary action by the Labor Party prior to 1910 would have been mean-

---

[58] Quoted in G. D. H. Cole and Raymond Postgate, *The British Common People* (New York: Barnes & Noble, 1961), p. 486.

ingless and ineffectual because of the overwhelming Liberal majority, while independent action after 1910 would have been disastrous for itself as well as the Liberal Party since it might have necessitated more elections. The expense of an election was the last thing the Labor Party could bear until the 1909 Osborne judgment of the House of Lords—which barred the use of trade union funds, the Labor Party's major source of financial support, for political purposes—could be overturned by legislation.[59]

The most celebrated criticism of the Liberal government, especially of Lloyd George, by the *Eye-Witness* centered about the Marconi controversy. This case seemed to afford clear-cut evidence of the validity of the Belloc-Chesterton view of the corrupt and plutocratic nature of British politics and to justify the *Eye-Witness*'s suspicions of the ultimate purposes of the ostensibly socially ameliorative new liberal legislation. The case involved a contract signed on March 7, 1912, by the Postmaster General, Herbert Samuel (one of the popularizing proponents of the new liberalism),[60] and the Marconi Company for the erection by the company of six wireless stations for an imperial communications system. Parliamentary action to approve

---

[59] Pelling, *Short History,* pp. 19–24.

[60] Herbert Samuel, *Liberalism* (London: G. Richards, 1902).

the contract was postponed on July 19 and further delayed on October 11, pending an inquiry by a select parliamentary committee. The delays and the inquiry were prompted by increasing parliamentary reservations about the terms of the contract and the surrounding circumstances—for instance, the managing director of the company, Godfrey Isaacs, being a brother of the Attorney General, Sir Rufus Isaacs; and members of the government perhaps being among the beneficiaries of an outstanding climb in the value of Marconi shares following the announcement of the contract. That three of the principals of a suspected deal, Samuel and the Isaacs brothers, were Jewish was a not unimportant factor kindling the ire of forces hostile to the world of high finance and speculation in general and to the role of Jews in that world in particular.

The main journalistic critics of the Marconi deal were Leopold J. Maxse's Unionist and imperialist *National Review* and the *Eye-Witness*. The latter began a series of articles in its issue for August 8, 1912 (more than a month after Belloc had turned the editorship over to Cecil Chesterton, although he continued to write for it), which insisted that it had "been secretly arranged between Isaacs and Samuel that the British people shall give the Marconi Company a very large sum of money through the agency of the said Samuel, and for the benefit of the said Isaacs." The contract, furthermore, was one characterized by "antiquated

methods, the refusal of competing tenders far cheaper
and far more efficient and the saddling of the country
with corruptly purchased goods."[61]

The select committee inquiry that was inspired by
such charges divided its mission in two. One inquiry
examined the more technical question of the compara-
tive competence of the Marconi Company for the
contracted project. It concluded that it was the most
capable, although the committee was not as certain that
the construction of the entire imperial wireless system
should be given to that company.[62] The second inquiry
examined the more sensational issue—allegations of
corruption. A most startling development grew out of
the testimony of Leopold J. Maxse before that committee. On February 14, 1913, a French newspaper,
Le Matin, inaccurately reported that Maxse had ac-
cused Samuel of having purchased shares in the Marconi Company before the settlement of the contract,
and of selling them at 400 percent profit when the
contract was publicly announced. Consequently, the
ministers Rufus Isaacs and Herbert Samuel engaged
the celebrated Unionist MPs F. E. Smith and Sir
Edward Carson to institute libel proceedings against
Le Matin. This was a step they had refrained from taking throughout the whole controversy against their

---

[61] *Eye-Witness,* August 8, 1912, p. 230.

[62] Frances Donaldson, *The Marconi Scandal* (New York: Harcourt,
Brace & World, 1962), p. 72.

principal journalistic accusers, especially against the *Eye-Witness,* partly because they were convinced, along with the Prime Minister, that such action would only secure notoriety and increased circulation for the papers.[63] *Le Matin* did not contest the suit and printed a retraction within three days. In their court statement the plaintiffs made a remarkable acknowledgment that they had in fact purchased Marconi shares and at a cheaper price than they cost when sold publicly. Purchases had also been made by Lloyd George and Lord Murray, the Liberal whip. But the purchases were of shares in the American Marconi Company, which action, they explained, made them completely innocent since that company did not benefit from the contract the English Marconi Company had made with the government. They further insisted that this admission did not contradict their emphatic denials during the discussion of the question in Parliament on October 11, 1912; then they had disavowed any dealing in the shares of the company with which the government had negotiated.[64] While such a fine distinction might spare them any charge of dishonesty or corruption, their prudence and frankness were questionable.

While the *Eye-Witness* had not been sued by the ministers in spite of its accusations, it did prompt a

---

[63] Jenkins, *Asquith,* pp. 281–82; Donaldson, *Marconi Scandal,* pp. 56–57.

[64] Donaldson, *Marconi Scandal,* pp. 131–32.

criminal libel suit by Godfrey Isaacs, the Marconi
director (who similarly engaged Smith and Carson),
because of an article in its issue of January 13, 1913,
that had examined his entrepreneurial record and suggested that his numerous unsuccessful business ventures
were spared from possible prosecution only because his
brother was Attorney General.[65] (By this date, Cecil
Chesterton had purchased complete control of the
paper and changed its name to the *New Witness*.)
Specifically, the libels were the suggestions that the
Marconi contract was corrupt and that Isaacs had been
guilty of criminal offense in the direction of the other
companies with which he had been connected. The
trial began on May 27, 1913, after the conclusion of
the select committee's hearings, but before the issuance
of its report or parliamentary action on such. The
Chesterton defense took the rather strange line that
the first alleged libel, that the Marconi contract was
corrupt, was directed against the ministers Rufus
Isaacs and Herbert Samuel and need not be defended
since the plaintiff was neither of them but Godfrey
Isaacs. The defense, therefore, mainly concentrated on
the second count. Cecil Chesterton appeared somewhat
indecisive in his own defense as he acknowledged on
the stand that he had no choice but to accept the denials
of Samuel and Rufus Isaacs of having acted dishonora-
bly or dishonestly in the Marconi matter, although he

---

[65] *New Witness,* January 2, 1913, pp. 257–58.

believed they had laid themselves open to such suspicions. He was found guilty and fined £100 and costs. His supporters regarded the nominal fine, instead of a possible imprisonment, as a moral victory and insisted that the decision of the jury simply implied that the *New Witness* was inaccurate in its analysis of the career of Godfrey Isaacs, but said nothing on the more serious question of the conduct of the ministers in the Marconi matter.[66] This, however, must be weighed against the remarks of the judge, when sentencing, that many of Chesterton's libels traced to "invincible ignorance—to ignorance of business and prejudice," and that he and his supporters "have been partly instigated by racial prejudice and partly blind to business matters."[67]

It is often the anti-Semitic flavor of the attacks by the *New Witness* that is most noted. The paper began to adopt a more shrill tone in this matter than it had under Belloc's editorship, and especially after its change of name. Belloc's anti-Semitism was undisguised, particularly as manifest in his novels and occasionally his poetry, but it had a more theoretical than personal basis. Although Belloc supported Chesterton in the libel trial as well as in his testimony on the Marconi affair before the select committee,

---

[66] G. K. Chesterton, *Autobiography* (New York: Sheed & Ward, 1936), pp. 210–11.

[67] Donaldson, *Marconi Scandal,* p. 182.

he privately "regretted the recent and increasing way the *New Witness* has got into of hitting blind." He had advised Chesterton that certain things the latter allowed to be published were "unwise and deplorable," for "the detestation of the Jewish cosmopolitan influence especially through finance, is one thing, and one may be right or wrong in feeling that detestation or in the degree to which one admits it, but mere anti-Semitism and a mere attack on a Jew because he is a Jew is quite another matter."[68]

In his own testimony Belloc had concerned himself primarily with the situation whereby a brother of a cabinet member was the recipient of a public favor or contract from another cabinet member, a favor that greatly increased the value of the shares of his enterprise. In other words, he was attacking the general situation in the world of high finance whereby the wealthier and well connected were able easily to increase their speculative values because of privileged information, while the smaller investor was heavily handicapped. When questioned as to anti-Semitic motives in his condemnation of the Marconi contract, he ironically wondered if there was "anybody less Jewish than the Chancellor of the Exchequer." Denying that the campaign was the result of prejudice, or an

---

[68] Hilaire Belloc to Maurice Baring, February 21, 1913, Robert Speaight, *The Life of Hilaire Belloc* (New York: Farrar, Straus & Cudahy), p. 311.

attack on "Jews as Jews," Belloc insisted it was aimed at "cosmopolitan finance . . . a power particularly dangerous to the separate nationalities of Europe." He recognized that "the racial Jewish element in cosmopolitan finance is a large element," and though he criticized that element, he was sympathetic to "a great mass of the Jewish race which is poor, and which is oppressed, and which is persecuted."[69]

On June 9, 1913, four days after the verdict in the Chesterton case, the select committee adopted, by a straight party vote of eight to six, a majority report which exonerated the ministers in the granting of the contract and insisted that the ministers' purchase of shares in the American Marconi Company was a matter completely unconnected with the controversial contract since neither that company nor the value of its shares benefited directly or indirectly by the contract.[70] Lord Robert Cecil issued a minority report which agreed that the ministers had not been influenced by personal interest in the performance of their duties. But he insisted that, in purchasing shares in the American company on the basis of advanced private information, the ministers had acted with great impropriety and could perhaps be put into a position of conflict of interest since the American Marconi Company was indirectly interested in the contract. He was also critical

---

[69] Donaldson, *Marconi Scandal*, pp. 164–67.
[70] *Ibid.*, pp. 266–67.

of the ministerial reticence and lack of frankness on the matter, especially in the October 11, 1912, discussion in the Commons.[71] On a strict party vote, however, the House of Commons rejected a motion embodying the criticisms made in Cecil's minority report.

In summary, Belloc's suspicion of and hostility toward the British party system, substantiated for him by the Marconi incident—an apparently real example of the theme of his political novels—made him incapable of believing that the Liberal government could act on domestic problems for any purpose other than to serve the interests of the plutocracy. He could interpret social legislation, like the Insurance Act, and efforts by the government to resolve labor disputes only in the worst possible light. From these suspicions he developed an analysis of the general direction in which government was moving, which he direly forecast to be in the direction of the servile state. In the next chapter we shall examine his analysis, and his proposed solution, which he called distributism, and compare them with the positions of other radicals also dissatisfied with the new liberalism, ranging from the Webbs to the guild socialists.

---

[71] *Ibid.*, pp. 294–96.

Chapter Six

The Servile State, 1912

The legislative program of the new liberalism, especially the Insurance Act, was criticized by many radicals, but from two different perspectives. On the one hand, the more conventional collectivists, like Sidney and Beatrice Webb, attacked the program for having been aimed at the alleviation of sickness and poverty rather than at their prevention. From the start of his public career Belloc had been hostile toward collectivism like that of the Webbs and their sometime Fabian associates, H. G. Wells and George Bernard Shaw, and by this time had come to view their ideas as accomplishing the same end as the new liberalism, the entrenchment of the plutocracy. On the other hand, a newer breed of radicals, specifically the guild socialists, viewed reform legislation with a distrustful attitude similar to that of Belloc, which one historian of political thought has called "a general reaction against 'the state.' "[1] But distributism, or the wide-spread ownership of capital, differed considerably from their solution.

The almost isolated position which Belloc's attitudes gave him in British thought partly resulted from their alien character—his curious dislike of capitalism and enthusiasm for property ownership reflected the paradoxical strains in his background of Victorian radicalism and Roman Catholicism. Both influences naturally made him very responsive to the iconoclastic historical interpretations of the Protestant Reformation, the Glorious Revolution, and the Whig supremacy current at the time. But the same influences restrained him from following the usual statist solutions inspired by the same historians. Indeed, the eccentricity of his views, coupled with his loss of faith in parliamentarianism, made him susceptible to a rightward turn, as he saw the only means of attaining his goals to lie in a system with a strong authoritarian executive, which he labeled monarchy.

In this chapter we will analyze Belloc's early hostility to socialism in general, his specific differences with other critics of the Liberal government, such as the Webbs and H. G. Wells, the similarities and differences

---

[1] Sir Ernest Barker, *Political Thought in England, 1848–1914*, 2d ed. (London: Oxford University Press, 1959; first published 1915), p. 197.

between him and the guild socialists, and, finally, his own program of distributism.

Belloc's hostility to socialism was closely connected to his religious position, as there was a close correspondence between his criticisms of it and those in the famous social encyclical *Rerum Novarum,* issued by Pope Leo XIII in 1891. In the encyclical the Pope was conscious of the "isolated and defenseless" position of the working class in the face of "the callousness of employers and the greed of unrestrained competition" and aware that monopolistic concentration of economic power had enabled "a small number of very rich men" to be "able to lay upon the masses of the poor a yoke little better than slavery itself." Notwithstanding, he urged restraint and limitations on state power and stressed widespread property ownership and private associations as the most suitable weapons for the alleviation of the plight of the working classes. Socialism, or the concept of community possession of property, received particular papal condemnation as "contrary to the natural rights of mankind." The Pope, instead, viewed the "stable and permanent possession" of individual property as necesary for man if he was to be the master of his own acts. This applied especially to families, whose privacy and liberty he was particularly anxious to preserve from state intrusion; indeed, he insisted that "the state must not absorb the individual or the family" and that "both should be allowed free and untrammeled action as far as is consistent with the common good and the interests of others." Leo XIII saw the main task of the state as one of impartiality and justice toward all portions of the community and solicitude for the welfare of all, a view suggesting that he regarded state favoritism toward, and patronage of, the wealthy and the capitalists as a major cause of the social problem. Therefore, rather than advocate special legislation for the workers, he held that "the more that is done for the working population by the general laws of the country, the less need will there be to seek for particular means to relieve them."[2]

The Pontiff did not object to state intervention in employer-labor relations to prevent unjust, degrading, or hazardous working conditions, and dangers to family life or morality. But even in such cases, "the law must not undertake more, nor go further, than is required for the remedy of the evil or the removal of the danger." Consequently he seems to have viewed the state's role as being primarily negative, that of protecting rights and preventing injustices—especially in the case of "the poor and the helpless," who are less able to protect themselves—rather than as one offering a positive program of social welfare. In this protective role "the chief thing to be secured is the safeguarding by legal

---

[2] Leo XIII, "The Condition of Labor," *Five Great Encyclicals* (New York: Paulist Press, 1939), pp. 2–7, 15–17.

enactment and policy of private property." But private property included the property and possessions of the workman, such as his spiritual and material interests. The protection of these interests necessitated cessation from work on Sundays and festivals, limiting the hours of daily labor lest it should endanger health and strength, and appropriate restrictions on child and female labor to protect from conditions dangerous to morality, health, education, and the very process of maturing. Last, the Pope challenged the view of wages as a thing to be settled by the labor market. While he preferred that wage contracts be arrived at by free arrangements between workmen and employers, he held that "there is a dictate of nature more imperious and more ancient than any bargain between man and man, that the remuneration must be enough to support the wage earner in reasonable and frugal comfort."[3]

But even on this last question, the Pope remained anxious about "undue influence on the part of the state," and looked more to workmen's associations as a source of relief and improvement of conditions. This improvement would, he hoped, result in a sufficiency in wages from which the worker could, by careful economy, begin to accumulate. In this regard, therefore, he thought not only that the law should favor ownership, but also that "its policy should be to induce as many people as possible to become owners." Such a develop-

---

[3] *Ibid.*, pp. 18–22.

ment, he believed, would prompt a greater distribution of property and a narrowing of the gulf between the few wealthy propertied and the impoverished multitude. In addition, possession by the many would stimulate even greater productivity, as well as inhibit excessive migration and all of the problems connected with it.[4]

This papal distrust of the state and the insistence on widespread property ownership were paralleled in some of Belloc's early strictures against socialism. In 1909, long before the Catholic-Bolshevik differences that would be emphasized so emphatically in Belloc's writings in the 1920s and 1930s, he envisioned a coming confrontation between Catholicism and socialism. Such was inevitable, he held, because of the increasing awareness by the socialists that their only serious opponent was the Catholic church, whose opposition was not grounded on "the vulgar capitalist arguments" which "take for granted the very postulates of socialism." Instead, the church based its hostility on the premise that

> human society is fulfilling the end of its being, is normal
> to itself, is therefore happier, when its constituent families
> own and privately control material things . . . that this
> institution of ownership is not merely a civil accident un-
> connected with the destiny of the soul . . . but a prior
> thing, connected with the nature of man, inseparable from
> him, and close in touch with the sense of right and wrong.[5]

---

[4] *Ibid.*, pp. 22–23.

[5] Hilaire Belloc, *The Church and Socialism* (London: Catholic Truth Society, 1909), pp. 7–8.

As evidence of this inherent Catholic antisocialism, he alluded to the tendencies toward widespread property distribution, especially peasant ownership in France, Southern Germany, Ireland, and the Catholic cantons of Switzerland. At a Catholic Truth Society conference in Manchester, he rejoiced particularly over how, under Wyndham's Land Act, "the Irish people have deliberately chosen to become peasant proprietors . . . when they could have become permanent tenants under far easier terms." This phenomenon proved to him that in "a universal Catholic society," there would develop "from the very sanctity in which it held property, a society in which the mass of citizens would own property."[6]

This act of 1903, which had been sponsored by the Conservative Chief Secretary for Ireland, George Wyndham, had all but settled the Irish land question as it continued and expanded the land purchase arrangements of earlier Unionist legislation aimed at "killing Home Rule with kindness." Under its provisions peasant tenants were given very favorable terms for state loans with which to purchase land from their landlords, who received a bonus over the sale price from the state as an encouragement to sell. Wyndham, who had served as Balfour's secretary, had been one of the "Souls," a young Tory set filled with an idealistic spirit of imperialist mission that somewhat offset the more practical political temper nourished in their party by

---

[6] *Times* (London), September 22, 1909, p. 8c.

Salisbury. He was one of the parliamentary colleagues with whom Belloc developed a very close friendship despite their great differences in political faith.[7]

Belloc had displayed his bias toward small property holding in *The Path to Rome,* noting how some of his friends agreed with him that it was preferable that craftsmanship and art be exercised for noncompetitive motives. Yet he was baffled when they proceeded "to the very strange conclusion that one should not own one's great noble house, nor one's pigsty, nor one's railway shares, nor the very boots on one's feet." When such friends argued that widespread ownership was impractical because of "the concentration of the means of production," he replied that even the ownership of highly concentrated capital could be widely distributed.[8]

A similar commitment to widespread property ownership as a solution for the social crisis of industrial capitalism was held by Belloc's close associate, G. K. Chesterton. Indeed, so close was their collaboration in espousing the alternative program of distribution, that, for all intents and purposes, this chapter could appropriately be regarded as an analysis of Belloc and Chesterton. But it must be noted further that Chester-

---

[7] Robert Speaight, *The Life of Hilaire Belloc* (New York: Farrar, Straus & Cudahy), p. 219.

[8] Hilaire Belloc, *The Path to Rome* (Garden City, N.Y.: Doubleday, Image Books, 1956; first published 1902), p. 75.

ton, whose first interests had been in literary, philosophical, and even theological matters, was very greatly indebted to Belloc in the formation of his opinions on political, sociological, and historical questions, and, in a sense, should be regarded more as the articulate disciple on these matters.[9] Striking the same note as the papal encyclical and Belloc's pronouncements about the appropriateness of property for human nature and its necessity for the family unit, Chesterton correlated property to human creativity, especially in the case of the average, not particularly talented man:

> Property is merely the art of the democracy. It means that every man should have something that he can shape in his own image, as he is shaped in the image of Heaven. But because he is not God, but only a graven image of God, his self-expression must deal with limits, properly with limits that are strict and even small.

Chesterton was aware that the word *property* had been defiled in his time by the corruption of the great capitalists, who were really "the enemies of property." Not knowing their own limitations, the capitalists "do not want their own land, but other people's." He, for his part, was interested only in defending that property which was desired by "every normal man." That would be "a house of his own" in which to put his family. The

---

[9] Maisie Ward, *Gilbert Keith Chesterton* (Harmondsworth, Middlesex: Penguin Books, 1958), p. 95.

desideratum Chesterton would set up to confront "the dehumanized poverty of modern industrialism" was "to give nearly everybody ordinary houses."[10]

This emphasis upon private ownership, especially by the family, and on the independence of the common man ran counter to the spirit of those other literary critics of the irrationalities and privileges of the Edwardian plutocracy, H. G. Wells and George Bernard Shaw. The clash was inevitable, given the collectivist premises of Wells, who, basing his socialism on a "faith in the order, the knowableness of things and the power of men in cooperation to overcome chance," called for "collective action" and the creation of "a comprehensive design" for "all the social activities of man."[11] This prompted him to put confidence, not in the common man, but in the rising and adaptable mechanical and engineering class, which possibly contained the "primary creative conditions of a new, numerous, intelligent, educated, and capable social element." He hoped this "great inchoate mass" of more or less capable people engaged in applying the growing body of scientific thought "to the general needs of society" would organ-

---

[10] G. K. Chesterton, *What's Wrong with the World* (New York: Sheed & Ward, 1956; first published 1910), pp. 35–36, 45–46.
[11] H. G. Wells, *New Worlds for Old* (New York: Macmillan, 1907), p. 21.

ize itself into "a system of interdependent educated classes with a common consciousness and aim."[12]

Shaw had similar elitist inclinations and a disregard for the common man idealized by Belloc and Chesterton. Asked Shaw, "If despotism failed only for want of a capable benevolent despot, what chance has democracy, which requires a whole population of capable voters?" He pointed to a solution—eugenics—whereby society could "either breed political capacity or be ruined by democracy," but was pessimistic that popular cowardice and sluggishness, "under cover of philanthropy," would block a policy of natural selection, and "under cover of delicacy and morality" neglect artificial selection.[13]

Wells also was very responsive to the idea of eugenics as a means for promoting a rational and organized society. He stated the first premises of his type of socialism, which premises reflected a spirit quite opposite to the Catholic social views already discussed:

> The community as a whole should be responsible . . . for the welfare and upbringing of every child born into that community. This responsibility may be delegated in whole

---

[12] H. G. Wells, *Anticipations* (New York: Harper & Brothers, 1901), pp. 97, 109.

[13] Bernard Shaw, *Man and Superman* (Harmondsworth, Middlesex: Penguin Books, 1946; first published 1903), p. 25.

or in part to parent, teacher or other guardian—but it is
not simply the right but the duty of the state—that is to
say, of the organized power and intelligence of the community—to direct, to inquire, and to intervene in any
default for the child's welfare.

Again:

The community as a whole should be inalienably the
owner and administrator of the land, of all raw materials,
of all values and resources accumulated from the past and
. . . all private property must be of a terminable nature,
reverting to the community; and subject to the general
welfare.[14]

From these premises Wells proceeded to argue that the
state should be concerned not so much with protecting
the property rights of as many families as possible, as
Belloc and Chesterton desired, as with encouraging
the development of a healthy, intelligent, and adaptable
race. He admitted that there was still insufficient scientific data to establish a positive policy for "the selective
breeding of individuals by the community as a whole."
But society should concern itself immediately with "the
wastage of such births as the world gets today," that is,
with providing the proper environmental conditions for
raising a healthy and educated populace. In accord
with the priority of responsibility he gave to society
over children, he would have the state provide the mini-

---

[14] Wells, *New Worlds,* pp. 52–53, 86.

mum standard of clothing, growth, nutrition, and education for those numerous neglected children, who, if left to their parents, would never attain the desirable health and educational standards. In turn for this care given to their children, the negligent parents would be held financially responsible to the state, under penalty of forced confinement in "celibate labor establishments." In this way, a kind of negative eugenics would operate whereby deficient parents would be discouraged from breeding, and "the worst fringe of this question, the maltreated children, the children of the slum, the children of drunkards and criminals, and the illegitimate," would be saved from wastage.[15]

Wells hoped that this combination—state interference to improve environmental conditions and negative eugenics to discourage the less qualified from breeding —would be applied on a much broader scale. This could be done by legislation penalizing parents who subjected their children to overcrowded and unhealthy conditions. In addition, minimum housing standards and minimum wage requirements could be set by law. The purpose of these laws would be primarily not to guarantee good housing and wages for the heads of poor families, but to make it impossible for parasitic landlords and employers to employ cheap labor profitably. Such practices had discouraged the construction

---

[15] H. G. Wells, *Mankind in the Making* (New York: Charles Scribner's Sons, 1904), pp. 61, 85, 94–95.

of suitable houses and had arrested "the development of labor-saving machinery" and the employment of "superior and socially more valuable labor." But minimum housing and minimum wages would deny over-crowded dwelling places and socially retrogressive cheap employment to those people who were "mainly unemployed because of a real incapacity in character, strength, or intelligence for efficient citizenship." With a home and employment denied them, mendacity laws inhibiting them from begging, and casual words catching and registering them,

> everything would converge to convince these people that to bear children into such an unfavorable atmosphere is an extremely inconvenient and undesirable thing. They would not have as many children and such children as they had would fall easily into our organized net and get the protection of the criticized and improved development of the existing charitable institutions.[16]

In summary, Wells saw the cause of the social problem to be the perpetuation of the educationally and technically unadaptable elements in the population. His solution was the breeding and raising of a more efficient race by increased state supervision of the conditions of child raising and the discouragement of propagation by the less efficient by removing their havens of over-crowded tenements and cheap employment. His position was in complete contrast to the aim of Belloc and

---

[16] *Ibid.*, pp. 95–103.

Chesterton, who were interested in transforming the proletariat into property holders rather than into an efficient race; they would indeed have sacrificed efficiency as a price. Chesterton distrusted the social dreams of middle-class reformers like Wells, and viewed them as part of the process of dispossession of the small man that had begun with the enclosures of the medieval commons and the seizure of the monasteries in the sixteenth century: "Now they are taking away the little that remains of his dignity as a householder and the head of a family, promising him instead utopias which are called (appropriately enough) 'Anticipations' or 'News from Nowhere.'" Chesterton was not as optimistic as Wells about the future, and preferred a past with "all the evils of democracy, variety and violence and doubt," to a future that would be "pure despotism." Striking at the theme of a Shaw play, he indicated his preference for "yesterday, when I knew I was a human fool," over tomorrow, when "I can easily be the Superman." Chesterton believed that the "real vision and magnet of mankind" were not any utopia but "the idea of private property universal but private, the idea of families free but still families, of domesticity democratic but still domestic, of one man one house." He set this against collectivism, which he believed would be imposed in England "by an instructed political class upon a people partly apathetic and partly hypnotized," and would be readily administered by an aristocracy, because "in some ways such a centralized political power is necessarily attractive to them."[17]

Belloc shared this suspicion of reform programs that were sponsored by the upper and middle classes and that regulated and interfered mainly with the lives of the poor. This suspicion prompted his opposition to the celebrated minority report of the Poor Law Commission, even though this brainchild of Sidney and Beatrice Webb was the yardstick by which many other radicals measured the insufficiency of the new liberal social legislation. The Webbs, for instance, disliked the Insurance Act as much as Belloc did, and the act's sponsors often justified it to conservative politicians by claiming it was a means of "dishing the Webbs." But Belloc could only interpret the alternative proposals of the Webbs in the same manner as he interpreted the Insurance Act, that is, as devices to ensure and increase the domination of English life by the plutocracy. Of course, the Webbs' use of the Fabian strategy of permeation, with its efforts to work through the existing power structure, gave him ample grounds for suspicion.

The Poor Law Commission, appointed by Balfour at the close of his ministry in 1905, sought over a period of three years to examine the inadequacies of the Poor Law system that had continued pretty much unchanged

---

[17] Chesterton, *What's Wrong with the World,* pp. 55–58.

since 1834. The majority report primarily urged changes in the machinery of administration of relief, such as transferring the management of poor relief from the *ad hoc* boards to the local governments. It also proposed unemployment and invalidity insurance for meeting distinct types of necessity, but it did not challenge the basic deterrence premise of the nineteenth-century system, which made the conditions for receiving assistance more unpleasant than the situation of the worst-off nonrecipient. On the other hand, the commission's minority, dominated by Beatrice Webb, issued a report calling for "the breakup of the Poor Law." In place of a system emphasizing the relief of the poor, the minority urged the establishment of local government committees that aimed at preventing destitution, or the very need for poor relief. So vital did the Webbs regard this shift in official philosophy that they temporarily abandoned both their scientific social research and their usual technique of permeation in order to commit their energies wholeheartedly to propaganda and agitation. In May 1909 they launched the National Committee for the Promotion of the Breakup of the Poor Law (later called the National Committee for the Prevention of Destitution) to promote legislative enactment of the proposals in the minority report.[18]

---

[18] Beatrice Webb, *Our Partnership* (London: Longmans, Green, 1911), pp. 422–23, 428.

The general aim of this reform campaign was to prevent destitution, which the Webbs defined as "the condition of being without one or other of the necessities of life, in such a way that health and strength, and even vitality, is so impaired as to eventually imperil life itself." Such a condition in modern urban life had occasioned not only disease and premature death, but "in the great majority of cases, the degradation of soul," whereby the mass of each generation below the "poverty line" grew up "in coarseness and bestiality, apathy and cynical skepticism." One step toward preventing destitution would be to prevent one of its major causes, sickness, which could be greatly lessened were local health authorities given increased powers for imposing health standards on the community, with the aim more of preventing than of curing illness. Along the same line of prevention, it was suggested that public authorities be able to "search out and permanently segregate, under reasonably comfortable conditions and firm but kindly control, all the congenitally feeble-minded," lest they should "continue to perpetuate their deficiency." The Webbs also held that thousands of children could be rescued from another cause of destitution—child neglect—by extended compulsory education, medical inspection of children, and provisions against the maltreatment of children. Another cause of destitution was sweating, which was the situation of workers receiving "earnings barely sufficient to sustain existence" and working "hours of labor such as to make their lives periods of almost ceaseless toil," and which took place under "sanitary conditions injurious to the health of the persons employed and dangerous to the public." To curb sweating the Webbs advocated a labor code imposing a national minimum with regard to wages, hours, and working conditions. For that other cause of destitution, unemployment, they called for a scientific unemployment program aimed at preventing, if possible, the discharge of workers, the rapid placing by labor exchanges of those who became unemployed, and, for those persons "demonstrably not capable of rendering any service that the community requires," temporary maintenance, "conditional on their submitting themselves to such training—physical and mental, general and technological—as may be found appropriate to their needs."[19]

These proposals suggested the assumption, which as we saw was held by Wells, that the poor had fallen into a state of degradation from which they could be rescued only by inspectors and regulators armed with the disciplinary powers of the state if they were to be made into more efficient members of society. Unlike Belloc, who desired the poor to become their own masters, the Webbs desired them to serve society efficiently. This attitude was manifest in their criticism of the Insurance Act. For instance, as early as October 1908 they had

---

[19] Sidney and Beatrice Webb, *The Prevention of Destitution* (London: Longmans, Green, 1911), pp. 1–2, 56–59, 88, 141.

sought to impress Lloyd George, Haldane, Churchill,
and other ministers that "any insurance scheme had the
fatal defect that the state got nothing for its money—
that the persons felt they had a right to the allowance
whatever their conduct." The Webbs regarded "doling
out weekly allowances . . . with no kind of treatment
attached" as "a most unscientific state aid." While the
unemployment insurance scheme had at least the
advantage, from their point of view, of opening the
door to compulsory labor exchanges, they evaluated
the health insurance system as "wholly bad." The
Webbs feared that the government had shirked "the
extension of *treatment* and *disciplinary supervision.*"
It seemed to them that the government wanted "merely
some mechanical way of increasing the money income
of the wage-earning class in times of unemployment
and sickness" without making any attempt "to secure
an advance in conduct, in return for the increased
income."[20]

It was this tone of their campaign that incurred
Belloc's hostility, as he wrote critically of the proposed,
but ultimately unsuccessful, legislation called the prevention of destitution bill. As to the Webbs, he noted,
" 'Running' the poor is their hobby, and the occupation
of the ample leisure which their own position as
capitalists affords them." He was particularly critical
of the arbitrary power the proposed bill would give

[20] B. Webb, *Our Partnership*, pp. 417, 468.

to the committees of the local government councils over those who were to be saved from destitution, especially in such matters as imposing compulsory vaccination, and determining who was mentally defective or an excessive drinker. He received the impression from the bill that those who were incapable of assisting themselves by their own labor, and were completely dependent on the assistance of society to stay alive, would "be kept alive with as much fuss, registration, running, and restraint generally, as can be crammed into the system."[21]

Belloc was particularly distressed at the "last-resort" solution which the Webbs had for those whose lack of ability made them unemployable even with the assistance of the labor exchanges. Such men could qualify for both an allowance for their families and meals for themselves by attending training camps from 6 A.M. to 7 P.M. every working day, at which they "would find their whole time mapped out in a continuous and properly varied program of physical and mental work, all of it being made of the utmost educational value," including "well-devised physical exercises." Those unemployed, who are of such "weak will," "slight defectiveness of mind or body," "irregular habits," or "mentally so far below par" that they "cannot respond to any sort of training," would, after a

---

[21] Hilaire Belloc, "The Prevention of Destitution Bill," *The New Age,* April 14, 1910, pp. 555–57.

period of trial, be medically certified as mentally or physically deficient and entitled to state assistance. However, for those who refused to work "because of moral obliquity . . . or determined recalcitrancy," there would be established "Reformatory Detention Colonies" that would be distinct from the ordinary prison.[22] Belloc believed the general objective of the bill on the question of unemployment was to put under the control of the politician "that margin of the able-bodied proletariat which is not absorbed by the labor market at any given time," with assistance available to their families only by this forced employment at labor colonies. He was outraged at "this scheme for putting citizens (or should I say comrades?) into compounds," especially since it "applies only to the very poor," and not "to the class to which the Webbs belong, nor indeed to anyone who, under the present capitalist system, is in possession of the means of production."

Belloc's dismay at the class basis of this reform legislation with the snobbish implications of special regulation and supervision of the poor rather than direct assistance with which they could manage their own affairs, caused a shift in his social criticism. No longer was he concerned about socialism as the major threat to the small man's property and independence. Instead, he feared ostensibly reformist legislation that

---

[22] Webb and Webb, *Prevention of Destitution*, pp. 141–51.

had absolutely nothing to do with the first principle of socialism—community control of the means of production—but that would establish "a political bond between master and man which recognizes the master as master and the man as his servant." That situation was what he called the servile state, and was "the negation of that state which socialists by definition demand."[23]

It was at about this time that Belloc began setting forth his celebrated thesis of the impending servile state. His theory appeared first in the independent radical political and literary weekly *The New Age,* edited since 1907 by A. R. Orage. Under Orage's direction the paper became a leading "presentive" journal, that is, one primarily concerned with introducing new ideas and engendering new points of view.[24] His tolerant editorial policy of complete freedom for contributors drew many of the foremost literary lights of the era to its columns. For example, from 1907 to 1909 Wells, Shaw, Belloc, and Chesterton conducted a running debate on the merits of socialism. During these exchanges Shaw contrived the four-legged pantomime creature, the "Chester-Belloc." Although the journal professed its loyalty to socialism, its radical

---

[23] Belloc, "Prevention of Destitution," p. 556.

[24] Wallace Martin, *The New Age Under Orage* (Manchester: Manchester University Press, 1967), p. 2.

independence led it to criticize groups such as the parliamentary Labor Party, for its subservience to the Liberal majority, and the Fabian Society, for its policy of permeation or collaboration with those in power. This independence made *The New Age* an appropriate journal for Belloc to initiate his criticisms of social reform programs on the grounds of their leading to a servile society.[25] As we have seen in the previous chapter, the same theme prevailed throughout 1911 and 1912 in the *Eye-Witness*'s criticisms of the New Liberal policies of social insurance and labor conciliation. Later Belloc set forth this thesis in book form in a seminal tract published in 1912, *The Servile State*.[26]

A preliminary point to be noted about this work is that it was not a criticism of socialism, for the servile state was not the socialist state. While he remained hostile to socialism, or collectivism as he interchangeably labeled it, he no longer feared it as a serious possibility. Instead, he was concerned, as he insisted in a debate with Ramsay MacDonald, that the political action of the collectivists "was beginning to have as its result—not the establishment of the collectivist or socialist state, nor an approach thereto," but, instead, a servile state, where the proletariat masses would be reassured as to their economic security and sufficiency,

---

[25] Hilaire Belloc, "The Servile State," *The New Age,* May 26, 1910, pp. 77–79.

[26] Hilaire Belloc, *The Servile State* (London: Constable, 1927; also Indianapolis: Liberty*Classics,* 1977; first published 1912).

and protected against cruelty by the owners of capital, but where at the same time they would be "permanently dispossessed of the means of production." There would be a legal differentiation between the two classes: "those who possess the means of production and those who do not," as the very reforms guaranteeing the well-being of the dispossessed would work toward their permanent dispossession, while the ownership class would be confirmed "in their possession of the means of production." This situation, he noted, would be the furthest thing from the ideal of "collectivizing or socializing the means of production."[27]

Central to Belloc's analysis was his view that the widespread ownership of the means of production was essential for a free society, since "to control the production of wealth is to control human life itself." Under capitalism, however, such ownership was confined to a very limited few, while the rest, the proletariat, although possessed of political rights, did not have "legal control over any useful amount of the means of production." These two factors—the limited number of owners of capital and the almost universal political freedom—created an "unstable equilibrium," which could logically be resolved either by extending economic freedom, that is ownership, to all or by legally, as well as

---

[27] Hilaire Belloc and J. Ramsay MacDonald, *Socialism and the Servile State* (London: South West London Federation of the Independent Labor Party, 1911), pp. 5–11.

economically, denying freedom. Probably an attempt would be made to avoid this dilemma resulting from the instability of capitalism by attempting collectivism, that is, the public ownership of the means of production. The reason for its apparent attractiveness was the great similarity between it and capitalism, especially from the point of view of the proletarian masses:

> Collectivism promises employment to the great mass who think of production only in terms of employment. It promises to its workmen the security which a great and well organized industrial capitalist unit . . . can give through a system of pensions, regular promotions, etc., but that security vastly increased through the fact that it is the state and not a mere unit of the state which guarantees it.[28]

In the eyes of the workers, collectivism would not appear very strange, except for offering "a promise of some increment in wages and a certainty of far greater ease of mind." Also, the owners of capital, to whom collectivism might appear as an enemy, could reach an understanding with it and permit themselves to be bought out by the collectivist state just as they would be bought out by other capitalists. In short, the collectivist system appealed "to no instinct, whether of cowardice, greed, apathy, or mechanical regulation, with which a capitalist community is not amply familiar."

---

[28] Belloc, *Servile State* (Indianapolis ed.), pp. 134–35.

But although collectivism would be attempted, what would result, Belloc feared, would not be collectivism at all, but something completely different—"the servile state: a state, this is, in which the mass of men shall be constrained by law to labor to the profit of a minority, but as the price of such constraint, shall enjoy a security which the old capitalism did not give them."[29] The reason this would happen, he explained, was the unwillingness and inability of the socialists, never mind the social reformer with more limited objectives, to follow through with the full implications of collectivism and confiscate the means of production lest such action should cause a complete breakdown in the economic system. They would settle for reforms providing security and sufficiency for the proletariat and establishing the "tabulation, detailed administration of men, the coordination of many efforts under one schedule," while acquiescing in the continued control of the means of production by the ownership class. Losing interest in "any scheme for socializing capital and land," the collectivist would turn his attention to schemes "for regulating, 'running,' and drilling the proletariat." Under this situation, the capitalist would scarcely be dispossessed, but, instead, be established in a legally defined relationship with his employers or the proletariat. This relationship would entail duties toward his employees, such as providing human treatment and

---

[29] *Ibid.*, p. 138.

adequate pay. But it would also permit compulsion of the employee. That very situation, whereby a few owners would have coercive authority over the masses, was the essence of the servile state.

Thus, the key features of the servile state, according to Belloc, were the continued ownership of the means of production by the capitalists and the legal stratification of the employer and employee classes. Furthermore, he asserted that the actual discussion, if not enactment, of this servility had already begun in England before World War I. He defined servile legislation as that which promoted "the reestablishment of status in the place of contract, and the universal division of citizens into two categories of employers and employed." Legislation was not servile simply because it interfered with the economic activity of citizens, as did the Factory Acts, or because it, in effect though not in wording, applied to only one class, such as the establishment of state educational institutions. It would be servile only when it specifically defined the status of employer and employee and regulated their relationship on a basis other than contractual. Specific laws which would do such fell into three categories: laws, such as the Insurance Act, compelling the insecurity of the proletariat to be relieved by itself or by the employers; laws, like minimum wage, compelling employers to compensate employees at not less than a certain minimum; and, last, laws compelling the nonowners to labor, which Belloc saw as an eventual result of compulsory labor arbitration, labor exchanges, and the labor colonies suggested by the Webbs.[30]

As for the continued maintenance of ownership of the means of production by the capitalists, Belloc noted that even when attempted, "all so-called socialist experiments in municipalization and nationalization were merely increasing the dependence of the community upon the capitalist class." This was because the original owners were guaranteed compensation for their property usually "at much more than their true value." Furthermore, they were compensated by bonds which, until they would accrue, received interest tantamount to a guaranteed profit, which in turn was reinvested as capital, often as a loan to the government to finance some other municipalization. Last, the municipalized property often was not productive or, at least, not profitable, even though interest still had to be paid to the bond-holding former owners by the state. Consequently,

> All these experiments up and down Europe during our generation, municipal and national, have resulted in an indebtedness to capital increasing rather more than twice, but not three times as fast as the rate of repayment. . . . Capitalism has seen to it that it shall be a winner and not a loser by this form of a sham socialism, as by every other.[31]

---

[30] *Ibid.*, pp. 179–80.
[31] *Ibid.*, pp. 194–97.

Corresponding to Belloc's unique forecast of the future course of political and economic developments was his distinct interpretation of European, and specifically English, history, which manifested both his hostility toward capitalism and his idealization of a period when he supposed there was almost the desired wide distribution of property owners. That period was the later Middle Ages, when the bonds of feudalism over the serfs had been greatly weakened, leaving the serf "secure in his position, and burdened only with regular dues, which were but a fraction of his produce"; when the freeholder of land was "independent save for money dues, which were more of a tax than a rent"; and when the guilds flourished, "in which well-divided capital worked cooperatively for craft production, for transport, and for commerce." All three "were making for a society which would be based upon the principle of property" owned by "all, or most—the normal family." But this distributist social system failed, not because failure was inevitable, but because of "the deliberate action of men, evil will in a few and apathy of will among the many."[32]

The failure occurred in England, he insisted, as a result of the transferal of ownership of the monastic lands seized by Henry VIII at the time of the Reformation to the wealthier of the landowners for nominal sums. This placed the latter in a position of control,

---

[32] *Ibid.*, pp. 79–82.

in many areas, of over more than half the land.
Coupled with this was their competitive rather than
customary management of their property, their domination of the universities and the judiciary, and the price
revolution of the time, which weakened the recipients
of customary revenue, like the Crown. All of these
factors resulted in a transformation of the English
state from a potentially powerful monarchy, capable of
working "for the weakening of the wealthier classes,
and to the indirect advantage of the mass of the
people," to "a powerful oligarchy of large owners over-
shadowing an impoverished and dwindled monarch."
Because this development had occurred before the Industrial Revolution, it was unavoidable that control
over the new means of production should also fall into
the hands of the same oligarchy. Belloc insisted, therefore, that the Industrial Revolution took on a capitalist
character because capitalism, that is, the ownership
by the few, preceded it. But capitalism, he argued, was
not essential for the Industrial Revolution, which could
have taken place under a system of well-divided
property.[33]

This view of early modern British history corre-
sponds to a revisionist position appearing at that time
often closely connected with the championship of
economic and social transformation of the capitalist-
industrial social structure of twentieth-century En-

[33] *Ibid.,* pp. 91–101.

gland. The basic themes stressed were both the rise of the new wealthy oligarchy in Tudor and Stuart times at the expense of monarchical, ecclesiastical, and old aristocratic power and wealth, and the essentially malevolent character of the eighteenth- and nineteenth-century Industrial Revolution with respect to the condition of the proletariat. The most celebrated exponent of the former view was the socialist historian R. H. Tawney, whose famous analysis *The Agrarian Problem in the Sixteenth Century* was published in the same year as *The Servile State*. In it, he depicted the dire fate of the small landowner before the rising gentry whose competitive and commercial spirit facilitated their climb. By the middle of the seventeenth century such economic forces had been set in motion that it was certain

the small holder will have a hard struggle to hold his own against the capitalist farmer. It is certain that . . . a great part of the fruits of economic progress will no longer be retained, as in the fifteenth century, by the mass of the peasants, but will pass in the shape of increased payments for land, into the pockets of the great landed proprietors. It is almost certain that to any new developments which may be detrimental to them the peasants will be able to offer a much less effective resistance than they have in the past. For the security of many of their class has been undermined; the gulf which separates them from the landed gentry, though still bridged by the existence of many prosperous freeholders, has been widened; and, above all, the destruction of the absolute monarchy has entrenched the great landlords inexpugnably at the heart of government, both central and local, and has made their power as great as their ambitions. Both from below and above they are unassailable. For a century and a half after the Revolution they have what power a government can have to make and ruin England as they please.[34]

The actual record of how those great landowners exercised this power in the late eighteenth and early nineteenth centuries was examined by the husband-and-wife historian team of J. L. and Barbara Hammond, who, the year after, published the first in a series of volumes on the further dispossession of the English peasantry and the development of industrialism. J. L. Hammond, who was one of Belloc's Oxford colleagues in the *Essays in Liberalism,* and Barbara Hammond shared Belloc's dislike of the landed establishment; they noted how "it has left dim and meager records of the disinherited peasants that are the shadow of its wealth; of the exited laborers that are the shadow of its pleasures; of the villages sinking in poverty and crime and shame that are the shadow of its power and its pride."[35]

Both Tawney's view of the Tudor-Stuart period and the Hammonds' view of the age of the Industrial Revolution have been severely criticized by more recent scholarship which tends to offset their one-sided appraisal. For instance, the cumulative effect of the work

[34] R. H. Tawney, *The Agrarian Problem in the Sixteenth Century* (London: Longmans, Green, 1912), pp. 403–4.

[35] J. L. Hammond and Barbara Hammond, *The Village Labourer, 1760–1832* (London: Longmans, Green, 1913), p. 332.

of historians like H. R. Trevor-Roper and J. H. Hexter has tended to make the political struggle of the Stuart era less exclusively a clash between rising new wealth and a weakened monarchy, and economic historians like J. H. Clapham and T. S. Ashton have sought to present the improving condition of the masses in the late eighteenth and early nineteenth centuries during the development of industrialism.[36] Nonetheless, a certain fondness for the Tawney-Hammond spirit, indeed even an idealization of late medieval peasant society comparable to Belloc's, persists among many historians, as is suggested in the prevailing tone of a relatively recent volume on the local history of a Leicestershire village:

> The peasant village had been swamped and then submerged completely, and the tide of industrialism rolled in over it unchecked. Fifteen times as many families now lived and got their living off the same area as had done so in the early fourteenth century, at the height of the medieval boom in farming. But a whole culture, a qualitative civilization, had perished to bring about this quantitative triumph.[37]

---

[36] H. R. Trevor-Roper, "The Gentry, 1540–1640," *Economic History Review,* supp. 1 (1953); J. H. Hexter, *Reappraisals in History* (London: Longmans, Green, 1961); J. H. Clapham, *An Economic History of Modern Britain,* 3 vols. (Cambridge: At the University Press, 1927–38), vol. 1; T. S. Ashton, *The Industrial Revolution, 1760–1830* (London: Oxford University Press, 1948).

[37] W. G. Hoskins, *The Midland Peasant* (London: Macmillan, 1957), p. 282.

Belloc's indictment of collectivism for failing to achieve its own purposes and his dire prediction about the future consequences of the new liberal social reform measures coincided with a widespread loss of faith in state action and traditional politics by the British left wing. We have already discussed the manifestations of syndicalism that appeared with the expansion of general labor unionism and the break with the parliamentary Labor Party by the more radical socialists. But perhaps even closer to Belloc's position was the guild socialist movement. The birthplace of the movement was the same periodical in which Belloc's servile state thesis originally appeared, *The New Age.* Furthermore, Belloc's writings had a considerable influence on the development of this particular disillusionment with traditional collectivism, especially of the Fabian administrative variety, although the ultimate solution that would be offered by the guild socialists differed somewhat from his small-holder proprietary ideal.[38] The independent socialist *New Age* had been suspicious, as had *The Eye-Witness,* of the Insurance Act. Curiously, it was also sympathetic to the Osborne decision (which denied labor unions the right to contribute out of their funds to political

---

[38] Indebtedness to Belloc's influence was acknowledged by one of the founders of the National Guilds League, Maurice B. Reckitt, in his memoirs, *As It Happened* (London: J. M. Dent & Sons, 1941), pp. 107–8.

causes). The basis for this position was the view that it was inappropriate for MPs who were ostensibly socialists and therefore theoretically anxious for the well-being of all of society to be the representatives of just one social group, as the union-sponsored MPs inevitably would be. Also, by being cut off from politics, the unions, *The New Age* held, could turn their exclusive attention to industrial action, which in view of the apparent futility of political action and social reform was the most appropriate means of improving the situation of the workers.[39]

In the opinion of A. R. Orage, an improvement in the condition of the workers was not just a question of increased wages and security, but a matter of the very status of the workers and their relationship to decision-making in the productive process. Orage was partly influenced by the ideas of a close friend, A. J. Penty, an architect and a disciple of the medievalist spirit of William Morris and John Ruskin. Orage and Penty had formed in 1906 a Guilds Restoration League, which championed a revival of craftsmanship. In his book *The Restoration of the Guild System,* Penty had suggested guilds like those of the Middle Ages, with an emphasis upon individual creativity and quality workmanship, as an alternative to the tedium of mass pro-

[39] S. T. Glass, *The Responsible Society* (London: Longmans, Green, 1966), pp. 26–28; Martin, *New Age Under Orage,* pp. 200–201.

duction and the shoddiness of its products.[40] However, while the guild socialist movement, as it developed in *The New Age* under Orage's direction, continued to emphasize the spiritually and psychologically de-humanizing status of the modern proletariat, especially its lack of authority over its own workmanship, the movement tended to divest itself of Penty's nostalgic medievalism and his hostility to modern industrialism.

This was especially the case with a series of articles that appeared in *The New Age* during 1912 and 1913 by S. G. Hobson. He was a Fabian journalist who had become disillusioned with the Fabian Society in 1910 for its failure to break with the opportunist Labor Party and seek to develop "a definite and avowed socialist party."[41]

His articles, when collected and published, became the first catechism of the guild socialist movement. He was critical, not of industrialism, but of the economic position of the workers, which he labeled the "wage system." That system, he held, transformed the worker's labor into a commodity, denying him any control over what he produced or any claim upon the surplus value he created. Furthermore, the price paid for the labor tended to remain at just about the subsistence

---

[40] A. J. Penty, *The Restoration of the Guild System* (London: S. Sonnenschein, 1906).

[41] S. G. Hobson, *Pilgrim to the Left* (London: Longmans, Green, 1938), pp. 117–19.

level, and where labor organization or skill was able to command higher wages, the costs for these increments were met by the denial of wages to the large number of laborers who were unemployed. Hobson was obviously indebted to Marxism for his analysis, but his solution was more in line with the antistate temperament of syndicalism. Also like Belloc, he depreciated both political reformism and state ownership of industry as futile unless the wage system should be abolished. He interpreted the Labor Party's position to be that "the state was economically a better capitalist than the private employer and far more humane." From this premise, he noted, it followed that the party would advocate "the continuance of the wage system." Its strategy was "to develop municipalism" and "acquire political power, with the avowed purpose of humanizing but not destroying the wage system." In Hobson's view, therefore, state socialism was basically "state capitalism," but "with the private capitalist better protected than when he was dependent upon voluntary effort."[42]

The only alternative for Hobson was to end the wage system, and thereby end profits, interest, and rent. The instruments for attaining this goal, he hoped, were national labor unions, which should pursue a strategy of a general strike organized and mobilized on an almost military basis with the specific goal of obtaining worker

---

[42] S. G. Hobson, *National Guilds* (London: G. Bell & Sons, 1914), pp. 8–9, 21.

control of the means of production. Unlike the medievalists, Hobson would not undo industrialism or mass production, but would place the control of the entire economy with decision over the production, exchange, and distribution of wealth into the hands of twenty-two national guilds, to which all workers would belong. These workers, no longer wage slaves, would democratically determine working hours and conditions of employment, compensation, costs, and the amount to be produced. Taking a page from the book of the laissez-faire school, he would separate the state from economic functions, leaving it with the tasks of law enforcement, defense, foreign affairs, education, government administration, and medicine. With the state being removed from economic questions, and with the problem of the production, exchange, and distribution of wealth solved, Hobson felt certain that then "a people thus materially emancipated will move up the spiral of human progress, and that out of that part of this movement will grow a purified political system, in which great statesmanship will play its part." He tended to identify human disputes almost exclusively with economic matters, and optimistically foresaw a moral regeneration under his system whereby "spiritual and intellectual problems" might "confidently be left to a body politic no longer dominated or biased by economic pressure of a sectional or selfish character."[43]

The theory of guild socialism was further developed

---

[43] *Ibid.*, pp. 263, 284.

and refined, although not without Hobson's opposition, by G. D. H. Cole, a Balliol graduate and later a fellow of Magdalen College. In 1914 a faction of his supporters unsuccessfully sought to convert the Fabian Society to the guild socialist cause (the semiautonomous Fabian Research Department was captured by the guildists), and subsequently they formed the independent National Guilds League, whose small membership list at times included such impressive names as R. H. Tawney, George Lansbury, and Bertrand Russell.[44] Cole was deeply impressed by the militancy of labor at the time and saw the trade unions as "tending to establish a sovereignty of their own," something like Hobson's vision of national guilds. Cole was also skeptical of traditional state socialism, and the emphasis placed by British collectivism "on distribution and consumption as opposed to production." He was critical of the collectivists' failure "to provide against the abuse of the new power they proposed to confer" and of their forgetfulness that "the extension of the powers of the state may be merely a transference of authority from the capitalist to the bureaucrat." However, Cole, whose approach and analysis were much more scholarly and balanced than Hobson's, perceived a number of flaws in the latter's system, the most notorious being its failure to take into account the position or the needs of the consumers of what the guild-managed enter-

---

[44] Glass, *Responsible Society,* pp. 38–39.

prises produced. Holding that "it would be dangerous to delegate absolute control of methods to any corporation which had not an interest in satisfying the consumer's needs," Cole took a more positive attitude toward the role of the state in the economy as a champion of the consumers. Consequently, he believed the state must have some role in determining production, preferably as part of a joint board with the various guild executives. This joint board and, "ultimately, the consumer would determine what was required to be produced, while the guild would be left to fulfill that requirement by whatever methods it saw fit."[45]

Despite the similarities in their distrust of ameliorative social legislation that did not change the servile status of the proletariat and their fondness for trade guilds as social institutions, there remained a considerable difference between Belloc and the guild socialists. Belloc's efforts at formulating a constructive alternative social program did not receive the same notoriety as did the dire forecasts of his *Servile State,* yet in the very year that it was published he wrote a program for reform that aimed at the restoration of the wide distribution of property, especially in capital. Although he approved of guild control of the process of production in preference to either plutocratic or state control, the

---

[45] G. D. H. Cole, *The World of Labor* (London: B. Bell & Sons, 1915), pp. 346–47, 365–67.

main emphasis in his program was on widespread individual or family control of the means of production in such forms as peasant proprietorships, small-scale enterprise, and widely distributed ownership of shares in larger enterprises.

Belloc realistically acknowledged the difficulty of his program being realized since it would involve a reversal of the whole current of social history for several generations. Furthermore, the British people, upon whose voluntary support a restoration of widespread property holding would ultimately rely, "have neither an experience of, nor an active appetite for possession." He noted that

> they think of themselves as wage earners. They only understand betterment as an improvement in the remuneration and the conditions of wage-paid labor. They prefer a certain gain in this field to any experiment involving the responsibilities and dangers of ownership.[46]

But even were there to be a substantial number of people interested in property ownership, certain powerful economic forces would militate against smaller owners, and perpetuate and augment large holdings. For instance, low interest rates, even though applying equally to all savers, worked to discourage the small saver but could mean formidable returns for the large

---

[46] Hilaire Belloc, "Reform: III—The Restoration of Property," *Oxford and Cambridge Review* 24 (October 1912): 57.

saver. Similarly the expenses in dealing in capital—commissions, clerical expenses, advocacy, registration fees, etc., even if levied at an equal rate—were proportionately more burdensome to the small investor. The high costs of legal expenses and the relatively higher costs of borrowing small sums were further examples of how "the whole mass of our forensic rules and commercial customs work against small ownership." Naturally, Belloc could scarcely avoid noting the privileged and advantageous information to which large owners of capital had access in the plutocratic Edwardian social structure, referring, particularly, to the Marconi affair.

Despite these obstacles, he was convinced that an experiment should be tried at the restoration of widespread property ownership, and the first step would be in landownership, since, in his opinion, landownership, regardless of the stage of economic development a society might have reached, would determine the type of state, either free or servile. However, contrary to what might have been expected of an ardent medievalist, Belloc did not expect the first experimental nucleus of small landowners, which he hoped could blossom into the prevalent pattern of society, to consist of agricultural holders. The possibility of successful small-scale farming had become all but impossible and unattractive given high interest rates and a lack of capital among small holders. Instead, he believed that

the great field . . . for experiments of this kind, paradoxical as it may sound, is the suburban field. So strong is
the desire for ownership on the part of men tolerably
secure of their livelihood, and expecting a sufficiency in
the same, in our great cities that, in spite of the anarchy
of present methods and of the fantastic toll in energy,
secrecy and hard cash which is levied upon the purchaser
and the seller alike by legal and other parasitical interests,
there is a universal tendency making for private ownership
of houses and small plots just outside our great urban
centers, and here a revolution upon a great scale could be
effected if the credit of the community were called into
play.[47]

Although public assistance would be essential in the
attainment of this development, Belloc would still
minimize the role of the state, giving it only the tasks
of raising and guaranteeing loans for small land purchases and providing wide advertisement for the
scheme. But the less the state would do beyond that
function, the more successful would the scheme be.
Otherwise, he envisioned no accomplishment other
than "expensive bungling jobs and oppression."

He believed that the ownership of homes and land,
however, was insufficient in itself, especially in an industrial society, because their owners, being interested
primarily in wages, would "still principally concern
themselves with employment," thereby leaving the
means of production in the hands of the capitalist class.
To achieve a widespread ownership of capital it would

---

[47] *Ibid.,* p. 65.

be essential that a significant number of citizens desire the possession of it. Also, there would have to be a number of what were "in the eyes of the modern industrial state . . . highly artificial and abnormal" steps aimed at making transference of capital property "more easy from the large man to the small and more difficult from the small man to the large." This meant a number of steps which presupposed "the state acting continually as the protector and nourisher of the *small man*." Examples of such action would be highly differential taxes on new companies and on the transference of capital which would rise rapidly in accord with the size of individual holdings in a company or of the holdings transferred by an individual; state purchase of capital financed by widely offered bonds which would be allotted preferentially to small purchasers; and the assumption by the state of the role of gratuitous broker and adviser for small purchasers of securities. Besides encouraging the accumulation of small holdings of capital, the state was looked to by Belloc to "perpetually cream large property to the advantage of the small" by imposing highly differentiated taxation on large property not only in the form of death duties and income taxes, but also in that of tolls on exchange.[48]

In summary, Belloc's program, which would even-

---

[48] Hilaire Belloc, "Reform: IV—Restoration of Property in Capital," *Oxford and Cambridge Review* 25 (November 1912): 87–96.

tually be labeled distributism, was more in the character of a people's capitalism than either guild socialism or medieval agrarianism. In a way, it recalled the social environment in which Victorian radicalism flourished, that is, the egalitarian situation of most involved in enterprise or production, such as yeomen, shopkeepers, and craftsmen. This equality among the "productive" class in mid-Victorian society was not contradicted by the unequal concentration of wealth in the hands of the upper class, especially the landed squires and the rentiers, for the wealth of the latter was often either idle or diverted to investments of a broad and national character, such as railroads or public bonds, which did not directly affect the normal localized pattern of economic life.[49] Just as the Victorian radicals were hostile to the "unproductive" aristocracy, Belloc despised the Edwardian counterparts of the latter, the finance capitalists. But perhaps even more than the spirit of Victorian radicalism, Belloc's proposals reasserted the basic postulates about the limitations on state power and the desirability of small-scale ownership proclaimed in the encyclical *Rerum Novarum.*

---

[49] J. R. Vincent, *Pollbooks, How Victorians Voted* (Cambridge: At the University Press, 1967), pp. 41–42.

Chapter Seven

Monarchism

Belloc's disgust with the party system and his anxiety about the impending servile state prompted his advocacy of a cause that was seemingly remarkable for an old-style radical: monarchism.

> The increase in the personal power of the monarch is the one real alternative present before the English state today to the conduct of affairs by organized wealth. To the end of increasing the personal power of the king should be directed the efforts of those who fear most what may be called, in one aspect, plutocracy, in another aspect, servitude.[1]

Because the English monarch was still a visible although powerless institution, he believed it potentially could be brought to play a role comparable to the American presidency, the Swiss referendum, or even

---

[1] Hilaire Belloc, "Reform: V—The Powers of the Crown," *Oxford and Cambridge Review* 26 (December 1912): 85.

French-style coups d'etat or peasant revolts in restraining the financial oligarchy. This development in Belloc's political thought can be better appreciated if one understands that his historical perspective for history, as one commentator noted, "stands out as his most ambitious field of endeavor."[2] The several currents prevailing in his work might best be summed up as anti-Whig history, that is, the reverse of what Herbert Butterfield noted as "the tendency in many historians to write on the side of Protestants and Whigs, to praise revolutions provided they have been successful, to emphasize certain principles of progress in the past and to produce a story which is the ratification if not the glorification of the present."[3] Whig historians generally applaud the Protestant Reformation and the Glorious Revolution and idealize the eighteenth- and nineteenth-century constitutional evolution of Britain. They sympathize with oligarchic constitutional systems like those of ancient Athens, the Roman Republic, the Dutch Republic, and Whig England, while empires, whether Roman, Bourbon, or Napoleonic, hierarchical and liturgical religions like Roman Catholicism, the Middle Ages, and popular or populist revolutions, whether

---

[2] Frederick Wilhelmsen, *Hilaire Belloc: No Alienated Man* (New York: Sheed & Ward, 1953), p. 49.

[3] Herbert Butterfield, *The Whig Interpretation of History* (New York: W. W. Norton, 1965; first published 1931), p. v.

Jacobite or Jacobin, are despised. Belloc's views were precisely the opposite.

Belloc's ideal of European civilization was what he saw institutionalized in the Roman Empire, within whose borders had been created a consciousness of civic unity and a single state regardless of ethnic, geographic, and even religious varieties, and where office rather than personality commanded.[4] The same empire was vitalized by the Catholic church. Its heritage was preserved despite the barbaric and Islamic assaults and gloriously revived in the High Middle Ages from the eleventh to the fourteenth century. The Protestant Reformation ruptured the unity of that civilization. With that disunity came the rise of oligarchic power and an increased reliance upon force rather than authority for the maintenance of institutions. In other words, the leviathan followed Luther! Consequently, from the fifteenth to the eighteenth century European —that is, Roman and Catholic—civilization had become "shut in with the bonds of lawyers" and princes waged quarrels that "were a mere insult to nature." In the seventeenth century pedants rationalized the ongoing struggle between princes and the upper classes to which the populace remained indifferent, whether

---

[4] For the best overall summations of Belloc's historical perspective, see Hilaire Belloc, *Europe and the Faith* (London: Burns & Oates, 1962; first published 1920); and Belloc, *The Crisis of Civilization* (New York: Fordham University Press, 1937).

that struggle be the Fronde or that "less heroic struggle
the Parliamentary Wars." By the eighteenth century the
ruling classes, who had lost interest in political and
theological struggles, sought to sanction their position
by invoking historical memories, that is, "the bones of
the Middle Ages" and "the relics of the saint and the
knight." But this ruse backfired, for it was not the
relics, but the medieval reality which they thought
dead, the spirit of the Middle Ages, the spirit of enthusiasm and of faith, the Crusades, that "came out of the
tomb and routed them."[5] In essence, the French Revolution was seen by Belloc as a reassertion of the European spirit and its fundamental premise of human
equality against the gross contradictions of "Christian
theory and the Roman Law" that had been allowed to
develop in the Old Regime.

Belloc's sympathy with the French Revolution was a
further manifestation of his anti-Whiggism. He believed
in democracy and egalitarianism as espoused by Jean
Jacques Rousseau. He insisted that Rousseau's principle of human equality—"that what is common to all
men is utterly beyond the accidents by which they
differ"—was the same premise used by the church in
discussing souls and by the Roman Empire in dealing
with citizens. Belloc was without Whiggish fears about
the totalitarian potential of Rousseau's theories on pop-

---

[5] Hilaire Belloc, *Danton* (New York: G. P. Putnam's Sons, 1928;
first published 1899), pp. 3–7.

ular sovereignty and the "general will." Rather, he celebrated them, since sovereignty by the whole community
meant "the executive was to become openly and by
definition its servant; the vague thesis of equality, upon
which jurisprudence reposed, was brought with exacti-
tude and vigor into every detail and made a test of
every law; the limits of individual liberty were to be
enlarged till they met for boundary the general liberty
of all." Thus Belloc accepted Rousseau's identification
of the exercise of popular sovereignty with the possession of liberty. Also, almost in anticipation of his own
disillusion with parliamentary politics, Belloc in 1901
remarked Rousseau's realization that "government by
deliberation was free in proportion as the community
was limited and its life autarchic" and his suspicion
of "representative bodies, that commonly proceed from,
that always tend toward, and that can only vigorously
coexist with plutocracy."[6] A decade later, after having
left Parliament, Belloc would hail Rousseau's warning
"against the possible results of the representative system," specifically "the general truth that men who
consent to a representative system are free while the
representatives are not sitting."[7]

[6] Hilaire Belloc, *Robespierre* (New York: G. P. Putnam's Sons,
1927; first published 1901), pp. 29–31.

[7] Hilaire Belloc, *The French Revolution* (London: Oxford University Press, 1960; first published 1911), p. 13; Jean Jacques Rousseau, *The Social Contract*, trans. and introd. by Willmoore Kendall
(Chicago: Henry Regnery, 1954), pp. 110–11: ". . . modern peo-

It is difficult to reconcile the French Revolution with the spirit of medieval Europe in view of the actual antagonism between the revolution and the Catholic church. However, Belloc sought to resolve this by insisting that "no quarrel can be found between the theory of the revolution and that of the church," but only "between the revolution in action and the authorities of Catholicism." The skepticism of a deistic hierarchy and the religious indifference of the eighteenth-century French population had caused nonreligious revolutionaries to view the church as an anachronism. They thought it ought to be allowed to die comfortably but under civil control. Hence the Civil Constitution of the Clergy. However, to their amazement the church was still vital, as proved by the refusal of nonjuring clergy to "admit the right of any other power exterior to its own organization to impose upon it a modification of its own discipline." Because this nonjuror resistance appeared simultaneously with the antirevolutionary reaction from other quarters, churchmen and revolutionaries, and their intellectual descendants, came to regard themselves as inherent enemies. Yet, Belloc insisted, "A man who knows both the faith and the republic will tell you that there is not

---

ples who regard themselves as free do have representatives, and ancient peoples did not. Be all that as it may, however, the moment a people gives itself representatives it ceases to be free; it ceases, indeed, to exist . . . only if the city is very small can the sovereign retain, in our day, the powers that belong to it."

and cannot be any necessary or fundamental reason why conflict should have arisen between a European democracy and the Catholic Church."[8]

Complementary to Belloc's enthusiasm for both the Roman Empire and the French Revolution was his Germanophobia, particularly of a Prussian-dominated Reich. This attitude was apparent in his distaste for the "Teutonic" school of popular historians prevalent in the England of his student days. That school attributed the constitutional strength of England to inherent Anglo-Saxon qualities and institutions and viewed the Anglo-Saxon invasions as a complete eradication of the older Roman and Celtic civilization. Belloc was completely revisionist on this question, denying that the Roman and Celtic foundations had been eliminated by the invaders. He attributed the ultimate prevalence of the Anglo-Saxon tongue not to any thorough conquest but to the reliance by the Roman missionaries on the cooperation of converted Teutonic courts in the reviving of Roman and Christian institutions. Had the reconversion of England been achieved by the Irish monks a Celtic tongue would have prevailed. Rather than deem England part of the Teutonic world, Belloc regarded it as an integral part of Roman and Catholic civilization. England contrasted with those much later converted areas that were "never sufficiently penetrated perhaps with the faith and the proper habits of ordered

---

[8] Belloc, *French Revolution,* pp. 169–201.

men—the outer Germanies and Scandinavia." Furthermore, the great tragedy of Roman Catholic civilization, the Reformation, would have remained limited to those "outer parts, which had never been within the pale of the Roman Empire." However, there was a defection by England that was caused by an unprincipled power grab by a wealthy class indifferent to the religious question. As a consequence England lent "the strength of a great civilized tradition to forces whose original initiative was directed against European civilization and its tradition," that is, "the barbarism of the outer Germanies."[9] From a very long perspective he saw the decisive securing of dominance by the Protestant and oligarchic-capitalist forces to have been the Anglo-Prussian alliance in the Seven Years War when "the French monarchy was mortally wounded," along with "the hegemony of Vienna over the Germanies," and "five generations of unquestioned mastery at sea fell to English sailors."[10] No wonder, then, that the pro-Boer, anti-imperialistic Belloc could enthusiastically support the British government's policy in World War I, for to him it was a return of England to Europe in a crusade against Prussian barbarism.

The war years saw a hiatus in his more creative

[9] Belloc, *Europe and the Faith*, pp. 94–129, 154.

[10] Hilaire Belloc and John Lingard, *The History of England*, 11 vols. (New York: Catholic Publication Society of America, 1915), 11:218–19; Belloc, *Marie Antoinette* (New York: G. P. Putnam's Sons, 1924; first published 1909), pp. 3–23.

work. This was partly attributable to personal grief caused by the premature death of his wife Elodie on February 2, 1914, at the age of forty-three, a grief that prompted his wearing black clothes and using black-bordered mourning stationery for the remainder of his life. Another cause of the suspension of creative work was his turning to military journalism following his failure to get a war office appointment, no doubt because of his controversial reputation. He wrote a regular analysis of military developments for the weekly journal *Land and Water*. Because of the vast circulation of the journal, these articles, which eventually appeared in book form, gained both a readership that had never read anything else written by him and a substantial financial remuneration. However, as is often the case with literary figures, that which brings them most remuneration and popular recognition is often their weakest work. Belloc's capacity, even as a military historian, should not, one hopes, be judged by what emerged in book form called *A General Sketch of the European War*.

During the war he even went on a semiofficial diplomatic mission to the Vatican, where he had an audience with Pope Benedict XV designed to induce more sympathy for the anti-Prussian crusade from a papacy probably much more sympathetic to Catholic Austria-Hungary than to the Free Masonic governments of France and Italy or Protestant Engand. The war itself saw further personal tragedy with the deaths of many close personal friends, including Cecil Chesterton, and Belloc's eldest son, twenty-year-old Louis, whose body was never recovered when he failed to return from a flying mission over German lines on August 26, 1918.

Belloc's hostility toward Germany, or more specifically Prussia, continued between the wars. He opposed disarmament and advocated greater rearmament when Germany began to challenge the Versailles terms in the 1930s. However, he would continue to think of a Prussia "who has gone mad again, as she does every generation" rather than of Nazism; he saw "the wretched Hitler," "who is a silly windbag," as "a figurehead" of the Junkers. Belloc preferred speaking of "the Germanies" to using "Germany." In October 1939 he noted that

> it is always the German herd which is the trouble. They have always stampeded and they always will, whether under a panic or under suggestion; whether moved by vanity, or by terror, or by sudden appetite. That is because they are immature. They do not reason, but they feel strongly and that is why they take refuge in music.

He remained convinced that it was impossible "to eradicate from the minds of dons and schoolmasters and the whole generation whom they brought up the old nineteenth-century doctrine that Prussia, which they call Germany, is a kind of God, twin to our Glorious Selves." English admiration for Germany, which "had been swelling ever since the advent of Frederick the

Great, . . . was enormously advanced by the defeat of Napoleon and was fantastically raised by the victories of 1864 to 1870." But he was hopeful that a defeat of the Germans, which he expected because of their "having fallen into incompetent hands," would result in their breakup as a united nation and end the "strange mood nourished from Oxford and Cambridge." He only regretted that the influence of British bankers and "the lethargic conditions of parliamentarism" had inhibited a British rearmament in 1935 or 1936 for then either "there would have been no war" or "the French and the English might have been able to get into Germany in the summer of '39."[11]

Belloc's anti-Whiggism was most apparent in his interpretation of English history. As we have already mentioned, he viewed the central tragedy in English history to have been the triumph of the oligarchy over the monarchy in the sixteenth and seventeenth centuries. This victory, which was attributable to the transfer of monastic lands to the gentry at the time of the Reformation, made permanent the separation of England from Roman Catholic Europe and established the oligarchy which would preside over the industrial

---

[11] Hilaire Belloc to Duff Cooper, March 14, 1932, to Lady Phipps, October 2 ,1933, to Evan Charteris, October 24, 1939, July 5, 1940, in Robert Speaight, ed., *Letters from Hilaire Belloc* (London: Hollis & Carter, 1958), pp. 226–27, 239–40, 280–81, 294–95; Belloc to Frothingham, July 31, 1934, Belloc-Lansdale Correspondence, Princeton University Library.

capitalism that was evolving into a servile state. Naturally, this view of English history turned on its head the prevailing orthodoxy of the nineteenth and early twentieth centuries that saw the Reformation and the triumph of Parliament in the Glorious Revolution as the reasons for the success of the British Empire, the industrial progress and prosperity of England, and its political liberty.

Belloc was scarcely unique in these maverick views. For instance, a most outspoken critic of the English Reformation as a cover for a land grab was the nineteenth-century radical pamphleteer William Cobbett. There were many similarities between Cobbett and Belloc: both were democratic or populist, hostile to the machinations of finance capitalism, and suspicious of government acting other than to enrich an oligarchic establishment or "system" or "thing." However, Belloc's ideas were much more systematic and reasoned in contrast to Cobbett's bluntness and impulsiveness.[12] The Conservative Prime Minister Benjamin Disraeli also uttered the same ideas, in his political novels *Sybil* and *Coningsby,* about the "plunder of the church," the identification of the monarchy with the people, and the Venetian-type oligarchy that controlled the country upon the accession of the House of Hanover. "The

---

[12] John W. Osborne, *William Cobbett* (New Brunswick, N.J.: Rutgers University Press, 1966); A. J. P. Taylor, "William Cobbett," *Essays in English History* (Harmondsworth, Middlesex: Penguin Books, 1976), pp. 49–54.

great object of the Whig leaders in England from the first movement under Hampden to the last most successful one in 1688, was to establish in England a high aristocratic republic on the model of the Venetian."[13] Such a combination of allies ought to prompt one to label the Bellocian view of English history as radical Tory. A more scholarly proponent of the same view was the Catholic priest-historian John Lingard (1771–1851), whose ten-volume *History of England,* written between 1819 and 1830, became the foremost alternative to the Anglo-Saxon and Whig orthodoxy.

Appropriately, Belloc was engaged to write a concluding eleventh volume to Lingard's work, which had come up only to the Glorious Revolution. In it Belloc spoke uncomplimentarily about the luminaries of the Hanoverian-Whig era. For instance, Robert Walpole, the first Prime Minister, was in character "tawdry but not vile; an intriguer and a corrupter of other men"; his "position was largely due to his great wealth" that had been "exceedingly ill-gotten." The elder William Pitt achieved historical greatness not because of any peculiar personal merit but by typifying "the intensely national oligarchy which was the foundation of England's greatness in the eighteenth century" and by desiring the very programs of naval supremacy, distant

[13] Benjamin Disraeli, *Coningsby* (London: John Lehmann, 1948; first published 1844), bk. 5, p. 240; Robert Blake, *Disraeli* (Garden City, N.Y.: Doubleday, 1968), pp. 186–88.

colonization, and expanded overseas trade that gave international supremacy to England. Edmund Burke "had all the Irishman's supreme political gift of rhetorical form," but was "essentially an advocate in mind; ready, when they had once been proposed to him or forced upon his masters, to undertake the defense of causes which he could never have discovered by his unaided genius." Naturally Belloc was sympathetic to the alleged aspirations of George III to revive the monarchy to a pre-1688 character. Unfortunately, for all of his intentions, the king, just a "young oaf" at his accession, with "obstinacy" being his most notable characteristic, was not up to transforming the oligarchic political structure into "a more popular thing." George III was a poor instrument to achieve the ideals of Bolingbroke, a Tory minister of Queen Anne who had tried to prevent the Hanoverian succession, a Jacobite, and a perennial critic of the oligarchic Whig system of the Walpole era. Belloc regarded Bolingbroke as "the most acute and one of the most generous intellects of English culture." Bolingbroke, although associated with the Jacobites and the 1715 effort at a Stuart restoration, advocated not a divine right or absolutist monarchy but a popular and active monarchy that would surmount factional and foreign influences. Significantly, his strategy in 1715 was to forge what today might be called a right-left link between the Jacobites and the Old Whigs, that is, the lower middle-class dissenters and the radical "commonwealth men" who had become disillusioned with the oligarchic character of the Hanoverian settlement.[14]

As much as he opposed oligarchy Belloc was not incapable of analyzing the functions of an oligarchy and, in particular, the specific strengths and characteristics of such a system. Most essential for the survival of an oligarchy or the rule by a few is that it transform itself into an aristocracy, that is, an elite which views itself as entitled to rule by right as well as being so regarded by those subject to its rule. Such a position had been attained by the English oligarchy in the eighteenth and nineteenth centuries. Specific characteristics of the populace of an aristocratic society were a "reverential attitude toward public persons" who were immune from suspicion and a jealousy "in restricting the power of government over their private lives." Institutional characteristics included the mixing of legislative, executive, and judicial powers, since "all three belong essentially to the aristocratic body," and an avoidance of "exact political definition," since an aristocracy must rely on "a large element of emotion which no formula can sufficiently contain." Its exercise of authority depended not on a specific written authorization, but on "the worship of those whom it governs, and . . . its own genius for commanding and retaining a mixture of awe and affection." A particular strength

---

[14] Belloc and Lingard, *History of England,* 11:159, 218–21, 234, 260.

of any aristocratic society is the ability to "coordinate all its interests" and "summon up its resources against a foreign menace" because of basic unity of the elite. Also its government is inhibited from "the extravagance of passion," allowing it to remain "cool in judgment in those periods of fever" which incapacitate both despotisms and democracies. The English aristocracy demonstrated this in its achievement of worldwide economic preponderance through capitalist production, industrialism, an adventurous temper in commerce, and control of the sea. Because of the "vast accumulations of surplus value into the hands of a small class," that same wealth could be easily summoned for national purposes. The same oligarchic solidarity could foster the development of credit whereby "millions not yet existent" could be promised to Continentals fighting England's battles.[15]

If a parliament or any representative body was to work, that is, "to legislate, to appoint magistrates, to administer and execute all the laws, to guide the general foreign policy of the country, and generally to act the prince," it must "necessarily turn into an oligarchy." Parliaments contrast with nearly democratic but nonsovereign assemblies whose meetings are of short duration and whose membership is continually changing. The longer-term members of a parliament meet in

---

[15] *Ibid.,* pp. vii–xxv; Hilaire Belloc, *The House of Commons and Monarchy* (New York: Harcourt, Brace, 1922), pp. 48–53.

one place, have a corporate life, and develop a common character as members of the "governing thing." The body inevitably becomes continuous, membership becomes a career, and it tends to renew itself "by choosing members who are related to, or patronized by, the old." Only by becoming a permanent body "slowly renewed, and renewed largely by its own volition," can the representative body "exercise the enormous powers of sovereignty." Like any oligarchy, a sovereign parliament can endure only by being an aristrocracy and enjoying "the popular worship of its fellow citizens." But to merit such "it should itself be worshipful." In short, the governed must possess an "aristocratic temper," or "a desire to be governed by a few," and the governing class must also have an "aristocratic temper," which requires "certain rules of conduct" and "a certain character which receives, nurtures, and maintains the respect given it from below."[16]

The aristocratic temper among both the rulers and the governed had decayed in late Victorian and early twentieth-century England. As a result, according to Belloc, the governing assembly of the aristocratic oligarchy, the House of Commons, would not be able to retain its sovereignty. Belloc wrote this as a statement of fact, not out of regret, for as a radical democrat he had no enthusiasm for aristocracy. The ruling class had begun to lose its principles or "norm of conduct."

---

[16] *Ibid.*, pp. 66–71.

That code, he insisted, was not necessarily a reflection of morality, as indeed its decline "often comes from something good in those who allow it to decline." Yet, it was the grounds for the survival of the aristocracy since it engendered respect and self-confidence. An example of decay of the aristocractic temper was the tolerance of "an easy domestic equality with adventurers and rascallions" (by which he meant financial operators) with whom "their fathers would not even have conversed in the street." Another example was the declining regular acquaintance of the aristocrat with the creative artist. In Belloc's time the aristocrat had become more interested in the acquaintance of people of wealth, "no matter how acquired or how ephemeral," and would have the artist or his entourage at his home more as an exhibit than as a guest. A vigorous aristocracy was capable of recognizing and selecting "proportion and order in creative power" and had "an instinct against chaos in the arts." But the declining aristocracy of Belloc's day sought "only novelty and even absurdity" as an example of creative power. It substituted "simple, crude, obvious and few passions for a subtle congeries of appetites." Last, the declining aristocracy had lost that most essential attribute, its national or representative character, because it had become quite alienated from the masses and no longer reflected the majority of the population.[17]

---

[17] *Ibid.,* pp. 93–106.

The governing organ of the English aristocracy, the House of Commons, had similarly lost aristocratic dignity. There had been an internal rot in the form of personal corruption and financial chicanery, that is, "the giving of secret contracts, the levying of blackmail, the immunity of even exposed and proved criminals from the criminal law, . . . the absurd sale of honors— a thing of no great practical importance save as a symptom." Originally this was known only by the few thousand directly involved in professional politics, but between 1905 and 1912 the general public had become acquainted with "what already everywhere filled private conversation in London." It was not so much the wrongs, for Belloc was scarcely one to think an aristocracy could do no wrong, as their "pettiness" which suggested the "decline of the aristocratic spirit in England" and in "its principal organ at Westminster." Although an aristocrat may "loot on a large scale" and "make his fortune too rapidly and almost openly through his political power," he must do it in "an aristocratic way." He might sell his own land to the state at a price excessive of the market value, or practice nepotism. But to accept a private bribe from a socially lower financial backer or to give a public position to an unqualified commoner was "unaristocratic" and symptomatic of the decay of the House of Commons.[18]

---

[18] *Ibid.,* pp. 82–89.

Last, the general population had lost the aristocratic temper. England could not help feeling, "however partially and however late," the egalitarian theory of the French Revolution, "a mood which has spread throughout Europe" and "a mood solvent of aristocratic government." But the greatest cause was the industrialization and urbanization of England, whereby the great masses had become "utterly divorced from the remnants and even the tradition of the old aristocratic organism." This loss of a desire for an aristocratic government by the masses, more than even the pettiness and loss of aristocratic dignity by the House of Commons itself, was what had deprived the Commons of moral authority. Therefore, even if the Commons were to be reformed, which he thought could no more practically be expected than could the eighteenth-century Bourbon monarchy have been expected "to shake off the habits of decline it had acquired," it could not be saved because "an oligarchy cannot long continue to govern in a country which has lost the appetite for aristocracy." The House of Commons' continued possession of sovereignty therefore promised nothing but "rapid national decline," for "nothing so surely saps the corporate strength of a nation as the continued rule of a prince who is despised." The only alternative for a modern large nation would be "the replacement of the perishing organ by the new organ of monarchy in some form: the establishment, or rather the growth, of a respected and strong power for which a known and personal magistrate—no matter what his term of office or his title—shall be responsible to the commonwealth."[19]

A replacement for the House of Commons frequently suggested in the early 1920s, especially by those influenced by guild socialism, was of a corporatist character, that is, councils representative of trades, professions, religious bodies, regions, and even subnationalities. While these might be supplementary and supportive of monarchy, Belloc held it would be a divorce from reality to expect such councils to possess sovereignty. Their functions and interests would not give to the combination and unity which an aristocratic chamber possessed.

However, such councils or corporate groups had already begun in the early 1920s, especially because of the decay of the sovereign assembly, the House of Commons, to exercise spontaneously and exclusively many of the subsidiary functions of the state. The trade unions had taken "a part in government; and a much more vital and real part than the House of Commons." The legal guild, which because "the modern administration of law is at once so complex, so ubiquitous, and so arbitrary," had achieved a position whereby it could only have "been challenged or controlled by a strong monarch." He anticipated that the medical guild, using the "excuse of national health," would achieve

---

[19] *Ibid.,* pp. 115–19, 133, 151.

the creation of a special department resulting in having "the children of the proletariat ticketed and numbered by doctors, recommended for particular employment by doctors, and their whole lives passed under medical supervision." The educational guild or teaching profession was another agency becoming increasingly conscious of its strength and, under the alleged motive of "greater instruction for the commonwealth," would work "to the progressive extinction—until reaction shall take place—of family and local control" over education. The other guilds were "the two combatant guilds," those of "the domestic police and of the armed forces." The development of corporate life among the police was "still embryonic" but that "general movement of our time which, for the moment at least, urges men to combine into professional associations," could not be permanently excluded from affecting the combatant forces. What must be expected to develop was "what may be called the praetorian character of the armed forces," that is, to be "not only the guard of Caesar, but also in part the master of Caesar." But without a real sovereign the development of these bodies would only contribute to national deterioration.[20]

England had ceased to be aristocratic and had become egalitarian. However, the ideal and nobler egalitarian society, the participatory democracy where

---

[20] *Ibid.,* pp. 161–67.

"citizens take part in their own government," would be incompatible with great population or great territory. Consequently, the other kind of egalitarian state, the monarchic, was essential, especially in a formerly aristocratic state where the citizenry, while having "lost their desire to be ruled by a special class," had not developed "any new desire . . . to govern themselves." Monarchy was not necessarily hereditary, nor a life appointment, and especially not purely symbolic. Ideally the term of office ought be for a considerable period, but all that was essential in the definition of monarchy was that there be "one real and attainable human head ultimately responsible in any moment for the fate of society." That notion of responsibility meant that the monarch ought be

> sufficiently removed from temptation by his own absolute position and vested with sufficient powers, able to act with sufficient rapidity. That one man is a concrete object. He can be got at by the people. He can be blamed or praised. He knows he is responsible. He cannot shift his burden on to some anonymous and intangible culprit.

The leading function of the monarch would be "to protect the weak man against the strong, and therefore to prevent the accumulation of wealth in a few hands, the corruption of the courts of justice and of the sources of public opinion." The restoration of monarchy might come in any of a thousand ways: perhaps (and ideally because it would be the most continuous) through the

return to sovereign power of the contemporary hereditary monarch, perhaps through election, or perhaps
through "the accidental popularity of one man in some
important crisis." Failing the restoration of monarchy,
the English state would either dissolve by "becoming
part of a larger federation, to be controlled from
abroad, or . . . lose its own character from within," and
thereby lose "the greatness and the homogeneity of the
nation," things "the English will not readily or easily
abandon."[21]

Belloc's conviction that a strong personal executive
or monarch was the only alternative to a decaying
parliamentary system prompted in him that injudicious
enthusiasm for "innovative" foreign rulers common to
intellectual critics. Hence he could celebrate Mussolini,
whom he had visited:

> What a contrast with the sly and shifty talk of your par
> liamentarian! What a sense of decision, of sincerity, of
> serving the nation. . . . Meeting this man . . . was like
> coming upon good wine in a Pyrenean village after com
> pulsory draughts of marsh water.[22]

Belloc's lack of faith in parliamentary regimes made
him very sympathetic to the memory of Napoleon. The
Corsican was the "man needed to control" against "the
breakdown of parliamentary government." Had he not
appeared France would have suffered an "economic

---

[21] *Ibid.*, pp. 174–88.

[22] Hilaire Belloc, *The Cruise of the "Nona"* (Westminster, Md.:
Newman Press, 1956), p. 164.

breakdown and invasion" that would have been "the end of that great affair which had begun in 1789."[23] However, the nation that provided for him a much better example of a democratic monarchy than did Fascist Italy or Napoleonic France was the United States. What must have startled superficial American democratic-isolationists and European legitimists was his assertion in 1924 that the basic political difference between Americans and Europeans was that the Americans had "retained in a very large degree the institution of monarchy and are daily increasing its scope." The specific monarchic offices were the mayors, the governors, and, most of all, the President. The American presidency was "in full force" the monarchy needed and craved for in Europe, as indicated by the enthusiasm for Mussolini, the Primo de Rivera regime in Spain, and the exercise of extraordinary presidential power in Weimar Germany. But in no way could he see the office of the English prime minister becoming a monarchic executive office. If anything that office had decayed, for its holders, like Lloyd George, were "made and unmade" by the "large international" financial forces and "the directors of the more vulgar press" of whom the prime minister had become "the poor servant."[24]

---

[23] Hilaire Belloc, *Napoleon* (Philadelphia: J. B. Lippincott, 1932), pp. 21–22.

[24] Hilaire Belloc, *The Contrast* (New York: Robert M. McBride, 1924), pp. 96–97, 104, 108–9.

He remained pessimistic about England's capacity to restore monarchy, as he understood the term, largely because of the continuation of the aristocratic character, no matter how decayed. "No society is less capable of reforming itself than an aristocratic society." The general spirit of such a society condemns "to oblivion" active criticisms and imposes "a uniform deadness of judgment and a general public ignorance." As a result England was "the only state where the sole alternative to aristocracy–active monarchy" was "forgotten and feels foreign." But one note of optimism was prompted in him by the crisis surrounding the abdication of Edward VIII in 1936, which, rather than symbolize the complete disappearance of "the last shred of any monarchical power," might just be the shock that would stimulate the "resurrection of such power."[25]

Belloc's desire for the establishment of monarchy, that is a strong personal executive, was intertwined with his opposition to the servile state and his advocacy of a proprietary society because the decaying parliaments only abetted the rise of servility. He was particularly alert to forces working to the destruction of widespread property ownership in general and, specifically, of the middle class. The latter case "grows up naturally in a society of many owners" and defines

---

[25] Hilaire Belloc, *An Essay on the Nature of Contemporary England* (London: Constable, 1937), pp. 39–42; Belloc, "English Monarchy: The Significance of the Abdication," *American Review* 8 (February 1937): 424–25.

and supports "the ideal of citizenship"; it "made" and "sustained" our culture. One such destructive force was the tendency since World War I "to raise taxation throughout Western Europe to levels which would have been thought, only a few years ago, fantastic and impracticable." Once society gets used to such taxation, it is not likely to be reduced, since governmental departments create functions and activities that if cut back would appear to "threaten disaster." The higher the rate of taxation the more burdensome it becomes, especially to the lower and middle classes, while those earning speculative income are often able to avoid the clutches of the tax collector. As a consequence there is instability in private fortunes and disinterest in investment for productive purposes. In addition, the numbers and strength of the bureaucracy increase while "civic action," that is, the involvement of the individual family or private group in controlling the state or exercising "self-government," declines. In summary, the evils of high taxation tend to

> eliminate what used to be the balance and heel of the republic—a large possessing class; because it tends to withdraw the tax-gathering and revenue-expending authority from public responsibility; and because it creates in larger and larger numbers citizens who are less and less full citizens and more and more the dependent salaried domestics of vast and concentrated monopolist powers.[26]

---

[26] Hilaire Belloc, "The Effects of High Taxation," *Fortnightly Review* 133 (April 1930): 471–80.

Besides the proprietary society and a strong monarchy, Belloc came to concern himself increasingly with a factor that the modern world had neglected, and that the middle class itself had "attacked, and all but dissolved." That was the "essential factor of a common religion or philosophy." Without a "common moral principle expressed in defined terms, the unity of society can never be achieved." The need for such had prompted the modern attempt to worship the state, the race, or the nation.[27] The alternative to such idolatries in Belloc's eyes was the Catholic faith, with which he identified the essential values of European civilization. However, Belloc the Catholic apologist, like Belloc the poet, or Belloc the traveler-sailor, would require another study as long as this study of his political theory.

World War II brought further immediate personal tragedy to Belloc; his son Peter died of pneumonia while on active duty in April 1941. And in January 1942 Belloc suffered a stroke, which impaired his powers of concentration and ended his literary career. He died on July 16, 1953, following a fall near his fireplace. He left no commentary on the changes in the world following World War II. One can only speculate as to what degree he would have regarded an Adenauer or a de Gaulle as meeting his monarchist ideal, or the Common Market as a return to his notions of a United Europe. Surely he would have shed no tears

---

[27] Hilaire Belloc, "The Death of the Middle Class," *Fortnightly Review* 151 (March 1939): 267–75.

over the disappearance of Prussia and the partitioning of the "Germanies," would have regarded the creation of a distinct Jewish national state as quite logical, and would have mourned the control of Eastern Europe by a socialistic and atheistic ideology. The post–Vatican II Catholic church would have broken his heart, as would probably the Americanization of Europe. Beyond a doubt, the continued growth of the state and its intrusion into more and more private spheres heretofore reserved to familial and local authorities, and the state's gargantuan indebtedness, would appear as confirmations of his forecast of impending servility. Last, he would certainly be in the front ranks of the right-to-life cause.

Recently Belloc has tended to be ignored. His friend G. K. Chesterton has fared somewhat better, possibly because of Chesterton's more jovial temperament in polemical encounters. Belloc's political and religious writings were too tightly reasoned to hold the sympathy of opponents in a way that the epigrams of Chesterton would. Naturally the elements of authoritarianism and anti-Semitism in his work have not helped Belloc. Especially devastating to him has been the inclination among post–Vatican II Catholic intellectuals to ignore distinctly Catholic literary figures, especially those who are apologists. It has been suggested that Belloc will endure only as a poet. Perhaps, but possibly this book will make some contribution to a revived appreciation of the prophetic and subtle character of so much of his social and political commentary.

Selected Bibliography

LEGISLATIVE DEBATES

Great Britain, Parliament, *Parliamentary Debates*

MANUSCRIPTS

Belloc Correspondence, New York Public Library
Belloc-Lansdale Correspondence, Princeton University Library

NEWSPAPERS AND PERIODICALS

Contemporary Review
Dublin Review
English Review
Eye-Witness
Fortnightly Review
International Quarterly
Living Age
New Age
New Witness
Oxford and Cambridge Review
Times (London)

WRITINGS BY BELLOC

This section includes only those writings that are relevant to an analysis of Belloc's social and political ideas. Consequently, only part of Belloc's writings are listed.

a. ARTICLES

Belloc, Hilaire. "The Argument for Protection." *Contemporary Review* 87 (June 1905): 835–43.

――――. "Audit the Party Funds." *Nineteenth Century* 101 (April 1927): 476–86.

――――. "The Battle of Sterling." *English Review* 61 (August 1935): 150–57.

――――. "Bribe the Coal Masters." *Eye-Witness,* February 22, 1912, pp. 304–5.

――――. "Capitalism and Communism—The Hellish Twins." *English Review* 54 (February 1932): 122–34.

――――. "The Change in Politics." *Fortnightly Review* 95 (January 1911): 33–45.

――――. "The Crown and the Breakdown of Parliament." *English Review* 58 (February 1934): 145–52.

――――. "Death Duties and Capital." *Fortnightly Review* 94 (August 1910): 213–23.

――――. "The Death of the Middle Class." *Fortnightly Review* 151 (March 1939): 267–75.

――――, and Shaw, Bernard. "A Debate on Distributism." *American Review* 8 (January 1937): 309–20.

――――. "The Economics of 'Cheap.'" *Dublin Review* 148 (January 1911): 69–84.

――――. "The Effects of High Taxation." *Fortnightly Review* 133 (April 1930): 471–80.

――――. "English Monarchy: The Significance of the Abdication." *American Review* 8 (February 1937): 418–26.

――――. "The English Revolution and the Press." *Harper's Monthly,* August 1925, pp. 367–73.

———. "The Export of Capital." *Dublin Review* 144 (April 1909): 378–95.

———. "A Few Kind Words on the Press." *Nineteenth Century* 120 (October 1936): 438–51.

———. "Honest and Dishonest Insurance." *Eye-Witness,* June 6, 1912, pp. 784–86.

———. "If They Were Honest." *Eye-Witness,* February 8, 1912, pp. 240–42.

———. "The Inflation of Assessment." *Dublin Review* 142 (April 1908): 351–62.

———. "The Limits of Direct Taxation." *Contemporary Review* 93 (February 1908): 191–206.

———. "The Measure of National Wealth." *Dublin Review* 144 (January 1909): 33–52.

———. "Modern Life." *English Review* 2 (March 1909): 799–808.

———. "The Modern Man." *English Review* 62 (January 1936): 58–65.

———. "Modern Thought." *New Age,* December 7, 1907, pp. 109–10.

———. "Neither Capitalism nor Socialism." *American Mercury* 41 (July 1937): 309–16.

———. "On Licensing." *English Review* 2 (June 1909): 600–608.

———. "The Party System." *English Review* 4 (March 1910): 706–18.

———. "Preliminaries." *Oxford and Cambridge Review* 22 (August 1912): 71–80.

———. "The Prevention of Destitution Bill." *New Age,* April 14, 1910, pp. 555–57.

———. "Property." *Oxford and Cambridge Review* 23 (September 1912): 65–77.

———. "The Protectionist Movement in England." *International Quarterly* 10 (October 1904): 181–89.

————. "A Question." *New Age,* March 21, 1908, p. 409.

————. "Reform III—The Restoration of Property." *Oxford and Cambridge Review* 24 (October 1912): 53–57.

————. "Reform IV—The Restoration of Property in Capital." *Oxford and Cambridge Review* 25 (November 1912): 87–99.

————. "Reform V—The Power of the Crown." *Oxford and Cambridge Review* 26 (December 1912): 72–86.

————. "The Servile State." *New Age,* May 26, 1910, pp. 77–79.

————. "The Strain of Transition." *Fortnightly Review* 95 (February 1910): 223–35.

————. "The Taxation of Rent." *Dublin Review* 145 (October 1909): 266–81.

————. "The Three Issues." *New Age,* May 2, 1908, pp. 8–10.

————. "Wheat Bounties." *Oxford and Cambridge Review* 17 (January 1912): 89–102.

————. "Whiggery." *Fortnightly Review* 152 (December 1939): 646–54.

b. BOOKS

Belloc, Hilaire. *Caliban's Guide to Letters.* London: Duckworth & Company, 1920; first published 1903.

————. *The Catholic Church and the Principle of Private Property.* London: Catholic Truth Society, 1920.

————. *A Change in the Cabinet.* London: Methuen & Company, 1909.

————. *The Church and Socialism.* London: Catholic Truth Society, 1909.

————. *The Contrast.* New York: Robert M. McBride & Company, 1924.

————. *The Crisis of Civilization.* New York: Fordham University Press, 1937.

————. *The Cruise of the "Nona."* Westminster, Md.: Newman Press, 1956; first published 1925.

———. *Danton.* New York: G. P. Putnam's Sons, 1928; first published 1899.

———. *Economics for Helen.* London: J. W. Arrowsmith, 1924.

———. *Emmanuel Burden.* New York: Charles Scribner's Sons, 1904.

———. *Essay of a Catholic Layman in England.* London: Sheed & Ward, 1931.

———. *An Essay on the Nature of Contemporary England.* London: Constable, 1937.

———; Hirst, Francis W.; Simon, J. Allsebrook; Phillimore, J. S.; Hammond, J. L.; MacDonnell, P. J. *Essays in Liberalism.* London: Cassell & Company, 1897.

———. *Europe and the Faith.* London: Burns & Oates, 1962; first published 1920.

———. *First and Last.* London: Methuen & Company, 1911.

———. *The Four Men.* London: Thomas Nelson & Sons, 1912.

———. *The Free Press.* London: George Allen & Unwin, 1918.

———. *The French Revolution.* London: Oxford University Press, 1960; first published 1911.

———. *The Great Inquiry.* London: Duckworth & Company, 1903.

———. *Hills and the Sea.* London: Methuen & Company, 1906.

———, and Lingard, John. *The History of England.* 11 vols. New York: Catholic Publication Society of America, 1915.

———. *The House of Commons and Monarchy.* New York: Harcourt, Brace & Company, 1922.

———. *The Jews.* London: Constable & Company, 1922.

———. *Lambkin's Remains.* London: Duckworth & Company, 1920; first published 1900.

———. *Letters.* Edited by Robert Speaight. London: Hollis & Carter, 1958.

————. *Marie Antoinette.* New York: G. P. Putnam's Sons, 1924; first published 1909.

————. *Mr. Clutterbuck's Election.* London: Eveleigh Nash, 1908.

————. *Mrs. Markham's New History of England.* London: Cayme Press, 1926.

————. *Napoleon.* Philadelphia: J. B. Lippincott, 1932.

————. *On Anything.* London: Constable & Company, 1910.

————. *On Everything.* London: Methuen & Company, 1909.

————. *On Nothing.* London: Methuen & Company, 1909.

————. *On Something.* London: Methuen & Company, 1910.

————, and Chesterton, Cecil. *The Party System.* London: Stephen Swift, 1911.

————. *The Path to Rome.* Garden City, N.Y.: Doubleday & Company, Image Books, 1956; first published 1902.

————. *Pongo and the Bull.* London: Constable & Company, 1910.

————. *The Restoration of Property.* London: Distributist Books, 1948; first published 1936.

————. *Robespierre.* New York: G. P. Putnam's Sons, 1927; first published 1901.

————. *The Servile State.* London: Constable & Company, 1927; first published 1912. Indianapolis: Liberty*Classics,* 1977.

————, and MacDonald, J. Ramsay. *Socialism and the Servile State.* London: South West London Federation of the Independent Labor Party, 1911.

————. *Sonnets & Verse.* London: Duckworth & Company, 1954.

————. *Survivals and New Arrivals.* London: Sheed & Ward, 1929.

————. *This and That.* London: Methuen & Company, 1912.

————. *The Verse of Hilaire Belloc.* Edited by W. N. Roughead. Holland: Nonesuch Press, 1954.

WRITINGS ABOUT BELLOC

This section includes only those writings relevant to the period of Belloc's life under discussion and to the general subject.

a. ARTICLES

Chesterton, Cecil. "Hilaire Belloc." *Living Age* 251 (December 15, 1906): 689–94.

Masterman, C. F. G. "After the Reaction." *Living Age* 244 (January 28, 1905): 202–4.

Payne, Burnell. "The Work of Mr. Belloc." *Living Age* 281 (June 6, 1914): 606–11.

Secombe, Thomas. "Life of Hilaire Belloc." *Living Age* 289 (April 8, 1916): 93–103.

Wells, H. G. "About G. K. Chesterton and Hilaire Belloc." *New Age,* January 11, 1908, pp. 209–10.

b. BOOKS

Creighton Mandell, C., and Shanks, Edward. *Hilaire Belloc.* London: Methuen & Company, 1916.

Hamilton, Robert. *Hilaire Belloc.* London: Douglas Organ, 1945.

Jebb, Eleanor, and Jebb, Reginald. *Belloc, the Man.* Westminster, Md.: Newman Press, 1957.

Lowndes, Marie Belloc. *I, Too, Have Lived in Arcadia.* London: Macmillan & Company, 1941.

————. *Where Love and Friendship Dwelt.* New York: Dodd, Mead & Company, 1943.

————. *The Young Hilaire Belloc.* New York: P. J. Kenedy & Sons, 1956.

Morton, J. B. *Hilaire Belloc: A Memoir.* London: Hollis & Carter, 1955.

Speaight, Robert. *The Life of Hilaire Belloc.* New York: Farrar, Straus & Cudahy, 1957.

Wilhelmsen, Frederick. *Hilaire Belloc: No Alienated Man.* New York: Sheed & Ward, 1953.

OTHER PRIMARY SOURCES

Bagehot, Walter. *The English Constitution.* Garden City, N.Y.: Doubleday & Company, Dolphin Books, n.d.

Beveridge, William H. *Unemployment, a Problem of Industry.* London: Longmans, Green & Company, 1909.

Blunt, Wilfrid Scawen. *My Diaries, 1888–1914.* London: Martin Secker, 1932; first published in 2 vols., 1919–20.

Braithwaite, William J. *Lloyd George's Ambulance Wagon.* Edited by Sir Henry N. Bunbury (with commentary by Richard Titmuss). London: Methuen & Company, 1957.

Chamberlain, Austen. *Politics from Inside.* New Haven: Yale University Press, 1957.

Charles Booth's London. Edited by Albert Fried and Richard Elman. New York: Random House, Pantheon Books, 1967.

Chesterton, Ada Elizabeth. *The Chestertons.* London: Chapman & Hall, 1941.

Chesterton, Cecil. *Gladstonian Ghosts.* London: S. C. Brown, Langham & Company, 1905.

Chesterton, G. K. *All Things Considered.* New York: John Lane Company, 1910.

————. *Autobiography.* New York: Sheed & Ward, 1936.

————. *Utopia of Usurers.* New York: Boni & Liveright, 1917.

————. *What's Wrong with the World.* New York: Sheed & Ward, 1956; first pubished 1910.

Churchill, Winston S. *Great Contemporaries.* London: Thornton Butterworth, 1937.

————. *Liberalism and the Social Problem.* New York: Hodder & Stoughton, 1909.

Cole, G. D. H. *Self-Government in Industry*. London: G. Bell & Sons, 1917.

————. *The World of Labor*. London: G. Bell & Sons, 1915.

Disraeli, Benjamin. *Coningsby*. London: John Lehmann, 1948; first published 1844.

Five Great Encyclicals. New York: Paulist Press, 1939.

Gardiner, A. G. *Prophets, Priests, and Kings*. London: J. M. Dent & Sons, 1914.

Green, Thomas Hill. *Lectures on the Principles of Political Obligation*. London: Longmans, Green & Company, 1941.

Hammond, J. L., and Hammond, Barbara. *The Village Labourer, 1760–1832*. London: Longmans, Green & Company, 1913.

Hirst, Francis W. *In the Golden Days*. London: Frederick Muller, 1947.

Hobhouse, L. T. *Democracy and Reaction*. 2d ed. London: T. Fisher Unwin, 1909.

————. *Liberalism*. New York: Oxford University Press, 1964; first published 1911.

Hobson, J. A. *The Crisis of Liberalism: New Issues of Democracy*. London: P. S. King & Son, 1909.

————. *Imperialism: A Study*. 3d ed. London: Duckworth & Company, 1938.

Hobson, S. G. *National Guilds*. London: G. Bell & Sons, 1914.

————. *National Guilds and the State*. London: G. Bell & Sons, 1920.

————. *Pilgrim to the Left*. New York: Longmans, Green & Company, 1938.

Lloyd George, David. *Better Times*. London: Hodder & Stoughton, 1910.

————. *War Memoirs*. Vol. 1. London: Toor Nicholsen & Watson, 1933.

Low, Sidney. *The Governance of England*. New York: G. P. Putnam's Sons, 1913.

Lowell, A. Lawrence. *The Government of England*. 2 vols. New York: Macmillan Company, 1916–17.

MacDonald, J. Ramsay. *The Social Unrest.* London: T. N. Foulis, 1924.

————. *The Socialist Movement.* London: Williams & Norgate, 1911.

————. *Syndicalism.* London: Constable & Company, 1912.

Masterman, Charles F. G., ed. *The Heart of Empire.* London: T. Fisher Unwin, 1902.

Masterman, Lucy, *C. F. G. Masterman.* London: Nicholsen & Watson, 1939.

Mill, John Stuart. *Autobiography.* Garden City, N.Y.: Doubleday & Company, Dolphin Books, n.d.

Morley, John Viscount. *Recollections.* 2 vols. New York: Macmillan Company, 1917.

Orage, A. R. *Political and Economic Writings.* Edited by Montgomery Butchart. Freeport, N.Y.: Books for Libraries Press, 1967.

Ostrogorski, M. *Democracy and the Organization of Political Parties.* Vol. 1. New York: Macmillan Company, 1902.

Oxford and Asquith, Earl of. *Fifty Years of the British Parliament.* 2 vols. Boston: Little, Brown & Company, 1926.

Penty, A. J. *Old Worlds for New.* London: George Allen & Unwin, 1917.

————. *The Restoration of the Guild System.* London: S. Sonnenschein & Company, 1906.

Reckitt, Maurice B. *As It Happened.* London: J. M. Dent & Sons, 1941.

Rousseau, Jean Jacques. *The Social Contract.* Translated and introduced by Willmoore Kendall. Chicago: Henry Regnery, 1954.

Rowntree, B. Seebohm. *Poverty: A Study of Town Life.* London: Macmillan & Company, 1901.

St. John, Henry (Viscount Bolingbroke). *The Idea of a Patriot King.* Edited by Sydney W. Jackman. Indianapolis: Bobbs-Merrill, 1965; first published 1749.

Samuel, Herbert. *Liberalism.* London: G. Richards, 1902.

Shaw, Bernard. *The Doctor's Dilemma.* Harmondsworth, Middlesex: Penguin Books, 1960.

————. *Major Barbara.* Harmondsworth, Middlesex: Penguin Books, 1966.

————. *Man and Superman.* Harmondsworth, Middlesex: Penguin Books, 1946; first published 1903.

Tawney, R. H. *The Agrarian Problem in the Sixteenth Century.* London: Longmans, Green & Company, 1912.

Wallas, Graham. *The Great Society.* New York: Macmillan Company, 1914.

————. *Human Nature in Politics.* New York: F. S. Crofts & Company, 1921.

Webb, Beatrice. *Our Partnership.* London: Longmans, Green & Company, 1948.

————, and Webb, Sidney. *The Prevention of Destitution.* London: Longmans, Green & Company, 1911.

Wells, H. G. *Anticipations.* New York: Harper & Brothers, 1901.

————. *Mankind in the Making.* New York: Charles Scribner's Sons, 1904.

————. *A Modern Utopia.* London: Thomas Nelson & Sons, 1905.

————. *The New Machiavelli.* Harmondsworth, Middlesex: Penguin Books, 1946.

————. *New Worlds for Old.* New York: Macmillan Company, 1907.

————. *Social Forces in England and America.* New York: Harper & Brothers, 1914.

SECONDARY SOURCES

a. ARTICLES

Adams, W. S. "Lloyd George and the Labor Movement." *Past and Present* 3 (April 1953): 55–62.

Bealey, Frank. "The Electoral Arrangement Between the Labor Representation Committee and the Liberal Party." *Journal of Modern History* 28 (December 1956): 353–73.

Brebner, J. Bartlett. "Laissez-Faire and State Intervention in Nineteenth-Century Britain." *Journal of Economic History,* supp. 8 (1948): 59–73.

Brown, W. F. "The Education Bill of 1906." *Dublin Review* 140 (January–April 1907): 128–38.

Cornford, James. "The Transformation of Conservatism in the Late Nineteenth Century." *Victorian Studies* 7 (September 1963): 35–66.

Drus, Ethel. "The Question of Imperial Complicity in the Jameson Raid." *English Historical Review* 68 (October 1953): 582–93.

Ensor, R. C. K. "Some Political and Economic Interactions in Late Victorian England." *Transactions of the Royal Historical Society,* 4th ser. 31 (1949): 17–28.

Fieldhouse, D. K. "Imperialism: An Historiographical Revision." *Economic History Review,* 2d ser. 14 (December 1961): 187–209.

Fletcher, T. W. "The Great Depression of English Agriculture, 1875–1896." *Economic History Review,* 2d ser. 13 (April 1961): 417–32.

Fraser, Peter. "The Growth of Ministerial Control in the Nineteenth-Century House of Commons." *English Historical Review* 75 (July 1960): 444–63.

Galbraith, John S. "The Pamphlet Campaign of the Boer War." *Journal of Modern History* 24 (June 1952): 111–26.

Glaser, John F. "English Nonconformity and the Decline of Liberalism." *American Historical Review* 63 (January 1958): 352–63.

Goodman, Gordon. "Liberal Unionism: The Revolt of the Whigs." *Victorian Studies* 3 (December 1959): 173–89.

Hanham, H. J. "The Sale of Honors in Late Victorian England." *Victorian Studies* 3 (March 1960): 277–89.

Herrick, Francis H. "The Origins of the National Liberal Federation." *Journal of Modern History* 17 (June 1945): 116–29.

Hobsbawm, Eric J. "General Labor Unions in Britain, 1889–

1914." *Economic History Review,* 2d ser. 1 (August 1948): 123–42.

————. "Twentieth Century British Politics: A Review Article." *Past and Present* 11 (April 1957): 100–108.

Howard, Christopher. "Splendid Isolation." *History* 47 (February 1962): 32–41.

Hyde, William J. "The Socialism of H. G. Wells in the Early Twentieth Century." *Journal of the History of Ideas* 17 (April 1956): 217–34.

Inglis, K. S. "English Nonconformity and Social Reform, 1880–1900." *Past and Present* 13 (April 1958): 73–88.

McGill, Barry. "Francis Schnadhorst and Liberal Party Organization." *Journal of Modern History* 34 (March 1962): 19–39.

Penson, Lillian M. "The New Course in British Foreign Policy, 1892–1902." *Transactions of the Royal Historical Society,* 4th ser. 25 (1943): 121–38.

Pumphrey, Ralph E. "The Introduction of Industrialists into the British Peerage: A Study in Adaption of a Social Institution." *American Historical Review* 65 (October 1959): 1–16.

Trevor-Roper, H. R. "The Gentry, 1540–1640." *Economic History Review,* supp. 1 (1953).

Wilson, Charles. "Economy and Society in Late Victorian Britain." *Economic History Review,* 2d ser. 18 (August 1965): 183–98.

b. BOOKS

Adamson, John William. *English Education, 1789–1902.* Cambridge: At the University Press, 1930.

Allen, Bernard M. *Sir Robert Morant.* London: Macmillan & Company, 1934.

Ashton, T. S. *The Industrial Revolution, 1760–1830.* London: Oxford University Press, 1948.

Ashworth, William. *An Economic History of England, 1870–1939.* London: Methuen & Company, 1960.

Barker, Sir Ernest. *Political Thought in England, 1848–1914*. 2d ed. London: Oxford University Press, 1959; first published 1915.

Beer, M. *A History of British Socialism*. 2 vols. London: George Allen & Unwin, 1919.

Beer, Samuel H. *British Politics in the Collectivist Age*. New York: Alfred A. Knopf, 1966.

Blake, Robert. *Disraeli*. Garden City, N.Y.: Doubleday & Company, 1968.

Briggs, Asa. *Social Thought and Social Action*. London: Longmans, 1961.

Bruce, Maurice. *The Coming of the Welfare State*. 3d ed. London: B. T. Batsford, 1966.

Buckley, Jessie K. *Joseph Parkes of Birmingham*. London: Methuen & Company, 1926.

Bullock, Alan, and Shock, Maurice, eds. *The Liberal Tradition*. London: Adam & Charles Black, 1956.

Butterfield, Herbert. *The Whig Interpretation of History*. New York: W. W. Norton, 1965; first published 1931.

Canovan, Margaret. *G. K. Chesterton: Radical Populist*. New York: Harcourt Brace Jovanovich, 1977.

Carpenter, Niles. *Guild Socialism*. New York: D. Appleton & Company, 1922.

Carter, Henry. *The English Temperance Movement: A Study in Objectives*. 2 vols. London: Epworth Press, 1933.

Clapham, J. H. *An Economic History of Modern Britain*. 3 vols. Cambridge: At the University Press, 1927–38.

Cole, G. D. H., and Postgate, Raymond. *The British Common People*. New York: Barnes & Noble, 1961.

Cole, G. D. H. *British Working Class Politics, 1832–1914*. London: Routledge & Kegan Paul, 1961.

———. *A History of Socialist Thought*. Vol. 3, Part 1: *The Second International, 1880–1914*. Vol. 4, Part 1: *Communism and Social Democracy*. London: Macmillan & Company, 1956.

Court, W. H. B. *British Economic History, 1870–1914, Com-*

mentary and Documents. Cambridge: At the University Press, 1965.

————. *A Concise Economic History of Britain, from 1750 to Recent Times.* Cambridge: At the University Press, 1954.

Curtis, S. J. *Education in Britain Since 1900.* London: Andrew Dakers, 1952.

Dangerfield, George. *The Strange Death of Liberal England, 1910–14.* New York: Capricorn Books, 1935.

Donaldson, Frances. *The Marconi Scandal.* New York: Harcourt, Brace & World, 1962.

Emy, H. V. *Liberals, Radicals, and Social Politics, 1892–1914.* New York: Cambridge University Press, 1973.

Ensor, R. C. K. *England, 1870–1914.* Oxford: Oxford University Press, 1936.

Faber, Geoffrey. *Jowett.* Cambridge: Harvard University Press, 1957.

Fraser, Peter. *Joseph Chamberlain.* London: Cassell, 1966.

Fulford, Roger. *Votes for Women.* London: Faber & Faber, 1957.

Garvin, J. L. *The Life of Joseph Chamberlain.* Vol. 3. *Empire and World Policy.* London: Macmillan & Company, 1934.

Gilbert, Bentley B. *The Evolution of National Insurance in Great Britain.* London: Michael Joseph, 1966.

Glass, S. T. *The Responsible Society.* London: Longmans, Green & Company, 1966.

Gollin, Alfred M. *Balfour's Burden.* London: Anthony Blond, 1965.

————. *The Observer and J. L. Garvin, 1908–14.* London: Oxford University Press, 1960.

————. *Proconsul in Politics.* London: Anthony Blond, 1964.

Gwyn, William B. *Democracy and the Cost of Politics in Britain.* London: University of London, Athlone Press, 1962.

Halévy, Elie. *The Era of Tyrannies.* Garden City, N.Y.: Doubleday & Company, 1965.

————. *Imperialism and the Rise of Labor, 1895–1905.* New York: Barnes & Noble, 1961.

————. *The Rule of Democracy, 1905–1914*. New York: Barnes & Noble, 1961.

Hamburger, Joseph. *James Mill and the Art of Revolution*. New Haven: Yale University Press, 1963.

Hay, J. P. *The Origins of the Liberal Welfare Reforms, 1906–1914*. London: Macmillan & Company, 1975.

Hexter, J. H. *Reappraisals in History*. London: Longmans, Green & Company, 1961.

Ho, Ping-Ti. "Land and State in Great Britain, 1873–1910." Ph.D. dissertation, Columbia University, 1952.

Hoskins, W. G. *The Midland Peasant*. London: Macmillan & Company, 1957.

James, Robert Rhodes. *Rosebery*. New York: Macmillan Company, 1963.

Jenkins, Roy. *Asquith*. London: Collins, 1964.

————. *Mr. Balfour's Poodle*. London: Heinemann, 1954.

Koebner, Richard, and Schmidt, Helmut Dan. *Imperialism*. Cambridge: At the University Press, 1964.

Koss, Stephen. *Nonconformity in Modern British Politics*. London: Batsford, 1975.

Lloyd, Trevor. *The General Election of 1880*. London: Oxford University Press, 1968.

Lyons, F. S. L. *The Irish Parliamentary Party, 1890–1910*. London: Faber & Faber, 1951.

McBriar, A. M. *Fabian Socialism and English Politics, 1884–1918*. Cambridge: At the University Press, 1962.

McClelland, Vincent Alan. *Cardinal Manning*. London: Oxford University Press, 1962.

Maccoby, S. *English Radicalism, 1855–1886*. London: George Allen & Unwin, 1938.

————. *English Radicalism, 1886–1914*. London: George Allen & Unwin, 1953.

————, ed. *The Radical Tradition, 1763–1914*. London: Adam & Charles Black, 1952.

MacColl, René. *Roger Casement*. London: Lonsborough Publications, 1959.

McDowell, R. B. *British Conservatism, 1832–1914*. London: Faber & Faber, 1959.

McEntee, Georgiana Putnam. *The Social Catholic Movement in Great Britain*. New York: Macmillan Company, 1927.

Macmillan, Gerald. *Honors for Sale*. London: Richards Press, 1954.

Martin, Wallace. *The New Age Under Orage*. Manchester: Manchester University Press, 1967.

Morris, A. J. A., ed. *Edwardian Radicalism, 1900–1914*. London: Routledge & Kegan Paul, 1974.

Morris, Homer Lawrence. "Parliamentary Franchise Reform in England from 1885 to 1918." Ph.D. dissertation, Columbia University, 1921.

Nicolson, Harold. *King George the Fifth: His Life and Reign*. London:-Constable & Company, 1952.

Nowell-Smith, Simon, ed. *Edwardian England, 1901–1914*. New York: Oxford University Press, 1964.

Oldmeadow, Ernest. *Francis Cardinal Bourne*. 2 vols. London: Burns, Oates & Washbourne, 1940, 1944.

O'Leary, Cornelius. *The Elimination of Corrupt Practices in British Elections, 1868–1914*. Oxford: Oxford University Press, 1962.

Osborne, John W. *William Cobbett*. New Brunswick, N.J.: Rutgers University Press, 1966.

Pearson, Hesketh. *Labby*. New York: Harper & Brothers, 1936.

——. *Lives of the Wits*. New York: Harper & Row, 1962.

Pelling, Henry. *A History of British Trade Unionism*. Baltimore: Penguin Books, 1963.

——. *The Origins of the Labor Party*. 2d ed. Oxford: Oxford University Press, 1965.

——. *A Short History of the Labor Party*. London: Macmillan & Company, 1965.

——. *Social Geography of British Elections, 1885–1910*. London: Macmillan & Company, 1967.

Phelps Brown, E. H. *The Growth of British Industrial Relations*. London: Macmillan & Company, 1959.

Pod, Jean van der. *The Jameson Raid.* Cape Town: Oxford University Press, 1951.

Postgate, Raymond W. *The Life of George Lansbury.* London: Longmans, Green & Company, 1951.

Richter, Melvin. *The Politics of Conscience.* London: Weidenfeld & Nicolson, 1964.

Robinson, Ronald, and Gallagher, John, with Alice Denny. *Africa and the Victorians.* New York: St. Martin's Press, 1961.

Rogger, Hans, and Weber, Eugen, eds. *The European Right.* Los Angeles: University of California Press, 1966.

Semmel, Bernard. *Imperialism and Social Reform.* London: George Allen & Unwin, 1960.

Shapiro, David, ed. *The Right in France, 1890–1919.* 2d ed. London: Chatto & Windus, 1962.

Simey, M. B., and Simey, T. S. *Charles Booth, Social Scientist.* London: Oxford University Press, 1960.

Sommer, Dudley. *Haldane of Cloan.* London: George Allen & Unwin, 1960.

Stansky, Peter. *Ambitions and Strategies.* Oxford: Oxford University Press, 1964.

Stern, Philip M. *The Great Treasury Raid.* New York: Random House, 1964.

Taylor, A. J. P. *Essays in English History.* Harmondsworth, Middlesex: Penguin Books, 1976.

————. *The Troublemakers.* London: Hamish Hamilton, 1957.

Thompson, F. M. L. *English Landed Society in the Nineteenth Century.* London: Routledge & Kegan Paul, 1965.

Thornton, A. P. *The Imperial Idea and Its Enemies.* London: Macmillan & Company, 1959.

Thorold, Algar Labouchere. *The Life of Henry Labouchere.* London: Constable & Company, 1913.

Vincent, John. *The Formation of the Liberal Party, 1857–1868.* London: Constable & Company, 1966.

Vincent, J. R. *Pollbooks, How Victorians Voted.* Cambridge: At the University Press, 1967.

Ward, Maisie. *Gilbert Keith Chesterton.* Harmondsworth, Middlesex: Penguin Books, 1958.

Wolf, Lucien. *Life of the First Marquess of Ripon.* 2 vols. London: John Murray, 1921.

Index

This book was linotype set in the Times Roman series of type. The face was designed to be used in the news columns of the *London Times*. The *Times* was seeking a type face that would be condensed enough to accommodate a substantial number of words per column without sacrificing readability and still have an attractive, contemporary appearance. This design was an immediate success. It is used in many periodicals throughout the world and is one of the most popular text faces presently in use for book work.

Book design by Design Center, Inc., Indianapolis
Typography by Weimer Typesetting Co., Inc., Indianapolis
Printed by North Central Publishing Co., Saint Paul